JUG

ON ALCHEMY

ENCOUNTERING

J U N G

JUNG ON ALCHEMY

JUNG ON EVIL

ENCOUNTERING

J U N G

ON ALCHEMY

SELECTED AND INTRODUCED BY NATHAN SCHWARTZ-SALANT

PRINCETON UNIVERSITY PRESS · PRINCETON, NEW JERSEY

First published 1995
by Routledge
11 New Fetter Lane, London EC4P 4EE

Simultaneously published in the USA and Canada
by Princeton University Press

Printed and bound in the United States of America by Princeton Academic Press

Library of Congress Cataloging-in Publication Data

Jung, C. G. (Carl Gustav), 1875–1961.
Jung on alchemy / C. G. Jung ; selected and introduced by Nathan Schwartz-Salant.
p.   cm. — (Encountering Jung)
Includes bibliographical references and index.
ISBN 0-691-01097-8 (pbk. : alk. paper)
1. Individuation (Psychology) 2. Alchemy. I. Schwartz-Salant, Nathan, 1938–   II. Title.
III. Series: Jung, C. G. (Carl Gustav), 1875–1961. Selections. English. 1995.
BF175.5.I53J86   1995
540'.'12—dc20   95-36790

10 9 8 7 6 5 4 3 2 1

Contents

Illustrations

JUNG

ON ALCHEMY

Introduction

ALCHEMY, SCIENCE AND ILLUMINATION

My first encounter with alchemy was a passing one as a student some thirty years ago in a course dealing with the scientific work of Sir Isaac Newton. When the professor, who had an interest in the history of science, discussed Newton he made a side reference to Newton's interests in alchemy, and he seemed both amused and embarrassed by how this legendary figure could be enchanted by such nonsense. And all of us followed suit, 'implanted' by the professor's attitude, as no doubt he had been by his teachers before him. The subject was soon dropped, cast aside as an obvious aberrant behavior of the times that could affect even the great Newton, but certainly not his 'real' work as we knew it. While his alchemical studies are now more well known and available, the alchemical aspect of Newton's work at that time were like books on the 'Index' of the Catholic Church; they were difficult to find, and one wondered if they really existed. None of us, most likely the professor included, had any inkling that over four decades of Newton's life were, in significant measure, spent in serious alchemical pursuits (Taylor, 1956; Geoghegan, 1957; McGuire, 1967; Dobbs, 1975, 1992), including a quest for the 'true philosophical mercury' (Dobbs, 1992, p. 195). But even now one can encounter an aversion among scholars to accepting the role of alchemy in Newton's life (Hall, 1992).

Today, a very great majority of educated people still regard alchemy with disdain. This modern attitude of distorting and maligning 'the sacred art' of alchemy seems almost adolescent, especially when seen against the fact that alchemy occupied some of the best minds for thousands of years. Indeed, alchemy's impressive beginnings reach back into prehistory, with its conceptual foundation in Greek and Stoic thought in the centuries prior to our present era. Why has this distortion occurred, and why is this remarkable body of thought still dismissed as an embarrassment that was only 'corrected' by the emergence of science? The historian of religion Mircea Eliade suggests:

> Having for so long (and so heroically!) followed the path which we believed to be the best and only one worthy of the intelligent, self respecting individual, and in the process having sacrificed the best part of

our soul in order to satisfy the colossal intellectual demands of scientific and industrial progress, we have grown suspicious of the greatness of primitive cultures.

(Eliade, 1962, p. 12)

Certainly, this attitude of suspiciousness, if not superiority, was what I and most people were once taught concerning alchemy. But, as Eliade also tells us, 'Alchemy is one of those creations of the pre-scientific era and the historiographer who would attempt to present it as a rudimentary phase of chemistry or, indeed, as a secular science, would be treading on very shaky ground' (ibid., p. 13). 'From the alchemist's point of view, chemistry represented a "Fall" because it meant the secularization of a sacred science' (ibid., p. 11).

C. G. Jung, perhaps more than any other modern researcher of alchemy, is responsible for resurrecting this body of thought as a respectable field of study. In alchemy, as we shall see, Jung found a mine of symbolism that he recognized to parallel the way a human being, with a correct use of will and imagination, and the assent of fate, can enter a process whose goal is the creation of an internal structure he called the self. The self, created through what Jung termed the individuation process, yields an inner stability and sense of direction for the ego even amidst stormy, emotional and en- vironmental conflict. But the self is filled with paradox, and it too can create chaotic states of mind that can endanger a person's sense of identity. Usually, this has a greater goal of enriching and widening the scope and values of the personality. But it also has its dangers. 'Many have perished in the work' is an alchemical saying that Jung quotes to offer a balance to any overly optimistic attitude. Jung found that alchemy mirrored the complexities of the process of the creation of the self in ways far superior to any other body of thought. I shall discuss such issues in greater detail in this introduction to *Jung on Alchemy*, after which I shall present excerpts from his writings on alchemical symbolism. But to begin with let us try to give some answers to the question: what is alchemy?

The alchemists worked with materials that they tried to change from base to more elevated forms, or they attempted to tincture substances to change their appearance, an endeavor that owed much to the Egyptian craft of dyeing fabrics. In general, alchemy attempted to deal with the complexities of change, the transformation from one state or form to another, from a seed to an embryo, or from an ore of little value to silver or gold, transformed, they believed, in the bowels of the earth under intense pressures and heat. The alchemical art attempted to imitate such processes in a laboratory. But this outer or mundane work with materials was intimately linked to an inner or arcane work on the human personality. For example, the alchemical fire, which is often called the secret of the *opus*, is clearly a physical fire, controlled within an actual vessel, but it is also the heat-producing quality of meditation and imagination. Some alchemical texts will often deal with an outer or inner form of fire, and others will combine them so that it is difficult to know which form is meant. This makes one wonder if this situation is a result of the confusion of a mind not yet capable of dealing with linear, discursive thinking and causality. But the situation is more interesting, and more complex.

Given the acute awareness of 'inner' and 'outer' that we find among certain practitioners of magic in the Renaissance, and the fact that alchemy attracted great scientists such as Newton, Thomas Aquinas and Roger Bacon, it is possible that the linking between 'outer' and 'inner' dimensions – which is anathema to our sense of science and its foremost need for objectivity – was also recognized and valued by some alchemists, without their necessarily losing sight of its dangers of confusing subject and object. Like the so-called 'primitive' logic of traditional cultures, alchemy may have been employing a different rather than a lesser form of thought (Lévi-Strauss, 1966, p. 15). Still, there was a tendency to obscure 'inner' and 'outer' in ways that did, at times, lead to considerable confusion. In some texts it is clear that an inner development is a conscious goal of the alchemist, while in others it is clear that the psychological or spiritual component is minimal; and one wonders if the alchemist is not lost in a maze of operations that are being mystified, rather than informed by mystery. As with science over the last three hundred years and today, one finds exceptional alchemists, mediocre ones and frauds. While we should remain cognizant of the fact that the alchemical mind was a product of its time and its historical past, and that it did tend to blur the distinction between inner and outer in ways that are different from our present consciousness, this should not lead us to a hypothesis of inferiority for that mind. In fact, alchemists were probably more aware of the use of *conscious projection* (Jung, 1988, pp. 1495–6) than we are today. In this regard one should also take note of Henry Corbin's work on the 'autonomous Imagination' and the Sufi notion of *himma* (1969, pp. 220–1), an idea that is akin to the alchemical *projectio*.

The alchemist's understanding of and transformation of matter were surely far inferior to what has been accomplished by modern science. His lack of interest in quantitative measurements contributed to this, as did his conceiving material processes in terms of their purpose or final cause. Historically speaking, the alchemical endeavor has been far more useful for reflecting upon psychological changes than for understanding physical processes. But as science expands the problems it addresses and attempts to tackle – for example, the complexities of how form develops – alchemical thinking may appear in a more interesting light, even to scientific thought. Newton's interest was far from an aberration. And, generally, it is a common mis-understanding that alchemy was a pseudo-science that gave way to the enlightened discoveries of chemistry. It is true enough that much of chemistry as it initially developed was an extension of alchemical ideas, but the tale of alchemy's fate is far more complex. It is indissolubly linked with the control and limitation of the imagination at the instigation of the Reformation (Couliano, 1987, p. 193) and, of course, with the development of science.

The demise of alchemy was probably ordained by two factors. On the one hand, it chose to address problems that are so difficult – issues of the qualitative transformations through which substance takes on new forms – that modern science has yet to truly explore them, let alone master them. On the other, the early fourteenth- and fifteenth-century practitioners of alchemy lived in a world that was entirely animated, one in which matter was not dead or chaotic but had a living soul. This kind of consciousness sees relationships between all levels of existence, animate and inanimate, spiritual and profane, but it does not deal with distinctness and separable entities within a causal process. It was an approach to the world that gave priority to a background sense of oneness. But this kept it from ever successfully separating from, and adequately evaluating, its most potent tool, the imagination. In a strong sense, alchemy, like the Renaissance, had to retreat to allow the individual ego to develop, an ego that could believe it was separate from other people and the world and from God, and an ego that could believe in the usefulness of understanding nature as a process in historical time.

During the time of the emergence of alchemy in the Renaissance, when it began to flourish once again after its birth in the second or third century BC and its communication to the West by the great Arab copyists and alchemists, ego-consciousness had barely developed. But, without the careful discrimination of the ego, a sense of what is inner and outer union states between people readily regresses into a hopeless muddle of fusion that blurs any subject–object differentiation. The mind in the Renaissance, and before, was characterized by an immersion in images, a lack of critical reflection on fantasy, and the use of fantasy to prove anything in an idiosyncratic way (Huizinga, 1954, p. 225 *et passim*). Scientific objectivity in any experimental sense did not exist. Relationships and disputes were subject to being resolved through appeal to mythical and philosophical precedence. Everything was based upon prior models, not on discerning the significance of events in the historical moment. The latter development came about later, with Descartes's separation of mind and body as two qualitatively different entities, and the exclusion of God and finality in theorizing about nature. This was a radical split, but a necessary one.

This great achievement in consciousness – an objectivity about nature and the development of self-awareness – which began to consolidate in the seventeenth century (Whyte, 1960, pp. 42–3), made possible the modern scientific approach. With it came as well the attitude, which became habitual, of separating processes into distinct parts, and focussing attention on the parts even to smaller and smaller units. Eventually, wholeness and a unitary background to existence, a mainstay of alchemical thinking, was lost sight of altogether, even to a degree that brought fragmentation into the life of modern-day people. Today, alchemical thinking holds out a way of return to wholeness without abandoning separation and distinctness of process. In a way alchemy's time has come. Perhaps we can now return to those mysterious realms or 'third areas' that are neither physical nor psychic, domains whose existence must be recognized if we are to re-connect orders of reality such as mind and body. It was such 'third areas' that were a major concern of alchemy. Like the notion of the ether, they were left behind by scientific thinking, but it is possible that even in science they may have to be re-introduced (Bohm, 1980). And if we are to gain a true sense of what relationship is, especially under the eye of psychotherapy, then such 'third areas' must, I believe, definitely be re-introduced (Schwartz-Salant, 1989, 1995).

The alchemists knew, from their own and from the accumulated experience of centuries of traditional cultures, that their personalities could be trans-formed. Through initiation rites they felt different, behaved differently, and grew in new ways. No longer bound to the compulsion of adolescent states of mind, or to the flights into promiscuity that wasted their sexual energies, people in traditional cultures learned that they could 'die' and be 'reborn.' And in their reborn form they actually did see the world differently. They could, in fact, *see* in ways they never could before. Their imagination could become a guide to truth instead of being a capricious trickster. And some alchemists could feel a guiding center that formed in their innermost being and which was strangely linked in feeling to experiences of their most ecstatic journeys. Alchemy developed within this respect for a human concern for the sacred. As a consequence, its very methods were intrinsically bound to the power of illumination and the imagination, and it especially applied the ideas of death and rebirth, so central to initiation rites and mystical experience, to material and psychological change. To understand the alchemical quest we must recognize the intimate relationship that existed between its methods and the transformation of the human personality, or else we shall miss its essential mystery.

I use the term 'mystery' with care. It is not possible to understand alchemy in the same way as one can understand scientific theories. There, one's limitations, whatever they may be, will largely be found in one's capacity for abstraction and in one's knowledge of certain mathematical methods. This is not to say that modern science does not deal with problems that are mysterious, for example, with black holes, chaos and the basic constituents of matter. But the nature of this mystery is that the more we know, the less mystery one finds, and then new problems, new mysterious frontiers open up, once again to be eventually better understood and lose their sense of being enigmatic. Science becomes familiar with problems in ways that seem to be able to take for granted as well known or understood issues that, at a prior time, were filled with mystery. In science, notions such as mass or energy become parts of equations, and cease to hold a sense of awe. This can be recovered when some scientists ask questions like 'What is energy?', and then we again recognize that we are, in fact, not dealing with simple issues at all. But in general the mystery of scientific concepts is hidden away in the equations that govern them, and one can do science without pausing very much to wonder about just what basic entities such as mass, energy or entropy actually are.

This quality of becoming abstract or distant from the concepts one works with is the strength of scientific approaches. One learns to operate with abstractions, and in the process one can solve real problems. Complicated technological advances that could never be accomplished with the magical or so-called primitive logic and attitudes of alchemy are a testimony to this triumph. Alchemy is very different. Here is a body of thought that requires that one be open to an Other dimension of existence in order both to understand the basic concepts, and to operate with them in an attempt to transform material life and the human personality as well. This Other dimension, which is often referred to as God in alchemical thinking, is that domain of human experience that, in early cultures, was mediated by the shaman, or priest, and was eventually codified into dogma in later religions. This codification was always balanced or opposed by a counter-movement of mystics who were determined not to lose a more immediate link with the sacred. Many alchemists were such people, informed by their visions and by being 'killed and reborn' through their experiences of the *numinosum*.

It is this mystery of death and rebirth that never gives way to more profane understanding, as is the case with scientific ideas that were once filled with awe. Whoever has known the *numinosum* in a deep enough way for his or her life to have been unalterably changed by it – changed in such a way that they now *see* differently and now experience the center of personality as existing outside the ego – such a person never *understands* this process. It for ever remains a mystery, one that he or she has been graced to participate in, and survive. And those who have been so changed can then become part of a process of change, for such experiences of death and rebirth are the beginning of the individual *opus*, not the end.

Alchemy depended upon such states of mind, and the art attempted to change not only the human personality but matter as well. Certainly there were many alchemists who had little immediate sense of the true mystery of their art. They were the 'puffers' that tried to transform matter or find the Elixir of Life, without recognizing that the endeavor was hopeless unless they themselves were transformed. But even in the most illuminated of alchemists, such outer goals were probably hopeless of achievement. For the nature of the experience of human transformation takes place, so to speak, in a state of mind and a sense of space that are peculiarly different from the external world in which we can grasp things as being outside of us, or inside of us. This is a critical point, and my own belief is that in a significant measure, aside from their ignorance of atomic structure and quantitative methods, alchemists' heroic effort to deal with matter failed because it was not possible to construct actual, chemical vessels that were analogous to the vessel or *vas hermeticum* in which human personality transforms (Rosen, 1995). I mention this in passing to highlight the fact of the difficult nature of the alchemical quest, rather than to see alchemy as some dumb pursuit of 'pre-scientific' people. Alchemy receded because the problems it set were too hard: problems such as the way the internal structure and outer form of an object change.

Science could advance because the problems it addressed were relatively simple. Science only has an embryonic mathematical understanding of how things take on a particular or changing form.

In good science there is always an interplay between experiment and theory, each enhancing and checking the other. Alchemy, as it was developed by many groups and individuals from Egypt, Arabia, Iran, Greece, India, China, England, Germany and France, was a kind of applied mystico-philosophical system. But instead of equations that ordered Nature, the background of alchemical thinking was a set of principles derived from reflections upon human nature and society, and, as I have stressed, the knowledge gained through mystical visions. We frequently read in alchemical texts that one who has not been illuminated, who has not known God through the *unio mystica*, cannot but be led into error and despair by trying to follow the texts; he will inevitably go astray.

Now this alone would seem to qualify alchemy for the dungheap of ideas. After all, how can we possibly consider with any respect a so-called science that relies upon illumination? There are several ways to discuss this criticism. On the one hand, it can be argued that the greatest failing of our world today, probably encouraged by the abstracting nature of science and technology, is the alienation from the *numinosum*. But, on the other hand, one can also look to the limitations of the alchemical world-view. Perhaps its greatest failing is that it encourages the inflation, which can become megalomania, of *knowing about God* by those who have never 'died.' The latter person is always humble, at least as long as his 'death and rebirth' is a living experience. But in a culture in which the numinous has a very high value, indeed is *necessary* for activities such as attempting the alchemical art, the tendency to behave as if one were illuminated, or to pull on strands of partial illumination as gained from dreams and minor visions, is very strong. This leads to inflations, fraudulence and unsubstantiated claims. The experimental thrust of modern science is also a major corrective and nourishing source that stands against the often, far too often inflated approaches, of a visionary science.

But alchemy was far too subtle to easily fall victim to this pitfall. While only a few were truly illuminated, this did not mean that an alchemical art could not be developed on a sound and humble footing, and still require illumination in some way. On the one hand, faith played a great role. To this was added an awareness of the vices of arrogance and pride. On the other hand, the alchemists recognized that the central illumination of mystical life, the union with God, had a corollary in Nature and, in our terms, in the human psyche. For through a particular quality of the imagination, one could experience a guiding light that was akin to the Light of greater illuminations. These levels of illumination are different from each other in extremely significant ways, and it is the mistaken road of inflation to totally identify the two. But there are also similarities, and because of this the alchemists could speak of 'true' versus 'false' imagination. Always, the central, life-

and death-dealing vision of God was held as the highest value, but it was also believed that other, 'lesser' but 'true', visions could also be a guide. Knowing the pitfalls of such a procedure the alchemists are forever stressing that one must study the masters, and that 'one book opens another.' It was a hazardous journey, filled with failure, but so worthy a one that it lasted for thousands of years.

ALCHEMY, UNION STATES AND THE TRANSFORMATION OF FORM

It is precisely in the issue of vision and relation to the *numinosum* that we find one of alchemy's remarkable achievements and services to modern-day people. For it was a body of thought that carried with it much of what was abused and rejected by the collective religions of the last two thousand years. Central to this is a peculiar form of illumination that focusses not only upon a person and a transcendent deity, but one which is encountered between two people. The experience I am referring to is known as the *hieros gamos* in the history of religion, and translates as the 'sacred wedding'. It is this image of relationship and union, which reflects an experience of the sacred that was cast aside by the patriarchal religions, that is central to alchemical thinking. They conceived of change in terms of the union of different substances. This union process, the alchemical *coniunctio*, was a marriage that, at its highest level of completion, the so-called stage of the *rubedo*, was filled with desire.

To see how the issue of union was applied to work with outer substances, we can turn to a fundamental alchemical principle frequently found among alchemical writers, the 'Axiom of Ostanes': *A nature is delighted by another nature, a nature conquers another nature, a nature dominates another nature.* This triadic formula underpins much alchemical thinking, from its earliest forms in Bolos-Demokrites (200 BC), who lived in Egypt and is often called the founder of alchemy, up through the next seventeen hundred years (Lindsay, 1970, p. 103).

The historian Jack Lindsay's reflections upon this formula offer us an invaluable perspective on alchemical thinking about the topic of transformation.

> The change in quality (of an object) was also change in inner organization, (and) was linked or identified with colour changes. Lead, a primary common metal, had to be broken up, changed, driven up the scale, towards silver or gold; it had to change its colour. So fire was invoked; and under its action the lead was reduced to a fluid state. The fluidity thus brought about was what constituted the primary level, in which new potentialities were actively present. . . . Also the liquefaction of lead involved its blackening. So the blackness of the liquid condition above all expressed the attainment of a primary level, a state of chaos. Having produced chaos, the alchemist was in a position to act the role of demiurge and drive matter up its hierarchical ladder, with gold as the highest step. To bring about this

upward-movement the principle of sympathy or attraction was invoked. Somehow the Primary Black had to be transformed into White or Yellow, which expressed the nobler metals. This could be done, it was believed, if one could find a metal which had certain affinities with both the lower and higher substances, which sympathized with both of them and which exerted its attractive power in both directions (downwards and upwards).

By using the right kind of metal, in the right kind of proportions, one could swing the balance towards the upper levels and thus transform the material into the higher. The principle of this operation was expressed in the famous triadic formula of Ostanes which Bolos-Demokritos discovered. The two materials, that of primary matter or liquid blackness and that of the alloying and transforming addition, must have something in common, some element of harmony. That is, they delighted in one another. But if that were all, a state of equilibrium was created and nothing happened; the first level was not transcended. So one nature must conquer the other. The conquering act was the moment of transformation, when the equilibrium was broken and a new relationship established.

The new fused substance existed at a higher level and involved the creation of a new quality, which revealed itself in the colour-change. But that was not enough. The new state must be stabilized, so that it might provide the basis for yet another upward-movement. Hence, the third section of the formula: one nature must dominate another. The three stages of the alchemic act might then be defined: mixture on the original level, introduction of a dynamic factor which changes the original relations and creates a new qualitative level, then stabilization of this level. In an Arab text the process [is] described as three marriages, the two substances acting on one another being called male and female.

(ibid., pp. 116–17)

The 'axiom' can be seen most clearly as an image of processes between two people in psychotherapy. To see this we may first note Lindsay's remark that transformation depends upon finding a metal which has certain affinities with both the lower and higher substances, which sympathizes with both of them and which exerts its attractive power in both directions (downwards and upwards). This 'metal' is the alchemical *lapis*, or what Jung denoted as the self. The logic follows the alchemical notion that it takes gold to make gold. Thus an analyst, for example, must have a sufficiently stable self, one that can allow the processing of internal experiences in which affects and ideas 'move upwards and downwards', from a spiritual–mental perspective towards an emotional–instinctual one, and vice versa. This internal act of 'sublimation' is what in turn helps the patient to process his or her own disordered material. Both analyst and patient have aspects of the same issues to process, but the analyst, ostensibly, will either have or discover a stable transformative agent within their interaction. He or she has a form of the 'gold' to begin with – or, what is more to the point, the capability to discover it within their interaction. This is what generally differentiates analyst and patient in the analytical process, although there is also room, at times, for these roles to be reversed. It is also interesting to note that the patient may have far more of a link to the *numinosum* than the analyst; but generally it is scattered, unable to exist in a stable manner under the impact of an emotional experience or outer stress. It is the analyst's 'gold' in the form of the capacity to process confusing issues of projection, and especially to survive emotional attacks from the patient in an intact manner, that matters, not his or her exalted awareness. It is likely that the awareness of processes imaged by the Axiom of Ostanes – a required consciousness for anyone practicing magic, which was so central to 'primitive' thought and to the Renaissance – was then projected into work with matter. As I have noted, there is reason to wonder if, at least among some alchemists, this was not an intentional act, while for others it was largely an unconscious process of fusion between matter and psyche.

The issue of illumination through union is pressing up from the depths of the human unconscious, having been cast out by nearly two thousand years of patriarchal forms of insight and vision. Perhaps this form of vision found a home in the interests of the alchemists. As an endeavor, alchemy developed largely as a result of its interest in the union experience. Consequently, it provides us with a mine of information on this issue which is fundamental to human relationships in life and in psychotherapy. Nowadays, the 'sacred marriage' has been lost from scientific pursuit, but finds itself in the analyst's consulting-room in the form of the unconscious union of psyches of analyst and analysand, the so-called transference and counter-transference.

ALCHEMY, HISTORY AND JUNG'S MODEL OF THE PSYCHE

It should be noted that historians of religion have recognized Jung's approach to alchemy as one very worthy of further study and application. Mircea Eliade (1962, pp. 221ff.) is one of these scholars. Historians of science as well, notably the Newton scholar Betty Jo Teeter Dobbs, have recognized the value of Jung's approach. Professor Dobbs writes:

> There has always been something of an historical problem in the very existence of alchemy. Its evident appeal to generation after generation of adepts does little to elucidate the grounds of the fascination it once exerted, even though its relation to innumerable scientific, technical, religious, and philosophical currents has been carefully explored. In recent years, how-ever, the insights of twentieth-century analytical psychology as applied to alchemy by C. G. Jung have come to provide a really promising approach to the problem, allowing as they do for an understanding of the many factors in alchemy which are not only obscure but patently irrational. Jung was not only very historically minded . . . but his views offer a comprehensive and comprehensible model of alchemy as a field of human endeavor.
> (Dobbs, 1975, p. 26)

Dobbs also calls attention to the fact that the value of Jung's approach to alchemy was 'long ago recognized by that eminent exponent of non-scientific motives in the history of science, Walter Pagel, and also by the historian of alchemy, Gerard Heym' (ibid., p. 27).

There are many ways of viewing the writings of the alchemists. On the one end of a spectrum of approaches there are those who see in alchemy nothing more than a projection of an inner developmental process that can be understood in Freudian, Kleinian or other developmental terms. Johannes Fabricius' work *Alchemy* (1976) is an example of this approach, as was Herbert Silberer's before him. On the other end of the spectrum are those who see alchemy as a divine science in which great mysteries are intentionally hidden from the uninitiated; they are encoded in chemical operations. Far from viewing alchemy as a a fledgling science dealing with matter and confused with projections, this approach sees it as a conscious system engaged in by centuries of adepts who passed their knowledge on to one another. From this point of view any assumption that links alchemy with the unconscious and its projections is totally off the mark. Instead it is a divine, spiritually illuminated science. Titus Burkhardt's book *Alchemy* (1967) is an excellent example of this attitude. Many occultists also take this point of view, but some are far more aware of the importance of the psychological approach than is Burkhardt, who can be quite intense in his opposition to any analysis based upon projection. The important work of Adam McLean is in this more reasonable category. We are indebted to him for his translations of alchemical works, and his fine commentaries (see the bibliography). There are many other contributions along this spectrum. Needless to say, these widely different approaches are often in great conflict, even creating an atmosphere of strife. Jung's work can be said to occupy a middle ground on this spectrum. He is well aware of the genuine illumination involved in the work of some alchemists, but also of the nearly random degree of projection in the work of others. He is aware of the fact that a developmental process is at work, but the sense of self (the *lapis*) aimed for far transcends the notion of self generally found among developmental theorists of various psychological schools of thought. I believe that his work is a remarkable testimony to the best of modern science. It shows a concern for what is observable by any capable and careful person, certainly in a non-idiosyncratic manner, but also for the wisdom of the imagination and the unfathomable depths of the psyche.

The Greeks, under Alexander the Great (356–323 BC), routed the Persians, conquered much of the ancient world, and occupied Egypt, where Alexandria, named after the great conqueror, was founded. It was there that much of the scientific basis of alchemy began to develop, a synthesis of the wisdom of Greek and Stoic thought as these combined with Egyptian technology in metallurgy, dyeing fabrics and perfume-making.

Alchemical thinking reflects and reminds one of the symbolism of the purpose and the oneness of process. An ancient craftsman from these times, attempting to dye a piece of cloth, would by no means be simply performing a technological act. He would be psychically involved with the object, which was not viewed as merely inanimate, for his spirit gave it life, and both of them would be part of a greater psycho-physical unity. The dye he applied would have to join with the fabric, which reminds us of the Axiom of Ostanes, in which 'A nature is delighted by another nature'. This was conceived as a union. But then this union state would have to overcome all the fabric's resistance to holding the dye, and the dye's tendency to lose color. To accomplish this, one would require another union and a new nature for the cloth: 'A nature conquers another nature.' And then one would require that the dyed fabric be stable over time through another union in which 'A nature dominates another nature.' Throughout, the craftsman's art would be dependent upon his state of mind and spiritual awareness. His own spirit was put into his work along with the dye itself. And one might well imagine the similar processes that attended perfume-making and its renowned secrecy. Was a perfume in those times ever reproduced exactly, or would it not also be dependent upon the *kairos*, the particular time in which it was prepared, and also upon the state of mind as well as the art of the maker?

By the first century AD, as Lindsay tells us, alchemical ideas in a limited scope were beginning to be widely known in the ancient world of the Near East. By the third century they were at their phase of most powerful expansion, and interconnected with a large number of kindred developments in the religious and philosophic spheres (Lindsay, 1970, p. 67). Prior to this, alchemical practices were often a secret affair, hidden away out of a fear of persecution rooted in charges of counterfeiting gold and precious metals.

The exoteric, or what may be called the extraverted side of the alchemical art, was largely informed by established Greek thought, which was essentially Aristotelian at this time. As the scholar of the exoteric alchemical tradition E. J. Holmyard tells us, the world, according to Aristotle, was comprised of a prime matter that only had a potential existence. To be actually manifest it had to be impressed by 'form'. This meant not only shape, but something that gave a body its specific properties. In the Aristotelian cosmology form gave rise to the 'four elements', fire, air, water and earth. Each of the elements is further characterized by the 'quality' of being fluid (or moist), dry, hot or cold; each element has two of these qualities. Hot and cold, and fluid and dry are contraries and cannot be coupled. The main thrust of the theory, to which the reader is referred to Holmyard for an in-depth presentation, is that any substance is composed of each and every 'element'; the difference between one substance and another depends upon the proportions in which the elements are present. And since each element, as the theory goes, can be transformed into another, any substance can be transformed into any other kind by changing the proportion of the elements in it. For example, in the Aristotelian theory the element fire is hot and dry, and the element water is cold and fluid. If one could combine them in a way that resulted in the dry and cold qualities leaving, one would have an element that was hot and fluid, the attributes the theory assigns to the element air. In such a way the form of things changes. In the same way one should, by being able to alter the qualities and thus the form of things, be able to transform any substance into another. 'If lead and gold both consist of fire, air, water, and earth, why may not the dull and common metal have the proportions of the elements adjusted to those of the shining, precious one?' (Holmyard, 1990, p. 23) The alchemical search for the right form of the 'prime matter' to work on – which, incidentally, was one of Newton's concerns – and the alchemist's relentless and often futile but sometimes successful laboratory efforts, informed as best they could be by divine revelation and moments of grace, make up much of the exoteric tale of alchemy.

Along with this theory of the four elements, a more introverted or esoteric basis for alchemy is found in related ideas from Greek thought and, as Lindsay tells us, was laid between the seventh and fourth centuries BC. These are: (1) the idea of a unitary process in nature, of some *ultimate substance* out of which all things are built up; (2) the idea of a *conflict of opposites* which are held together by the overriding unity, as the force driving the universe onwards; (3) the idea of a *definite structure* in the ultimate components of matter, whether this structure is expressed by varying aggregates of atoms (*atomon*, indivisible unit) or by the combination of a set of basic geometrical forms at the atomic level (Lindsay, 1970, p. 4). To this was added the Stoic position that the psyche was material, that there was a mutual penetration of soul and body, of *physis* and the world of plants, of *hexis* and the world of inorganic matter. Stoic physics consistently saw all the more solid or specific elements as permeated and held together in the infinite network of pneumatic tensions (ibid., pp. 22–3).

It is striking to note that in Jung's view of the psyche we meet the same propositions. These are: (1) the idea of a unitary process – the self – which operates by creating equilibrium through manifesting compensatory images; (2) the idea of a conflict of opposites held together by this unitary and compensatory process; (3) the idea of the archetypes, which provide an underlying structure for the psyche's components; and (4) the belief that through projection and the imagination – akin to the Stoic *pneuma* – psyches could connect to and affect one another. Furthermore, Jung's approach is identical to alchemical science in the sense of connecting two orders of reality, the 'metals' or 'chemicals' in their 'ordinary' and 'philosophical' forms. This point of view is found in Jung from the beginning of his scientific work on the complex in which an archetypal core organizes numerous associations from life's personal experiences. But in the following quotation from his *Mysterium coniunctionis* the alchemical point of view and Jung's come out especially clearly:

> The causalism that underlies our scientific view of the world breaks everything down into individual processes which it punctiliously tries to isolate from all other parallel processes. This tendency is absolutely necessary if we are to gain reliable knowledge of the world. . . . Everything

that happens, however, happens in the same 'one world' and is a part of it. For this reason events must possess an *a-priori* aspect of unity.

(Jung, 1963, para. 662)

The essence of Jung's approach to psychotherapy is contained in this quotation. It posits the necessity of both understanding a person's process in terms of causal interactions, whether they stem from childhood or present situations, and linking these processes to their a priori aspect of unity. This is precisely the function of the alchemical *coniunctio*: it resides in a 'third' or 'in-between' space of relations, akin to the alchemical *pneuma*, which links the unitary and discrete, separable, realms.

It was the study of alchemical symbolism, a labor of love for over forty-five years, that continually refreshed Jung and expanded his own individuation quest and development of his psychological system. Like the alchemical *vas hermeticum* and its contents, these two aspects of Jung's life were one.

WHY SHOULD WE STUDY JUNG'S WORK ON ALCHEMICAL SYMBOLISM?

Alchemical symbolism provided Jung with his basic idea of the individuation process and the associated awareness that there was a *process* in the unconscious, indeed one that had a *goal* beyond discharging tension and hiding pain. This process created new structures from old ones, with the self, the alchemical *lapis*, being the ultimate creation.

But if alchemy provided Jung with material which somehow fitted his 'personal equation' and the visions that shaped his life, what do we gain by investigating his alchemical studies? One might wonder if it would not be sufficient to gather up and examine the concepts (archetypes, individuation, transcendent function, causality, finality, complexes, symbols, imagination, opposites, *anima*, *animus*, shadow, self) that alchemy mirrored and deepened for him. There has to be some justification for a work that asks the reader to consider Jung on alchemy, and especially when that reading includes often abtruse quotations from alchemists.

A significant justification for a book quoting from Jung's research into alchemical symbolism is that one cannot rely solely on Jung's conceptual apparatus to truly understand his thought. His conceptual apparatus is his attempt to contain scientifically his investigations into the life of the psyche. Consulting Jung's alchemical works is a way of coming closer to the spirit of his approach to the unconscious, closer than his conceptual apparatus allows. For the psyche, as Jung would be the first to insist, cannot ever be adequately described in a scientific way. The concepts are intended to guide, to aid one on the path, but they can also retard one's investigation. Theory, as Jung was fond of saying, is the very devil. For example, Jung called the process which provides the link between conscious and unconscious 'the transcendent function'. He held that it was developed through the process he called 'active imagination', whereby one consciously enters a dialogue with unconscious images. This is an accessible technique for working with the unconscious through the use of material supplied by dreams or fantasies. But what a world of depth and richness we enter when we engage the alchemical referent to this process, the *coniunctio*. There we see the many different forms of linking that can exist between conscious and unconscious, and between people. These forms create an entire array that spans possibilities from states of total fusion that obscure difference, to those that tend toward fusion but then rhythmically separate, to states that destroy all forms of linking. And any of these states can include the vexing role of desire: does it destroy union or enhance it? The multiple forms of union and disunion combine in forging the bridging, transcendent function, with the goal that it will endure throughout emotional, physical and environmental stress. As another example, Jung describes the contrasexual components of the psyche, *anima* and *animus*, in many descriptive and penetrating passages. Yet when we see these two 'lights' in their alchemical guise, as the symbols *sol* and *luna*, and their many interacting transformations, then *anima* and *animus* take on far richer, and also less culture-specific, forms. And in the same spirit his concept of the shadow can be looked at: for Jung its personal variation is the repressed, inferior side of the ego, and its transpersonal form is the dark side of the self and collective evil. In alchemy this concept corresponds to the *nigredo*, which includes not only the imagery of the shadow and the chthonic side of life, but also the shadow's mysterious purpose in dissolving old structures so that new ones can be created. And when we reflect upon the self through the alchemical symbolism of the *lapis* and the many transformations it undergoes, especially as it changes to include the body and the 'lower depths' of instinctual processes, the self is returned to its matrix of mystery, against which conceptual descriptions quickly pale.

In his studies of alchemical symbolism we find Jung's most insightful and valuable reflections on the body. In distinction to most of his other works, Jung's alchemical studies often present the self as having an embodied, material aspect. While Jung often takes references to the body in alchemical texts to mean the realization of consciousness in behavior or daily life, he also follows another path of inquiry, that of the body and its transformations, and also that of the mental–spiritual self's embodiment. In alchemy the *lapis* has a 'spiritual' and a 'material' aspect. It can 'raise and lower' matter, as part of the transformation of the relation between mind and body (as is its role in the Axiom of Ostanes). As Jung tells us, just what the alchemists mean by 'matter' is not always clear, but it often includes the body, albeit in ways that recognize a subtlety in conception of body that our culture has all but lost sight of. When the alchemist Paracelsus says 'destroy the bodies', he is probably referring to an experience of body in which character armour is transformed, but also to a transformation of more subtle features that would lead to the body being experienced as a source of information and consciousness. G. R. S. Mead believed that alchemy was primarily about dealing with transformations of a 'subtle embodiment of the mind' (1919, pp. 1 and 14), also called the 'subtle body'. And Jung says 'the ultimate aim of alchemy was [to] produce a *corpus subtile*, a transfigured and resurrected body, i.e. a body that was at the same time spirit' (1953, para. 511).

We find this *corpus subtile* in an untransformed and dissociated form in split-off complexes. I think it is reasonable to suggest that Jung's notion of the complex as a feeling-toned cluster of associations that has an archetypal core also has a body aspect. Jung recognized that every time a complex is constellated there are associated physiological responses such as changes in galvanic skin resistance, blood pressure, etc. This was the basis for the polygraph. But aside from these representations of the body, one can note a more subtle form. It is possible to say that *every complex has a body*. That is, when one's mind is affected by a complex (so that concentration is disturbed and one's responses to a situation become, to one degree or another, maladaptive), so too one's sense of body changes. One's body feels different from its accustomed, normal state; for example, it feels more rigid, less friendly, ugly, despised, dangerous or non-existent. One's body-image changes just as one's mental self-image changes. In its unintegrated state the mental and physical aspect of the complex is split in the sense that ego-consciousness experiences them as conflicting opposites. To connect to, or be engulfed in, one opposite is to exclude awareness of the other. Or else the two realms, mind and body, are mixed together and one cannot distinguish one's ideas from affective, turbulent states of the body. In an alchemical treatise this mixture is equated with the alchemical chaos with which the *opus* begins (Waite, 1973, vol. 2, pp. 167–8). Differentiating this chaos into a mental and bodily component, 'making two from one', is the initial step the alchemist must accomplish.

When it comes to 'the self', it is a term used so widely in other schools of thought, each with their own formulation, that it is important to emphasize that Jung connects it to the depths of the collective unconscious and the *numinosum* in ways that other approaches usually do not embrace. He says:

> The unconscious does indeed put forth a bewildering profusion of semblances for that obscure thing we call . . . 'self'. It almost seems as if we were to go on dreaming in the unconscious the age-old dream of alchemy, and to continue to pile new synonyms on top of old, only to know as much or as little about it in the end as the ancients themselves. . . . It is easy enough to say 'self', but exactly what have we said? That remains shrouded in 'metaphysical' darkness. . . . True, [the self] is a concept that grows steadily clearer with experience – our dreams show – without, however, losing anything of its transcendence. Since we cannot possibly know the boundaries of something unknown to us, it follows that we are not in a position to set any bounds to the self. . . . The empirical manifestations of unconscious contents bear all the marks of something illimitable, some-

thing not determined by space and time. This quality is numinous and therefore alarming, above all to a cautious mind that knows the value of precisely limited concepts. . . .

All that can be said about the symbolism [of the self] is that it portrays an autonomous psychic fact, characterized by a phenomenology which is always repeating itself and is everywhere the same. It seems to be a sort of atomic nucleus about whose innermost structure and ultimate meaning we know nothing.

(Jung, 1953, paras 247–9)

Alchemical literature is a mine of symbolism of the self originating in the depths of the collective unconscious, so that its imagery is significantly unaffected by cultural biases.

This relative independence of symbolic forms from the imagery of the prevailing culture was an important reason for which Jung investigated alchemical symbolism. But perhaps, as Jung says, a more pressing reason was that

it is only possible to come to a right understanding and appreciation of a contemporary psychological problem when we can reach a point outside our own time from which to observe it. This point can only be some past epoch that was concerned with the same problems, although under different conditions and in other forms.

(Jung, 1954, p. 166)

There are also psychotherapeutic applications to be gained from exploring the seemingly bizarre imagery of alchemy. This brings us face to face with an aspect of Jungian thought which truly sets it apart from all other psycho-therapeutic endeavors; for an individual is capable of experiencing imagery that has no relationship to his or her previous experience. Such encounters with the unconscious are often explained away as distorted recollections of previous experience, and the strangeness of any image can often be seen as a result of the workings of ambivalence and unconscious defense mechanisms. Or imagery that it is totally inexplicable to the observer can be seen to be, if not actually a bizarre product of psychotic process, denuded of meaning. But while both of these possibilities are clinically important, a knowledge of the symbolism and attitudes of past eras, especially alchemy, can often reveal the hidden meaning in what might otherwise be seen as a secret sector of madness or a highly disguised image of an infantile trauma. Thus Jung says:

What the doctor can hear, when he listens attentively, of fantasies, dreams, and intimate experiences is not mentioned in the Encyclopedia Britannica or in textbooks and scientific journals. These secrets are jealously guarded, anxiously concealed, and greatly feared and esteemed. They are private possessions, never divulged and talked about, because they are feared as ridiculous and revered as revelations. They are numinous, a doubtful treasure, perhaps comical, perhaps miraculous, at all events a painfully vulnerable spot, yet presiding over the crossroads of one's individual life. They are officially and by general consent just as unknown and despised as the old parchments with their indecipherable and anaesthetic hieroglyphics, evidence of old obscurantisms and foolishness. We are ignorant of their contents, and we are equally ignorant of what is going on in the deeper layers of our unconscious, because 'those who know do not talk, those who talk do not know' (*Tao-te-ching*, ch. 56). As inner experiences of this kind increase, the social nexus between human beings decreases. The individual becomes isolated for no apparent reason. Finally this becomes unbearable and he has to confide in someone. Much will then depend on whether he is properly understood or not. It would be fatal if he were to be misinterpreted. Fortunately, such people are instinctively careful and as a rule do not talk more than necessary. . . .

. . . historical comparison is not a mere learned hobby but very practical and useful. It opens the door to life and humanity again, which had seemed inexorably closed. It is of no ultimate advantage to deny or reason away or ridicule such seemingly abnormal or out-of-the-way experiences. . . . One should be aware of the high esteem which in past centuries was felt for such experiences, because it explains the extraordinary importance that we moderns are forced to attribute to them in spite of ourselves.

(Jung, 1991, paras 1267–9)

Jung usually approaches the psyche as an archaeologist, sifting through and comparing its symbolism to previous periods of thought. But his work is always oriented towards clinical practice, and the spirit of this work is extremely helpful in everyday work. Consider the following brief example from my own practice.

A man, a scientist in his fifties, with great trepidation and after a year of establishing my reliability, began a session by telling me that he really felt there was no point to human relationships. Immediately my inner 'clinical register' sprang up and, as I wrestled with an intense field of dissociation in which it was all but impossible to focus upon what he was saying, notions of withdrawal, schizoid phenomena and psychotic process presented themselves to me. When he further described how a day of his own creative work as a physicist would often lead to a remarkable smell in the room, a perfume, I felt cautious, for still I could barely concentrate. With effort, I managed to become more focussed as he told more about his experiences. Little by little I began to understand that he was revealing an invaluably deep secret. The perfume-like smell was very real for him and, like the 'sweet smell of the Holy Ghost', brought him into a numinous realm. He knew it was very dangerous to share this. When, however, he saw that I understood, his dissociation vanished, and it became clear that we were not dealing with anything like psychotic process. Instead, this man was working through a terrible existential dilemma. His very early experiences were filled with fraudulent relatedness and that left him with a keen vulnerability to 'double-bind messages', messages in which what a person says and the feeling he communicates give contradictory messages. Many individuals who grow up in families where such double-bind messages also accompany physical or emotional abuse have this extreme sensitivity to human interaction. Whenever he had attempted non-superficial communication with anybody else in his life, his sensitivity to anything non-authentic in the other kept him from being able to divulge deeper, more delicate experiences. This was the first time he had ever risked revealing his extraordinary encounters with the perfume-like spirit which had been sustaining him throughout his entire life. My Jungian training in respect for the *numinosum* helped establish the atmosphere which could receive this.

Jung's work, and especially his alchemical researches, embodies an attitude of respect for the psyche's mystery that is enormously helpful in dealing with clinical material. But its scope does not end there. Alchemy is an old science, but also a new science that is only now beginning to unfold. It reflects upon the mystery of *relations* between things, and upon one's relationship to the cosmos. It has only been a relatively short time since this kind of awareness has re-emerged. Up to the last few decades there were few voices of concern for the health of our planet, and the state of the environment. Alchemical thinking embraces humankind in relation to the macrocosm.

To summarize, the main reasons for studying Jung's researches into alchemical symbolism are:

1 the relative independence of its alchemy imagery from cultural bias;
2 the historical and psychotherapeutic vantage-points that alchemy provides;
3 the way in which alchemy offers elaboration and augmentation of Jung's thought.

Many other instances of ways that alchemy elaborates his conceptual formulations, besides transcendent function, *anima/animus*, self and shadow noted before, could be added. These include Jung's alchemical works that elaborate upon the archetypes and the creation of new forms, the importance of finality in understanding psychic processes, the mystery of the body, the imagination, and the ego and its relationship to the self. But, most important, Jung's alchemical studies offer us an *attitude* towards psychic transformation in greater scope and depth than any of his other works offer. Here we learn of the mystery of chaos and evil; of the ways in which processes of disorder couple with ordering ones; and how the creation of order can lead to the darkest night.

As I see it, there are two main criticisms that have been leveled at Jung's alchemical studies. The first concerns what relevance texts from nearly one thousand or more years ago – especially medieval alchemy – may have for a modern person, and in particular for psychotherapy today. I have already addressed this concern, noting the usefulness of Jung's method of critically reflecting upon the contents and methods of a prior era. But we should note that Jung's method, which is to regard these texts as products of the unconscious that are created through projection, is an hypothesis that can certainly be challenged. A great deal of conscious care and mystico-philosophical reflection went into the work of the better alchemists, just as considerable conscious effort goes into a literary creation. But still, there is no doubt that a great deal of unreflective projection was also present, and Jung's thesis about alchemy being free of cultural overlays is a largely workable hypothesis.

Another criticism one encounters is that alchemy was developed within a patriarchal structure. Why, then – especially since this approach, the argument goes, sees the world through the eyes of a man and not of a woman, and certainly not a contemporary woman with a critical mind – should alchemy interest us? In other words, why should we see it as anything like a guide, precisely the role it played for Jung?

It is true that by and large alchemy was developed by men. There were female alchemists, notably two by the names of Maria Prophetissa and Kleopatra in the third century, and then there are male–female pairs of workers in the sixteenth and seventeenth centuries. But by and large men worked out the various systems. Does this mean that alchemy has little relevance today? I don't think so, because the basic structures of alchemical thought, which largely revolve around the issue of the union and separation of opposing states of mind or unconscious qualities, are far more deeply rooted in the collective unconscious than they are informed by issues of gender. But an important question, it seems to me, is whether the way medieval alchemy thought about archetypes such as the *coniunctio* is workable and useful, and whether the patriarchal emphasis can, when appropriate, be filtered out. Jung skirted this issue when he claimed that alchemy primarily applied to masculine psychology. But how can union states, especially ones whose archetypal form goes back to the religion of the Great Goddess, be reserved for male psychology? The *coniunctio* is an archetypal pattern that is extremely pertinent for both men and women. Jung found it to be the foundation of the transference. But what we can question is whether men and women will approach it in the same way. For women (unless they have been victimized by emotional or sexual abuse) often appear to be less threatened by union states than do men. Perhaps this is because a man is inherently different and 'other' from his mother from the very first.

To consider this a bit further. When we look at the archetypal imagery of the *Rosarium philosophorum*, which is the most influential of the alchemical texts, we find that after a union state there inevitably follows a state of death, the *nigredo*. Is this a male construction? Does there have to be a death-like experience of loss and despair, or is this a result of a man's greater need to separate from the union state rather than stay with it more fully as a woman might be better able to do? If this need to leave a union state more quickly were dominant in the construction of alchemical ideas about union, then the alchemical imagery Jung uses would be highly suspect and not useful today. But this, in my experience, is hardly the case. Women will also suffer a *nigredo* after the *coniunctio*, but my experience is that they will often have a greater natural capacity than a man to stay with the resulting sense of loss and despair. As a consequence these affects can be more integrated, with the result that the union experience can become internalized as a structure that links conscious and unconscious through a field of desire. In my work supervising male analysts I have, on numerous occasions, discovered that a *coniunctio* experience had occurred with a female patient, and the analyst then denied the emotions of despair and grief that followed, with the result that the analysis either collapsed or could only be salvaged when it was recognized that the woman was carrying the analyst's share of the feelings as well as her own. It seems to me that further research in this area will be especially fruitful. But the underlying archetypal schemata, laid out in alchemical imagery, are valid and useful for helping us to chart our way in a sea of possibilities in which our subjectivity can drown us rather than enhance our uniqueness.

Thus alchemy today has a great significance for both men and women. A man can not only learn to allow a woman's different experience of the archetypes, but his individuation can be furthered in the process. The same is true for a woman experiencing a man's relationship to the archetypes such as the *coniunctio*. To allow *difference* is a frightening thing. A woman is 'Other' to a man, and a man 'Other' to a woman. Alchemical approaches to nature and human interaction can be a vehicle for allowing the 'Other' to exist, with all its terror; and at the same time alchemical attitudes, especially their respect for 'third areas' that are beyond gender, helps us to recognize common structures that bind us together.

ALCHEMY IN JUNG'S LIFE

The study of alchemy was profoundly important for Jung. The significance of his investigations of this arcane, two-thousand-year-old body of literature goes back to that fateful time in Jung's life when, in 1913, he parted ways with Freud. He knew he was plunging into the unknown: 'Beyond Freud, after all, I knew nothing; but I had taken the step into darkness' (Jung, 1973, p. 199). The break with Freud was a trauma. It caused Jung to have to deal with intense abandonment issues, which – because he delved so deeply into the psyche – led even into psychotic areas. The ensuing four years, 1913–17, were filled with emotional turbulence. Jung was faced with the possibility of being mad, for the states of mind he experienced were unfathomable and overwhelming. Yet it was from this time in his life that the next forty-five years of his scientific work were cast. 'It all began then; the later details are only supplements and clarifications of the material that burst forth from the unconscious, and at first swamped me. It was the *prima materia* for a lifetime's work' (ibid.). It was alchemy that only later provided some illumination into these experiences of the unconscious.

Jung knew nothing of alchemy during those years immediately after the break with Freud. In 1917 he had read Herbert Silberer's *Problems of Mysticism and its Symbolism*, but even though he valued Silberer's work and communicated with him, he still 'regarded alchemy as something off the beaten track and rather silly' (Jung, 1973, p. 204). As with all of his creative pursuits, Jung had a dream which preceded his involvement in alchemy. At the end of that dream (which occurred in 1926, and which he records in its entirety in his autobiography) he finds himself entering a courtyard when the doors slam shut behind him and a voice says: 'Now we are caught in the seventeenth century.' Jung noted that upon awakening he felt resigned to being 'caught for years', but then had the thought, 'Someday, years from now, I shall get out again' (ibid., p. 203).

Jung tells us that it was only much later that he realized that the seventeenth century referred to alchemy. This understanding followed a great deal of study of 'ponderous tomes on the history of the world, of religion, and of philosophy' (ibid., p. 203). He says he had forgotten what Silberer had previously written on the topic, and also that the material Silberer used was from late alchemy and very difficult to decipher. For Jung, 'Light on the nature of alchemy' came only after reading *The Secret of the Golden Flower*, 'that specimen of Chinese alchemy which Richard Wilhelm sent me in 1928' (ibid., p. 204). After reading this Taoist treatise on alchemy Jung commissioned a bookseller to find any alchemical books for him, and he soon received the *Artis auriferae volumina duo* (1593), a collection of classic Latin treatises on alchemy.

> I let this book lie almost untouched for nearly two years. Occasionally I would look at the pictures, and each time I would think, 'Good Lord, what nonsense! This stuff is impossible to understand . . .' Finally, I realized that the alchemists were talking in symbols – those old acquaintances of mine. 'Why this is fantastic', I thought. 'I simply must learn to decipher all this.' By now I was completely fascinated, and buried myself in the texts as often as I had time. One night, while I was studying them, I suddenly recalled the dream that I was caught in the seventeenth century. At last I grasped its meaning. 'So that's it! Now I am condemned to study alchemy from the very beginning.'
>
> (ibid., pp. 204–5)

Jung studied these texts for the next decade. This was no mean task as it meant refining his knowledge of Greek and Latin, and especially of their complicated medieval forms. He managed to decipher these texts by carefully comparing the manner in which different authors used phrases containing obscure words such as *lapis*, *prima materia*, *Mercurius*, etc. In the process he saw that 'analytical psychology coincided in a most curious way with alchemy' (ibid., p. 205):

> When I poured over these old texts everything fell into place: the fantasy-images, the empirical material I had gathered from my practice, and the

conclusions I had drawn from it. I now began to understand what these psychic contents meant when seen in historical perspective. . . . The primordial images and the nature of the archetype took a central place in my research, and it became clear to me that without history there can be no psychology, and certainly no psychology of the unconscious . . . as soon as we wish to explain a neurosis we require an anamnesis which [goes beyond personal history and] reaches deeper than the knowledge of consciousness.

(ibid., pp. 205–6)

The importance of alchemy to Jung is further indicated by his comments that alchemy showed him how the unconscious is a *process*, and that through studying alchemical symbolism he arrived at the central concept of his life's work, *the process of individuation* (ibid., p. 209). Further, he tells us that through Paracelsus

I was finally led to discuss the nature of alchemy in relation to religion and psychology. . . . This I did in *Psychology and Alchemy* (1944). Thus I had at last reached the ground which underlay my own experiences of the years 1913–1917; for the process through which I had passed at that time corresponded to the process of alchemical transformation as discussed in that book.

(ibid., p. 209)

Jung's alchemical investigations reached their apotheosis in 1955 with the completion of *Mysterium coniunctionis*, his *magnum opus*. There, he tells us, he again took up the problem of the transference, having previously dealt with it in 1946 in his 'Psychology of the Transference' (see Jung, 1954). The *Rosarium philosophorum* provided him with an 'Ariadne thread through the complexities of the transference' (Jung, 1954, p. 165). *Mysterium coniunctionis*, however, had a larger intent; primarily it concerned his

original intention of representing the whole range of alchemy as a kind of psychology of alchemy, or as an alchemical basis for depth psychology. In *Mysterium Coniunctionis* my psychology was at last given its place in reality and established upon its historical foundations. Thus my task was finished, my work done, and now it can stand.

(Jung, 1973, p. 221)

Alchemy's primacy in Jung's life evolved from its answering his personal quest for understanding. It illuminated his own personality for him, and it also served his professional desire for gathering an historical context and symbolic amplification for the individuation process. In a way, it even functioned as a psychological container for the experiences of the years after his break with Freud, in which the unconscious was often dangerous and emotionally flooding. Beyond this, in his explorations of alchemy we find

Jung discussing areas of personality that he was often reticent to advance as his own thoughts. Psychological insights and propositions which many of his contemporaries found unscientific or too outrageous to accept, Jung could slip in while discussing the odd qualities of an alchemical text. This freed him up to speak on difficult topics as well: the power of projections and the imagination, and the complexities of the body and sexuality, are often commented upon in his alchemical studies.

Jung's exploration of alchemical symbolism is both an invaluable resource to anyone interested in this remarkable body of thought, and also the best representation we have of his own *opus*, in which one finds his most mature thoughts about psychotherapy. While alchemical imagery and texts are often obscure and bizarre, Jung found within this body of thought (which represents experiment and reflection among the best minds of centuries that cover two thousand years, beginning in the fourth century BC), a remarkable mine of information for the process of healing and the nature of the archetypes that was, for him, at the center of his efforts as a psychotherapist. But therapeutics was not necessarily always his main concern.

As he wrote in *Mysterium coniunctionis*:

> Investigation of alchemical symbolism, like a preoccupation with myth-ology, does not lead one away from life any more than a study of comparative anatomy leads away from the anatomy of the living man. On the contrary, alchemy affords us a veritable treasure house of symbols, knowledge of which is extremely helpful for an understanding of neurotic and psychotic processes. This, in turn, allows us to apply the psychology of the unconscious to those regions in the history of the human mind which are concerned with symbolism. *It is just here that questions arise whose urgency and vital intensity are even greater than the question of thera-peutic application.* Here there are many prejudices that still have to be overcome. Just as it is thought, for instance, that Mexican myths cannot possibly have anything to do with similar ideas found in Europe, so it is held to be a fantastic assumption that an uneducated modern man should dream of classical myth-motifs which are known only to a specialist. People still think that relationships like this are far-fetched and therefore improbable. But they forget that the structure and function of the bodily organs are everywhere more or less the same, including those of the brain. And as the psyche is to a large extent dependent upon this organ, presumably it will – at least in principle – everywhere produce the same forms. In order to see this, however, one has to abandon the widespread prejudice that the psyche is identical with consciousness.
>
> (Jung, 1954, pp. xviii–xix; italics added)

In a sense, this attitude, which looks to the psyche's creative potential rather than primarily embracing personal issues of human suffering, is a truly healing one. It represents an Eros for the psyche rather than the human ego. While Jung surely had compassion for the individual, he knew that a respect for the soul – the inner life that has its own autonomy to produce images – was essential to healing humankind's dissociation from the sacred realms of body and spirit.

THE *PRIMA MATERIA*

The alchemical process began with a much-prized and often obscure basic substance. Jung described this *prima materia* in a number of his works on alchemical symbolism. It is important to recognize that various modern writers on alchemy describe the mysterious starting-point in differing ways. And if one reads the alchemists themselves one will not find Jung's description that I shall soon quote. Indeed, what he says is his own reading of alchemy, and as such it is his own subjective statement. Some of its elements can be found amidst alchemical writings, but Jung's extraction is a remarkable understanding of the *prima materia*. It is fruitful to retain the view that he holds, which can be lost sight of when immersed in the hundreds of pages of commentary on alchemy that he wrote over some forty-five years. For the ways one actually meets the *prima materia* in alchemy are so varied that we constantly read of its nature as being hidden, existing everywhere, despised, recognizable only by those who have been illuminated, poisonous, healing, and hundreds of other contradictory definitions. But in *Psychology and Alchemy* he pinpoints the key nature of the *prima materia* in a remarkably succinct manner:

> Alchemy is rather like an undercurrent to the Christianity that ruled on the surface. It is to this surface as the dream is to consciousness, and just as the dream compensates the conflicts of the conscious mind, so alchemy endeavors to fill in the gaps left open by the Christian tension of opposites. [The fundamental idea] of alchemy points back to the . . . primordial matriarchal world which [was] overthrown by the masculine world of the father. This historical shift in the world's consciousness towards the masculine is compensated first by the chthonic femininity of the unconscious. In certain pre-Christian religions the differentiation of the masculine principle had taken the form of the father–son specification, a change which was to be of the utmost importance for Christianity. Were the unconscious merely complementary, this shift of consciousness would have been accompanied by the production of a mother and daughter, for which the necessary material lay ready to hand in the myth of Demeter and Persephone. But, as alchemy shows, the unconscious chose rather the Cybelle–Attis type in the form of the *prima materia* and the *filius macrocosmi*, thus proving that it is not complementary but compensatory. This goes to show that the unconscious does not simply act *contrary* to the conscious mind but *modifies* it more in the manner of an opponent or partner. The son type . . . calls up another son. . . . The mother, who was anterior to the world of the father, accommodates herself to the masculine principle and, with the aid of the human spirit (alchemy or 'the philosophy'), produces a son – not the

antithesis of Christ but rather his chthonic counterpart, not a divine man but a fabulous being conforming to the nature of the primordial mother. And just as the redemption of man the microcosm is the task of the 'upper' son, so the 'lower' son has the function of a *salvator macrocosmi*.

(Jung, 1953, para. 26)

Although [this 'lower son'] is decidedly hermaphroditic he has a masculine name – a sign that the chthonic underworld, having been rejected by the spirit and identified with evil, has a tendency to compromise. There is no mistaking the fact that he is a concession to the spiritual and masculine principle, even though he carries in himself the weight of the earth and the whole fabulous nature of primordial animality.

(ibid., para. 29)

This answer of the mother-world shows that the gulf between it and the father-world is not unbridgeable, seeing that the unconscious holds the seed of the unity of both.

(ibid., para. 30)

The extraordinary breadth of vision which allowed Jung to grasp the identity of dream on the personal, and alchemy on the transpersonal, level is truly awesome. As M.-L. von Franz, Jung's collaborator and expert on alchemy has noted, this is a description of the relationship between the two worlds of alchemy and Christianity 'that cannot be bettered' (Franz, 1975, p. 216). Jung's understanding of the unconscious as a teleological entity, perpetually seeking to balance and harmonize the unfolding of incarnated life, is truly moving, if not reassuring. And if one accepts Jung's proposition that alchemy holds the solution through compensation to the patriarchal suppression of the feminine, the importance of alchemy for our troubled world becomes obvious, even pressing.

Whatever the path may now be to a new relationship towards the feminine and between the sexes, the attitude of consciousness towards this goal is one that can greatly benefit from the alchemical image of the *filius philosophorum*, the 'philosopher's son', meaning the spirit born out of the alchemical art. In other words, what was once an unconscious compensation can and indeed must now become a conscious attitude. Then, the greater depth of the feminine can be approached, as it cannot be with a patriarchal or solely Apollonian attitude. Just as the ancient myth of Dionysus shows that this god, and perhaps this god alone, can co-exist with the Great Goddess Cybelle–Rhea, and survive amidst persecutory affects without being killed or reduced to a consort, so too a new kind of consciousness, yet to be achieved but envisioned by alchemy, is a necessary component of a future order.

The new consciousness, symbolized by the *filius philosophorum*, has, in its most penetrating aspect, forms which Jung associates with 'the fiery, chthonic Mercurius [which unites the opposites] from *below*, i.e. in the water which is the counterpart of the spirit' (Jung, 1954, para. 455). This chthonic spirit, which lives in the depths of the body and matter, was cast aside by the 'upper spirit' of centuries of patriarchal rule, but it can no longer be denied. We, perhaps, see the results of such repression emerging in extremely negative forms nowadays in the terribly widespread accounts of incest abuse. The alchemist knew of the dangers of engaging this 'older brother' of Christ (as the chthonic spirit of alchemy was sometimes called), but they also knew that the future of the soul, in both a micro- and a macrocosmic sense, demanded its integration. Rather than the *numinosum* being known through an ecstatic ascent to a heavenly Father in the *unio mystica*, now the same *numinosum* was to be encountered through the mystery of union, the *coniunctio*, which would have an object or partner that was both personal and divine.

Such chthonic depths (as well as those of ascent mysticism and its illuminations, which were also essential to alchemy) are ever-present in alchemy: they are omnipresent today in our daily lives. Consider the reflections of the French psychoanalyst Luce Irigaray in her book *Elemental Passions*:

> Man is divided between two transcendencies: his mother's and God's – whatever kind of God that may be. These two transcendencies are doubtless not unrelated but this is something he has forgotten. . . . His mother is transcendent to him because she is a different genre and she gives him birth. He is born of an other who is always Other-inappropriable. For centuries, at least in the so-called Western tradition, that transcendency has seldom been recognized as such.
>
> (Irigaray, 1992, p. 1)

Alchemy, however, is passionately involved with these 'two transcendencies'. They are the two domains known as solar and lunar, two forms of revelation and vision whose union was always sought after, leading to the creation of the *lapis* or the hermaphroditic *filius philosophorum*. But the union of the solar and lunar, the *coniunctio*, which was the focus of Jung's studies, remains shrouded in mystery. Perhaps we have not yet achieved the necessary consciousness to deal with such realms. But if we continue to fail in this regard, what will become of civilization, of the relation between the sexes, and what will become of the planet we live on?

Part of the process of embracing this new hermaphroditic consciousness involves understanding what is meant by 'the feminine'. This phrase needs defining, else it tends to become a 'thing' rather than a process, and thus can become a reification of something that is actually very fluid and subtle. An interesting formulation can be found in the French psychoanalyst Julia Kristeva's notion of forms of *jouissance*, which she discusses in *Black Sun*:

> Two forms of jouissance . . . seem possible for a woman. On the one hand there is phallic jouissance – competing or identifying with the partner's symbolic power. . . . On the other hand, there is an *other jouissance*

that fantasy imagines and carries out by aiming more deeply at psychic space, and the space of the body as well. That other jouissance requires that the melancholy object blocking the psychic and bodily interior literally be liquefied.

(Kristeva, 1989, pp. 78–9)

This description of two forms of *jouissance* is, as in Irigaray's notion of 'two transcendencies', an aspect of what the alchemist means by Sol and Luna. 'The feminine', or *luna*, refers to psychic space and the space of the body, and the workings of the imagination within it. Kristeva's description is also alchemical, for it describes the transformation of the *nigredo*, the 'melancholy object' that must be 'liquefied'. We often read in alchemy that everything must be reduced to water, to a primal chaos, that is prior to the imposed forms of historical life. In alchemical terms, Kristeva describes the emergence of Luna out of the captivity of the despair and depression of the *nigredo*.

It is characteristic of Jung's awareness of the psyche's multiple faces and its maze-like structure that his studies of the *prima materia* amplify it with many differing forms from alchemical texts. This can easily cause one to forget his central awareness of its compensatory relationship to thousands of years of Western culture, and its primary form in the son–lover mythologem.

The son–lover dynamic is found at the basis of Freud's conception of the Oedipus complex. But here a triangular relation exists, with the father representing the factor of conscience or the super-ego. It is a more specific and limited version of the son–lover mythologem, which is itself far more complex and primitive, and lacks the structural 'third' factor of the oedipal relation. The 'third' element can modify and protect against the passions of the son–lover mythologem.

An analogy from the Freudian drama of the Oedipus complex may help clarify why the *prima materia* can take so many different forms. A classical, Freudian analyst working with a patient places a high premium on working through the Oedipus complex and has done so in his or her own work and training. This corresponds to the end-product of the *opus*, the gold, some of which at least the alchemists insist one must have in order to begin the work of creating more: 'It takes gold to make gold.' The analyst's consciousness will discover the ways in which the Oedipus complex has either failed to form or failed to resolve in the patient. From this, he or she will be able to note the numerous so-called defense mechanisms that hide the memories linked to early forms of the complex. Any of these discovered memories or the defenses that hide them can be a starting-point for the work. In this way one can enter the path of the libido at numerous points as it twists and turns towards and away from the goal of creating and resolving the Oedipus complex. Any of these points can be the *prima materia*, for example, a process may focus upon earlier zonal fixations of a so-called oral or anal nature. By the same token, any of the defenses against experiencing one's incestuous urges, such as regression or repression or sadomasochistic dynamics, can be the *prima materia*. Even the unconscious link between analyst and analysand through which early childhood experiences are recreated, the transference, can be a starting-point. Therefore, the *prima materia*, as this simple example of the Oedipus complex shows, can take on many forms other than the explicit one of the family romance. The situation is far more complex when we turn to the alchemical *prima materia*, as seen in the Attis–Cybelle-type myth. For then many other features (as will be made clear when I discuss the myth), including madness or chaos, can be the *prima materia*.

The alchemists in their work combined material, practical experience with actual chemicals and substances to help them elucidate and clarify their abstract thinking, and vice versa. It is difficult for us, whose thinking has developed in ways radically separated from matter and the imagination, to put these two – abstraction and practical experience – together. Our minds resist the combination. But the alchemists believed that any substance had its own nature – we might say energy grade or pattern – and that this nature existed not only on the concrete, material plane but on the emotional, mental and spiritual planes as well. By tracking how the properties of the substances they worked with behaved on the physical plane, the alchemists could experience and imagine, as real events, the same interplay of energies on the other levels. Thus while the alchemist maneuvered the properties on the physical plane in our space/time world, he was also contacting and interacting with other dimensions characterized by timeless oneness. It is for this reason that the names and terms the alchemists use are not only actual chemicals but are, in their terms, 'philosophical' as well.

Alchemy's *prima materia* has many unexpected names, for example, sulphur which is not only an actual chemical but is 'philosophical', for us a symbol; what it represents cannot be conceptually exhausted. Jung's masterful analysis of sulphur shows us that it has two faces, that of God and that of the Devil. As such it has the power to be God at one extreme: one can be gripped by the positive *numinosum* and have a mystical experience. At the other extreme one can be dragged into the dregs of a demonic compulsion, acting out destructive impulses. This is but a passing example of why descriptions of the *prima materia*, here as symbolic of the mystery of compulsion, are so varied and can cause one to lose focus so easily. In a sense the alchemical sulphur is a component of the Attis–Cybelle myth, seen in various alchemical parables of the roving charms of sulphur in the garden of Venus. But one cannot reduce the *prima materia* to any one form, even to the Attis–Cybelle myth, although that is probably its central image. Rather, as in alchemical logic, each form is a face of a hologram, and as such each contains all other forms.

But certain authorities on alchemy, notably Johannes Fabricius, state that Jung never made clear just what the *prima materia* was, and Fabricius boldly states that it is nothing other than adolescent sexuality. But he has not read Jung carefully enough on this point. Adolescent sexuality, with its powerful aggressive and erotic currents, and its central problem of managing regression, is certainly part of the *prima materia*. But it is only an aspect, a face: for example, of the alchemical sulphur. Jung's researches threw out a far wider net, and it is not possible truly to understand alchemy if one requires the pinning-down of notions such as the *prima materia* to distinct things or processes. It is not alchemy, and it is not Jung's way.

Since Jung places such value on the relation of the son–lover and the Great Goddess as an aspect of the *prima materia*, especially upon one of the earliest forms of this myth in the tragic drama of Attis and Cybelle, we would do well to explore this myth in some detail.

THE ATTIS–CYBELLE MYTH

The myth of Attis and Cybelle is part of a thread running throughout Western culture, probably dating from the end of the Neolithic Age. It represents a state of mind and body that has never been adequately addressed. The alchemical approach is the most detailed and serious attempt in the last two thousand years to integrate the forces this mythologem presents.

Ovid's telling of the myth is in service of explaining the rite of castration of the priests of Cybelle. But it contains the main issue of the 'impossible passion' that never resolves. In Ovid's tale, Attis, at the outset, has attracted Cybelle to him by his vow of 'chaste passion' in service to the goddess. But upon falling in love with a nymph named Sagaris, Attis breaks his vow, and Cybelle takes vengeance, killing the nymph. This causes Attis to go mad. He flees to the top of Mount Dindymus, raving in hallucinatory terrors. He then turns upon himself in the most terrible way: 'He mangled, too, his body with a sharp stone.' And in the midst of his self-mutilation, he cries out as one whose guilt is overbearing: 'I have deserved it! With my blood I pay the penalty that is my due' (Ovid, *Fasti*, IV. 237–9).

It is curious to note that while psychoanalysis was for years guided by the vicissitudes of infantile sexuality and the various forms of 'perversion' that arose from failures in development, nowadays madness is a more important cornerstone (Green, 1975). Beyond this, it is worth mentioning that the dismemberment Attis suffers is part of the fragmentation and dissociation of psyche that Jung, departing from Freud, believed to have a greater significance for development and pathology than did repression. We see the role of dissociation and ways in which it is overcome discussed by Jung in his alchemical studies, often with reference to mythical figures that bear certain similarities to Attis, notably the Egyptian Osiris and his dismemberment by Seth. Mankind's greatest dilemma is envisioned in the Attis–Cybelle myth, and to this day it lingers as civilization's basic problem. It is still our *prima materia*, and it still contains a spirit of union that has not been extracted.

The Attis–Cybelle myth, especially since it portrays the son–lover of the Great Goddess, can at first appear to represent only the trials of separation from the mother world, and especially of males from their mothers. From this limited perspective, the mother-goddess, or a real women, is seen as dangerous to a man: he must gain the capacity to separate. Women then become pushed into a corner, and the demand made that they be *anything but* Cybelle. That is, they should be understanding, loving, giving, but not people with their own needs and patterns of existence. In a sense, that is the scenario this seminal myth has been reduced to, and at great cost to both sexes.

But the myth can more productively be understood as representing both an intrasubjective drama and the vicissitudes of union states between two people. Jung demonstrated this when he used the *Rosarium* in his study of the transference. For convenience, consider a man and a woman, although gender does not limit the applicability of the myth to any relationship. Either person, the male or the female, can experience the dynamics which the Attis–Cybelle myth puts forth as an intrasubjective drama. A man's consciousness, and his capacity to enter and discover new psychic territory, will be experienced by him as if it were in the grip of another force that prevents such discoveries. He may project this force on to the woman, or he may, which is of course preferable, experience it as an inner conflict. Aggressive inquiry, new or independent acts, incur anxiety because they imply a leaving of the world of fantasy and eternal possibilities. Also, on an intersubjective level, he will be frightened about becoming engulfed in a relationship. A woman will experience a similar intrasubjective field: an inner force, which has a male image to it and feels to be 'Other', compels her into involvement and fusion with others. Her own desire for separation and autonomy and her active, separating capacity is terribly hindered because it is Attis-like. The male-dominated culture wants the Cybelle aspect of woman to be controlled. The Cybelle factor can also lie in men, and especially in their feminine sides and irrational moods which can be projected into women. A woman's controlled, weak and terrified Attis-like side can project into a man. Each will hold the other in secret contempt. Then the woman has, in a sense, become like Cybelle to a man, and he like Attis to her. The myth has then projected outward and turned especially destructive.

Another possibility, and more in the alchemical way of thinking, is to envision the Attis–Cybelle dyad as a force-field experienced in a way as an imaginal, unconscious couple. This is a field that two people can partake of in the sense of being moved by its currents of energy and inherent pattern of behavior. They would experience this field as a 'transitional space' in Winnicott's sense, which would mean that it would be, paradoxically, something that they were both inside of and also observing as though it were also an object between them that also contained them (Winnicott, 1971). The Attis–Cybelle field, in the primitive form in which the myth portrays it, would be one that tended towards fusion and literalization, in distinction to being experienced as an 'Other', a 'third thing', with its own dynamic that is itself linked to the projections and imaginations of both people. The alchemists worked on such fields to transform them from a dominant fusion dynamic (in which one person fears, or actually is overwhelmed by the emotions of the other) into a field that had a rhythmical dynamic of separation and fusion, with neither polarity dominating. The famous alchemical dictum of 'slay the dragon' represents this kind of transformation, the dragon representing the field in the negative fusion mould. The goal of this transformation was the *lapis*, that self-structure whose basic rhythm was the *coniunctio* purified of all negative fusion dynamics as well as its other side, soul-less distancing.

Desire, with its powerful, compulsive quality, is the single most dominant element which impedes the purification of the Attis–Cybelle field. Yet, in its transformed state – the transformation signified in another alchemical image by the cutting-off of the paws of a lion – desire is the key ingredient, the fire which drives the process. Irigaray provides a profound insight into desire and the space, or 'interval', in which union can be experienced when she says:

> Desire occupies or designates the interval. A permanent definition of desire would put an end to desire. Desire requires a sense of attraction: a change in the interval or the relations of nearness or distance between subject and object.
>
> (Irigaray, 1987, p. 120)

In discussing desire she speaks eloquently of the dynamics of what we would term the *coniunctio*. She notes that if there is a 'double desire', man and woman capable of desiring and being desired, then

> the positive and negative poles divide themselves among the two sexes . . . creating a chiasmus or double loop in which each can move out towards the other and back to itself.
>
> (ibid., p. 121)

> In order to keep one's distance, does not one have to know how to take? or speak? It comes down in the end to the same thing. Perhaps the ability to take requires a permanent space or container, a soul maybe, or a mind?
>
> (ibid.)

The *coniunctio* is not without its dangers. Irigaray continues:

> The subject who offers or permits desire transports and so envelops, or incorporates, the other. It is moreover dangerous if there is no third term. Not only because it is a necessary limitation. This third term can show up within the container as the latter's relationship with his or her own limits: a relationship with the divine, death, the social or cosmic order. If such a third term does not exist within and for the container, the latter may become *all-powerful*.
>
> (ibid., p. 123)

In the initial four woodcuts of the sixteenth-century alchemical text the *Rosarium philosophorum*, which formed the backbone of Jung's major study of the transference, 'Psychology of the Transference', one finds this 'third term' as the descending holy ghost. Later, the *coniunctio* forms and becomes

Ænigma Regis.

ẞie iſt geboren der Keyſer aller ehzen/
Kein höher mag vber jn geboren werden.

Figure 0.1 Hermaphrodite with three serpents and one serpent. Below, the three-headed Mercurial dragon.

Source: From the *Rosarium philosophorum* (1550); reproduced in Jung's *Collected Works*, Vol. 12.

the third thing itself, for it has, to a workable degree, internalized the rhythms of separation and nearness. But fusion, the collapse of the gap or interval, is a constant threat. In woodcut seventeen (Figure 0.1) we have a symbolic portrayal of this final overcoming of negative fusion states. And the woodcuts that follow address the issue of further transforming the *coniunctio* into a container–contained form that holds out the consummation of desire for its greater goal: harmony between the sexes and between an individual's male and female polarities. In woodcut eighteen (Figure 0.2) we reach a stage of such a transformed field of relations and a sense of container with the paradoxical feature of its inside being identical with its outside: in this woodcut, often said to hold the key to the entire series, it is intentionally ambiguous whether the lion is devouring or releasing the sun.

If the vicissitudes of desire are to be understood in terms of early object relations, then states of abandonment, despair and loss, to mention a few,

Figure 0.2 The 'green lion' devouring the sun.

Source: From the *Rosarium philosophorum* (1550); reproduced in Jung's *Collected Works*, Vol. 12.

which can arise in the transference or any relation, will be understood as repetitions of what occurred, or failed to occur, in early life. But Jung's approach, as mirrored by the alchemical tradition, was different. He took such states to be aspects of the alchemical *nigredo* and as always being goal-oriented. Of the many functions of the *nigredo* we may single out its role in the dissolution of defenses on a psychic and bodily level, so that a new self-structure, the *lapis*, could be created. Alchemy knew of the mystery of terror, often seen as the dark side of God and reckoned as a transformative agent that could dissolve rigid defenses and allow for new archetypal levels of psychic structure to embody. The alchemists sought out the *nigredo*, and embraced it as 'our *nigredo*'. This is all the more remarkable when we recognize the soul's torment that was thus invited, even including states of madness. Far from only being a result of early trauma or a lack of 'good enough mothering', the *nigredo* was understood to follow a prior experience, the *coniunctio*. The affects that the *nigredo* brought with it were thus thought to have their own necessary, transformative quality. Yet in the *nigredo* one meets the individual and collective history of incestuous fusion states, humankind's 'impossible passion', as seen, for example, in the Attis–Cybelle myth. Hence the *nigredo* had to be transformed. 'Cleanse our minds of this horrible darkness', exclaims an alchemist, echoing the cry of so many of

Figure 0.3 The *coniunctio* in a gruesome form.
Source: From the *Turba philosophorum* (ca. ninth century); reproduced in Jung's Collected Works, Vol. 12.

these suffering workers of the art. An alchemical engraving associated with a text from the *Turba philosophorum*, from probably the ninth century, and hence one of the older alchemical texts, illustrates the complexity of such states of union (Figure 0.3).

By experiencing the *coniunctio* and resulting *nigredo* over and over again, a new state could be reached, the 'whitening' of the *albedo*. This was part of the qualitative transformations of alchemy which were signified by color changes. In the *albedo*, the despair, madness and fears of abandonment were overcome to the extent that these states no longer created a radical splitting from union or a regressive fusion into total identity loss. In Mylius' alternative engraving of woodcut ten of the *Rosarium philosophorum* there is a hermaphroditic figure, resurrected from a previous dead state, and supported by a crescent moon (Figure 0.4). This signifies not only a union of opposites, the male–female polarities of the hermaphrodite, but also an overcoming of psychic death related to the dread and terror of despair and abandonment.

Figure 0.4 Mercurius as the sun-moon hermaphrodite (*rebis*), standing on the (round) chaos.

Source: From Mylius, *Philosophia reformata* (1622); reproduced in Jung's *Collected Works*, Vol. 12.

The changing quality of the moon, oscillating between a full light and periods of darkness, represents a new consciousness no longer inimical to the constancy demands of solar-rational quests. Change becomes a cradle of stability rather than its enemy. And change that previously meant despair and fear of loss can be seen, now, as part of a process with a source – a previous union – and a goal – the purification of fusion states and the eventual creation of a stable structure of union. This purification of desire and fusion from a captivating and compulsive form is, as has been noted, signified by woodcut seventeen of the *Rosarium* (Figure 0.1), while the last woodcut, number twenty, portrays the final, stable structure (Figure 0.5). It is depicted here as the resurrected Christ, and in other alchemical works as the resurrected Osiris, portrayed by the mysterious Egyptian symbol of the Djed column, which waxes and wanes like the moon.

This structure that alchemy aims to create, the *lapis*, lives in a 'third realm' between space–time and *a*temporal worlds. To create it finally in a stable form requires that one come to terms with desire. No longer something to be heroically overcome, now desire can be an integral part of the process, a fire that drives the creation of an embodied self. This stage, in which the passions

Figure 0.5 The Risen Christ as symbol of the *filius philosophorum*.

Source: From the *Rosarium philosophorum* (1550) reproduced in Jung's *Collected Works*, Vol. 12.

are engaged, follows the 'whiteness' of the *albedo* and was known as the *rubedo*. As Jung said:

> [In the] state of 'whiteness' one does not *live* in the true sense of the word. It is a sort of abstract, ideal state. In order to make it come alive it must have 'blood', it must have what the alchemists called the *rubedo*, the 'redness' of life. Only the total experience of being can transform this ideal state into a fully human mode of existence. Blood alone can reanimate a glorious state of consciousness in which the last trace of blackness is dissolved, in which the devil no longer has an autonomous existence but rejoins the profound unity of the psyche. Then the *opus magnum* is finished: the human soul is completely integrated.
>
> (McGuire and Hull, 1977, p. 229)

In his non-alchemical studies, Jung's approach to the Attis–Cybelle myth follows his libido theory and the heroic mode of overcoming death. He takes

Attis' self-castration as representing the sacrifice of instinctual feelings that would regressively cling to the Great Mother. These feelings are represented by the animal that must be sacrificed, the animal in us 'which fights with all his instinctive conservatism' against the individuation urge (1953, para. 653). For Jung, castration signifies the sacrifice of the libido, both as the incestuous love of the son for the mother, and of her incestuous love for him (ibid.).

This sacrifice is completely and thoroughly necessary: Jung sees it as a stage in the development of individual human consciousness. His choice example is Christ, who sacrificed not only instinctuality, 'but the entire natural man' (ibid., para. 673). The danger in this, of course, as Jung says, is that the body and instinctual life are made totally subject to the mind and its rule (ibid., para. 673). But only through this sacrifice 'will the dominating idea of consciousness be in a position to assert itself completely and mould human nature as it wishes. . . . The attempt must be made to climb these heights, for without such an undertaking it could never be proved that this bold and violent experiment in self-transformation is possible at all' (ibid., para. 674).

From this point of view the patriarchal suppression of the feminine is seen as a tragic but necessary step in humankind's reaching for an individual, rational consciousness. It does not see the time of the religion of the Great Goddess as a paradisiacal era. The capacity for separation from the negative fusion state was, and to a great extent continues to be, the major issue, the struggle which causes so much incalculable suffering in all relations.

The heroic approach is the one that has actually been played out in history. But the other approach – the alchemical one – survived and is still a potential option. In psychotherapy the issues raised by the transference and counter-transference relationship continually brings it to the fore in this contemporary guise. Are we 'heroically' to extract consciousness from the transference–counter-transference relation, thus regarding it as a means to this end, if not an obstacle to be overcome? Or does a field become created between two people, one whose archetypal energies and patterns can be experienced such that this encounter with the *numinosum* results in a new awareness and structural change?

Alchemy is thoroughly involved with such fields and often deals with their complex, dangerous qualities in terms of the notion of sin. In a highly novel departure from Christianity's notion of the Fall, Original Sin is depicted in an early alchemical myth as being the result of the castration of the originally bisexual Great Goddess Cybelle (Jung, 1963, para. 27 and n. 185). And this, humankind's Original Sin, results in a wound that is felt as a torment within union. Seen in the context of this myth, the wound is linked to a symbiotic field of desire that can be neither fulfilled nor relinquished. The myth actually portrays a terrible suffering that many people know and keep locked within their hearts in a rigidity of pessimism and despair that excludes faith. This suffering stems from moments of union, a felt I–Thou connection, perhaps known very early in one's life, that is quickly eclipsed. One is caught in the dilemma of wanting to stay within the beauty and renewing quality of the *coniunctio*, while also feeling how its fusion dynamics undercut the sense of separation indispensable to the individual ego. The term 'preoedipal disorder' can be something of an apotrapoaic device meant to deal with this level and force its energies and process into a linear-developmental model.

The 'wound' points to a level of human existence that can breed the most intense despair. Yet the alchemists suggested a panacea: they believed that suffering the state of failed union could be relieved, even terminated, through the mediation of a substance called the *balsam* (Jung, 1963, para. 27). Taking this term from the aromatic substance that flows spontaneously from plants, and perhaps as well from the balsam which played a role in the Egyptian art of embalming and preserving the dead, the alchemist believed that balsam was created by suffering through the affects of successive unions, that is, suffering through the darkness and madness of the ensuing *nigredos*. Through experiencing again and again the rhythm of the *coniunctio–nigredo*, a healing substance, the balsam. is produced. It goes through transformations and, in alchemical imagery, yields the possibility of transforming the chthonic life of the body. The alchemists depict this in terms of the imagery of the cold-blooded raven, snake and dragon, changing into that of the lion and then the eagle, representing illumination.

* * *

I hope this introduction aids the reader in his or her entry into Jung's alchemical studies. I have especially highlighted what I think of as Jung's special achievements, namely his awareness of the central feature of the *coniunctio*, the Attis–Cybelle myth as related to the *prima materia*, and his remarkable ability to decipher a goal-oriented process amidst the all but unintelligible maze of alchemical texts.

There have been many contributions from Jungian analysts on alchemy, and I should like to mention a few that seem to me to be especially important. M.-L. von Franz, Jungian analyst and philologist, was Jung's collaborator in research for many years; she is the leading authority on alchemy from a Jungian perspective. She has contributed many books on the subject, and these are especially important in that they clarify and complement Jung's own research. For example, she wrote an extended commentary to the *Aurora consurgens* (1966), a document she (as well as Jung) attributes to Thomas Aquinas; this was published as a companion work to Jung's *Mysterium coniunctionis*. Her book *Alchemy* (1980), one of several works on the subject that derived from lectures she gave at the Jung Institute in Zürich, is highly recommended as an introductory text on alchemy. It contains a wide-ranging historical survey of the origins of alchemy, and features an analysis of alchemical texts from Arabic, Greek and European alchemy. And, to note only one other seminal work, her *Alchemical Active Imagination* (1979) is a fine study of the alchemist Gerard Dorn's attitude towards imagination and the body. Anyone interested in alchemy can gain a great deal from her writings.

Concerning the contributions of several others who were closely connected to Jung, mention should be made of an anthology and introduction to the writings of Paracelsus compiled by Jolande Jacobi (1951). And Joseph Henderson has spent considerable effort upon the alchemical text *The Splendor Solis*. A video cassette of the interesting fruits of his research is available from the San Francisco Jung Institute.

James Hillman has written extensively on alchemy. He often has a poetic and refreshing insight into alchemical processes. In general, one can find inspiring and useful reflections on alchemy in many of Hillman's writings. I should like especially to single out his essay 'Silver and the White Earth' (Hillman, 1980, 1981), in which one can find important contributions to the meaning of the alchemical Sol, Luna and sulphur. Another important source for a Jungian view of alchemy is to be found in Edward Edinger's *Anatomy of the Psyche* (1985). This work is a systematic study of the meaning for psychotherapy of the various alchemical operations such as the *solutio*, the *coagulatio*, etc.

There have also been many essays by Jungians which attempt to bring his alchemical amplification of the transference into a closer connection with clinical practice. Noteworthy are Michael Fordham's 'Jung's Conception of Transference' (1974), in which Fordham reflects upon the critical stage of *coniunctio* and *nigredo* in terms of projective identification; Judith Hubback has used the image of the *coniunctio* in a paper on dealing with depressed patients (1983); Andrew Samuels has employed the imagery of the *Rosarium* in a novel and useful way in terms of metaphorical images of analytic interactions (1985); Barbara Stevens has used the same alchemical imagery in her study of ways that the feminine principle informs psycho-therapy (1991); Mario Jacoby's study of the transference in his *The Analytic Encounter* (1984) is a highly readable and important contribution to the transference as reflected through the alchemical imagery of the *Rosarium*; and I have contributed several papers on the theme of the application of alchemical imagery to understanding the abandonment depression (1990), projective identification (1988), issues of sexual acting-out in analysis (1984), and borderline states of mind (1989). Edward C. Whitmont has written extensively on healing and has a keen insight into alchemical thinking. Among other topics, his latest book, *The Alchemy of Healing*, relates alchemy to homeopathy and to the connection of psyche and soma.

Mention should also be made of an important review article 'Alchemy: Jung and the historians of science' (1987–8) by David Holt, who has made important contributions towards relating Jung's alchemical studies to the history of science. In his review article Holt summarizes articles in *Ambix*, the journal of the Society for the Study of Alchemy and Early Chemistry, and in the process attempts to widen the dialogue between Jungians and historians of science.

The following chapters of this book will comprise extracts from Jung's writings on alchemy. In Chapter 1, I shall survey alchemical images and thoughts concerning the *prima materia*. Chapter 2 will take up the 'Alchemical mind'. Chapter 3 will focus upon 'Projection and imagination in alchemy'. In Chapter 4 'Alchemy and individuation' will be the focus, and Chapter 5 will be concerned with the related material of 'Alchemy and religion'. Chapter 6 will represent alchemical writings on the 'Body and subtle body'; Chapter 7 will center upon the 'Opposites and the *coniunctio*'; and Chapter 8 will deal with 'Alchemy and psychotherapy.'

I would like to register my special thanks to my wife, Lydia Salant, for her efforts in helping me to put this introduction into an understandable form. She has assisted me in this process and, over many years, we have wrestled with understanding alchemical ideas. My understanding is often inextricably bound up with hers. My greatest debt is to C. G. Jung. My labor of choosing extracts from his *Collected Works* is, of course, like only a few drops compared with a sea that represents his efforts. I, and I think anyone seriously studying alchemy, will be for ever grateful to him. This introduction is dedicated to him and especially to his courage as an investigator of the psyche's mysterious depths. He was one who entered these depths and, in distinction to other great souls, did not perish.

REFERENCES

Bohm, David (1980) *Wholeness and the Implicate Order* (London: Routledge & Kegan Paul).

Burkhardt, Titus (1967) *Alchemy* (London: Stuart & Watkins).

Corbin, Henry (1969) *Creative Imagination in the Sufism of Ibn 'Arabi* (Princeton, New Jersey: Princeton University Press).

Couliano, Ioan P. (1987) *Eros and Magic in the Renaissance* (Chicago, Illinois: University of Chicago Press).

Dobbs, Betty Jo Teeter (1975) *The Foundations of Newtons's Alchemy, or 'The Hunting of the Greene Lyon'* (Cambridge: Cambridge University Press).

—— (1992) *The Janus Faces of Genius* (Cambridge: Cambridge University Press).

Edinger, Edward (1985) *Anatomy of the Psyche* (La Salle, Illinois: Open Court).

Eliade, Mircea (1962) *The Forge and the Crucible* (New York: Harper & Row).

Fabricius, Johannes (1976) *Alchemy* (Copenhagen: Rosenkilde & Bagger).

Fordham, Michael (1974) 'Jung's Conception of Transference', *Journal of Analytical Psychology*, 19:1.

Franz, Maria-Louise von (1966) *Aurora consurgens* (London: Routledge & Kegan Paul).

—— (1975) *C. G. Jung: His Myth in Our Time* (New York: Putnam).

—— (1979) *Alchemy* (Toronto: Inner City Books).

—— (1980) *Alchemical Active Imagination* (Irving, Texas: Spring Publications).

Geoghegan, D. (1957) 'Some Indications of Newton's Attitude towards Alchemy', *Ambix*, 6: 2.

Green, André (1975) 'The Analyst, Symbolization and Absence in the Analytic Setting', *International Journal of Psycho-Analysis*, 56.

Hall, Rupert. A (1992) *Isaac Newton, Adventurer in Thought* (Oxford: Blackwell).

Heym, Gerard (1938–58) 'Reviewing Jung's *Mysterium coniunctionis*', *Ambix*, 2 (1938–46); *Ambix*, 3 (1948–9); *Ambix*, 6 (1957–8).

Hillman, James, (1980) 'Silver and the White Earth', *Spring* (Texas: Spring Publications).

—— (1981) 'Silver and the White Earth', *Spring* (Texas: Spring Publications).

Holmyard, E. J. (1990) *Alchemy* (New York: Dover) (first publ. 1957).

Holt, David (1987–8) 'Alchemy: Jung and the Historians of Science', *Harvest*, 40–60.

Hubback, Judith (1983) 'Depressed Patients and the Coniunctio', *Journal of Analytical Psychology*, 28:4.

Huizinga, Johan (1954) *The Waning of the Middle Ages* (New York: Doubleday) (first publ. 1924).

Irigaray, Luce (1987) 'Sexual Difference', in Toril Moi, ed., *French Feminist Thought* (Oxford: Basil Blackwell).

—— (1992) *Elemental Passions* (New York: Routledge).

Jacobi, Jolande, ed. (1951) *Paracelsus* (Princeton, New Jersey: Princeton University Press).

Jacoby, Mario (1984) *The Analytic Encounter* (Toronto: Inner City Books).

Jung, C. G. (1953) *Symbols of Transformation* (*Collected Works*, Vol. 5) (Princeton, New Jersey: Princeton University Press).

—— (1954) *The Practice of Psychotherapy* (*Collected Works*, Vol. 16) (Princeton, New Jersey: Princeton University Press).

—— (1960) *The Structure and Dynamics of the Psyche* (*Collected Works*, Vol. 8) (Princeton, New Jersey: Princeton University Press).

—— (1963) *Mysterium coniunctionis* (*Collected Works*, Vol. 14) (Princeton, New Jersey: Princeton University Press).

—— (1973) *Memories, Dreams and Reflections*, ed. Aniela Jaffé (New York: Pantheon).

—— (1988) *Nietzsche's Zarathustra*, ed. James L. Jarret, 2 vols (Princeton, New Jersey: Princeton University Press).

—— (1991) *Psyche and Symbol*, ed. Violet de Laszlo (Princeton, New Jersey: Princeton University Press).

Kristeva, Julia (1989) *Black Sun* (New York: Columbia University Press).

Lévi-Strauss, Claude (1966) *The Savage Mind* (London: Weidenfeld & Nicolson).

Lindsay, Jack (1970) *The Origins of Alchemy in Graeco-Roman Egypt* (London: Frederick Muller).

McGuire, J. E. (1967) 'Transmutation and Immutability: Newton's Doctrine of Physical Qualities', *Ambix*, 14:2.

McGuire, William and Hull, R. F. C. (1977) *C. G. Jung Speaking* (Princeton, New Jersey: Princeton University Press).

McLean, Adam, ed. and comm. (1981a) *The Rosary of the Philosophers* (Edinburgh: Magnum Opus Hermetic Sourceworks).

—— ed. and comm. (1981b) *Splendor solis*, trans. Joscelyn Godwin, (Edinburgh: Magnum Opus Hermetic Sourceworks).

—— (1991) *A Commentary on the Mutus Liber* (Grand Rapids, Michigan: Phanes Press).

Mead, G. R. S. (1919) *The Subtle Body* (London: Stuart & Watkins).

Moi, Toril, ed. (1987) *French Feminist Thought* (Oxford: Basil Blackwell).

Ovid. *Fasti* (Cambridge, Massachusetts: Harvard University Press, 1989, trans. Sir J.G. Frazer).

Pagel, Walter (1948) 'Jung's Views on Alchemy', *Isis*, 39.

Prigogene, Ilya (1986) 'The Reenchantment of Nature', in *Dialogues with Scientists and Sages: The Search for Unity*, ed. Renée Weber (London: Routledge & Kegan Paul).

Rosen, Steven (1995) 'Pouring Old Wine into a New Bottle', in *Chiron: Interpretation and the Interactive Field*, ed. M. Stein (Wilmette, Illinois: Chiron Publications).

Samuels, Andrew (1985) 'Symbolic Dimensions of Eros in Transference–Countertransference: Some Clinical Uses of Jung's Alchemical Metaphor', *International Review of Psycho-Analysis*, 12.

Schwartz-Salant, Nathan (1984) 'Archetypal Factors Underlying Sexual Acting-Out in the Transference/Countertransference Process', in *Transference and Countertransference*, ed. N. Schwartz-Salant and M. Stein (Wilmette, Illinois: Chiron Publications).

—— (1988) 'Archetypal Foundations of Projective Identification', *Journal of Analytical Psychology*, 33.

—— (1989) *The Borderline Personality: Vision and Healing* (Wilmette, Illinois: Chiron Publications).

—— (1990) 'The Abandonment Depression: Developmental and Alchemical Perspectives', *Journal of Analytical Psychology*, 35.

—— (1995) 'The Interactive Field as the Analytic Object', in *Chiron: Interpretation and the Interactive Field*, ed. M. Stein (Wilmette, Illinois: Chiron Publications).

Sheldrake, Rupert (1986) 'Morphogenetic Fields: Nature's Habits', in *Dialogues with Scientists and Sages: The Search for Unity*, ed. Renée Weber (London: Routledge & Kegan Paul).

Silberer, Herbert (1917) *Problems of Mysticism and its Symbolism* (New York: Moffat, Yard) (trans. S.E. Jellife).

Stevens, Barbara (1991) *Psychotherapy Grounded in the Feminine Principle* (Wilmette, Illinois: Chiron Publications).

Taylor, F. Sherwood (1956) 'An Alchemical Work of Sir Isaac Newton', *Ambix*, 5:3.

Waite, Arthur E., ed. (1973) *The Hermetic Museum*, 2 vols (London: Robinson & Watkins).

Weber, Renée, ed. (1986) *Dialogues with Scientists and Sages: The Search for Unity* (London: Routledge & Kegan Paul).

Whitmont, Edward C. (1994) *The Alchemy of Healing* (Berkeley: North Atlantic Books).

Whyte, Lancelot Law (1949) *Unitary Principles in Physics and Biology* (New York: Basic Books).

—— (1960) *The Unconscious before Freud* (New York: Basic Books).

Winnicott, D. W. (1971) *Playing and Reality* (London: Tavistock).

1 The *prima materia*

From: *Nietzsche's Zarathustra* (1988), 2: 954

Now as long as things are in the state called by the alchemists *materia prima*, primal matter, it is dark and objectionable; nobody is convinced that the self will come from such a thing and therefore they don't find it. Psychologically it means of course that the mystery always begins in our inferior function, that is the place where new life, regeneration, is to be found. For we cannot finish perfect bodies, as the ancients say, we must work on imperfect bodies because only what is imperfect can be brought to perfection; a perfect thing can only be corrupted. This is perfectly obvious, so it cannot be done with the superior differentiated function. A very good, well-trained mind is the sterile field where nothing grows because it is finished. So you must take that which is most repressed by the mind, the feeling. And there you find the original chaos, a disorderly heap of possibilities which are not worked upon yet and which ought to be brought together through a peculiar kind of handling. You know we say psychologically that the inferior function, in this case the feeling, is contaminated with the collective unconscious; therefore it is disseminated all over the field of the collective unconscious and therefore it is mythological. So when you try to bring it up, a lot of archaic fantasies appear, the whole thing is unwieldy and utterly mistakable; you easily take it for something poisonous or wrong or mad on account of that mixture of unconscious material. You reject it altogether therefore; no decent individual would have anything to do with an inferior function because it is stupid nonsense, immoral – it is everything bad under the sun. Yet it is the only thing that contains life, the only thing that contains also the fun of living. A differentiated function is no longer vital, you know what you can do with it and it bores you, it no longer yields the spark of life.

From: 'Individual Dream Symbolism in Relation to Alchemy' (1936) (*CW* 12)

306   In alchemy the egg stands for the chaos apprehended by the artifex, the *prima materia* containing the captive world-soul. Out of the egg – symbolized by the round cooking-vessel – will rise the eagle or phoenix,

the liberated soul, which is ultimately identical with the Anthropos who was imprisoned in the embrace of Physis.

From: *Nietzsche's Zarathustra* (1988), 2: 886

Yet nobody has ever known what this primal matter is. The alchemists did not know, and nobody has found out what was really meant by it, because it is a substance in the unconscious which is needed for the incarnation of the god.

From: 'Religious Ideas in Alchemy' (1937) (*CW* 12)

425   The basis of the *opus*, the *prima materia* is one of the most famous secrets of alchemy. This is hardly surprising, since it represents the unknown substance that carries the projection of the autonomous psychic content. It was of course impossible to specify such a substance, because the projection emanates from the individual and is consequently different in each case. For this reason it is incorrect to maintain that the alchemists never said what the *prima materia* was; on the contrary, they gave all too many definitions and so were everlastingly contradicting themselves. For one alchemist the *prima materia* was quicksilver; for others it was ore, iron, gold, lead, salt, sulphur, vinegar, water, air, fire, earth, blood, water of life, *lapis*, poison, spirit, cloud, sky, dew, shadow, sea, mother, moon, dragon, Venus, chaos, microcosm (Figure 1.1). Ruland's *Lexicon* gives no less than fifty synonyms, and a great many more could be added.

426   Besides these half-chemical, half-mythological definitions there are also some 'philosophical' ones which have a deeper meaning. Thus in the treatise of Komarios[1] we find the definition 'Hades'. In Olympiodorus the black earth contains the 'accursed of God' ($\theta\epsilon o\kappa\alpha\tau\acute{\alpha}\rho\alpha\tau o\varsigma$). The 'Consilium coniugii' says that the father of gold and silver – i.e. their *prima materia* – is 'the animal of earth and sea', or 'man', or a 'part of man', e.g. his hair, blood, etc. Dorn calls the *prima materia* 'Adamica' and – basing himself on Paracelsus – *limbus microcosmicus*. The material of the stone is 'no other than the fiery and perfect Mercurius' and the true hermaphroditic 'Adam and Microcosm' (= man)(Figure 1.2).[2] Hermes Trismegistus is said to have called the stone the 'orphan'. Since Dorn was a pupil of Paracelsus his views are probably connected with the Anthropos doctrine of his master. For this I must refer the reader to my essay 'Paracelsus as a Spiritual Phenomenon'. Further connections between man and the *prima materia* are mentioned in other authors, but I cannot quote them all here.

427   The mercurial dragon of Greek alchemy, surnamed $\grave{\epsilon}\nu$ $\tau\grave{o}$ $\pi\bar{\alpha}\nu$, gave rise

Figure 1.1 The unfettered opposites in chaos. 'Chaos' is one of the names for the
prima materia.
Source: From Marolles, *Tableaux du temple des muses* (1655); reproduced in Jung's *Collected Works*, Vol. 12.

to descriptions of the *prima materia* as *Unum, Unica Res*[3] and Monad[4] and
to the statement in the 'Liber Platonis quartorum' that man is well qualified
to complete the work because he possesses that which is *simple*, i.e. the
soul.[5] Mylius describes the *prima materia* as the *elementum primordiale*.
It is the 'pure subject and the unity of forms', and in it any form whatsoever
may be assumed (*in quo retinetur quaelibet forma cum possibilitate*).[6]

428   In the second version of the *Turba*, Eximindus says:[7]

Figure 1.2 Earth as *prima materia*, suckling the son of the philosophers.
Source: From Mylius, *Philosophia reformata* (1622); reproduced in Jung's *Collected Works*, Vol. 12.

I make known to you, ye sons of the doctrine, that the beginning of all creatures is a certain primary everlasting and infinite nature which cooks and rules everything, and whose active and passive [aspects] are known and recognized only by those on whom the knowledge of the sacred art has been bestowed.

429   In Sermo IX of the *Turba*,[8] 'Eximenus' puts forward a theory of creation that corresponds to the Biblical one (creation through the 'Word') but stands in flagrant contradiction to the above, according to which the beginning is a *natura perpetua et infinita*. In the *Rosarium* the *prima materia* is called *radix ipsius* (root of itself). Because it roots in itself, it is autonomous and dependent on nothing.

444   According to Basilius Valentinus, the earth (as *prima materia*) is not a dead body, but is inhabited by a spirit that is its life and soul. All created things, minerals included, draw their strength from the earth-spirit. This spirit is life, it is nourished by the stars, and it gives nourishment to all the living things it shelters in its womb. Through the spirit received from on high, the earth hatches the minerals in her womb as the mother her unborn

child. This invisible spirit is like the reflection in a mirror, intangible, yet it is at the same time the root of all the substances necessary to the alchemical process or arising therefrom (*radix nostrorum corporum*).[9]

430   Being a *radix ipsius*, the *prima materia* is a true *principium*, and from this it is but a step to the Paracelsan view that it is something *increatum* (uncreated). In his 'Philosophia ad Athenienses', Paracelsus says that this unique (*unica*) *materia* is a great secret having nothing in common with the elements. It fills the entire *regio aetherea*, and is the mother of the elements and of all created things (Figure 1.2). Nothing can express this mystery, nor has it been created (*nec etiam creatum fuit*). This uncreated mystery was prepared (*praeparatum*) by God in such a way that nothing will ever be like it in the future nor will it ever return to what it was.[10] For it was so corrupted as to be beyond reparation (which presumably refers to the Fall). Dorn's rendering gives the sense of the original text.[11]

433   The *prima materia* has the quality of ubiquity: it can be found always and everywhere, which is to say that projection can take place always and everywhere. The English alchemist Sir George Ripley (*c.* 1415–90) writes: 'The philosophers tell the inquirer that birds and fishes bring us the *lapis*,[12] every man has it, it is in every place, in you, in me, in everything, in time and space.'[13] 'It offers itself in lowly form [*vili figura*]. From it there springs our eternal water [*aqua permanens*].'[14] According to Ripley the *prima materia* is water; it is the material principle of all bodies,[15] including mercury.[16] It is the *hyle* which the divine act of creation brought forth from the chaos as a dark sphere[17] (*sphaericum opus*).[18] The chaos is a *massa confusa* that gives birth to the stone. The hylical water contains a hidden elemental fire.[19] In the treatise 'De sulphure' hell-fire (*ignis gehennalis*) is attributed to the element earth as its inner opposite.[20] According to Hortulanus, the stone arises from a *massa confusa* containing in itself all the elements.[21] Just as the world came forth from a *chaos confusum*,[22] so does the stone.[23] The idea of the rotating aquasphere reminds us of the Neopythagoreans: in Archytas the world-soul is a circle or sphere;[24] in Philolaos it draws the world round with it in its rotation.[25] The original idea is to be found in Anaxagoras, where the *nous* gives rise to a whirl-pool in chaos.[26] The cosmogony of Empedocles is also relevant: here the σφαῖρος (spherical being) springs from the union of dissimilars, owing to the influence of φιλία. The definition of this spherical being as εὐ'δαιμονέστατος Θεός, 'the most serene God', sheds a special light on the perfect, 'round' nature of the *lapis*,[27] which arises from, and consti-tutes, the primal sphere: hence the *prima materia* is often called *lapis*. The initial state is the hidden state, but by the art and the grace of God it can be transmuted into the second, manifest state. That is why the *prima materia* sometimes coincides with the idea of the initial stage of the process, the *nigredo*. It is then the black earth in which the gold or the

lapis is sown like the grain of wheat. It is the black, magically fecund earth that Adam took with him from Paradise, also called antimony and described as a 'black blacker than black' (*nigrum nigrius nigro*).[28]

From: 'The Personification of Opposites', *Mysterium coniunctionis* (1955–6) (*CW* 14)

183   The chaos as *prima materia* is identical with the 'waters' of the beginning. According to Olympiodorus, lead (also the *prima materia*) contains a demon that drives the adept mad.[29] Curiously enough, Wei Po-yang, a Chinese alchemist of the second century, compares lead to a madman clothed in rags.[30] Elsewhere Olympiodorus speaks of the 'one cursed by God' who dwells in the 'black earth'. This is the mole, which, as Olympiodorus relates from a Hermetic book, had once been a man who divulged the mysteries of the sun and was therefore cursed by God and made blind. He 'knew the shape of the sun, as it was'.[31]

184   It is not difficult to discern in these allusions the dangers, real or imaginary, which are connected with the unconscious. In this respect the unconscious has a bad reputation, not so much because it is dangerous in itself as because there are cases of latent psychosis which need only a slight stimulus to break out in all their catastrophic manifestations. An anamnesis or the touching of a complex may be sufficient for this. But the unconscious is also feared by those whose conscious attitude is at odds with their true nature. Naturally their dreams will then assume an unpleasant and threatening form, for if nature is violated she takes her revenge. In itself the unconscious is neutral, and its normal function is to compensate the conscious position. In it the opposites slumber side by side; they are wrenched apart only by the activity of the conscious mind, and the more one-sided and cramped the conscious standpoint is, the more painful or dangerous will be the unconscious reaction. There is no danger from this sphere if conscious life has a solid foundation. But if consciousness is cramped and obstinately one-sided, and there is also a weakness of judgement, then the approach or invasion of the unconscious can cause confusion and panic or a dangerous inflation, for one of the most obvious dangers is that of identifying with the figures in the unconscious. For anyone with an unstable disposition this may amount to a psychosis.

253   The alchemists understood the return to chaos as an essential part of the *opus*. It was the stage of the *nigredo* and *mortificatio*, which was then followed by the 'purgatorial fire' and the *albedo*. The spirit of chaos is indispensable to the work, and it cannot be distinguished from the 'gift of the Holy Ghost' any more than the Satan of the Old Testament can be distinguished from Yahweh. The unconscious is both good and evil and yet neither, the matrix of all potentialities.

From: 'Rex and Regina', *Mysterium coniunctionis* (1955–6) (*CW* 14)

381   In order to enter into God's Kingdom the king must transform himself into the *prima materia* in the body of his mother, and return to the dark initial state which the alchemists called the 'chaos'. In this *massa confusa* the elements are in conflict and repel one another; all connections are dissolved. Dissolution is the prerequisite for redemption. The celebrant of the mysteries had to suffer a figurative death in order to attain transformation. Thus, in the Arisleus vision, Gabricus is dissolved into atoms in the body of his sister–wife. We have seen from the analogy with the Ancient of Days what the alchemist's goal was: both artifex and substance were to attain a perfect state, comparable to the Kingdom of God. I will not discuss, for the moment, the justification for this seemingly presumptuous comparison, but would remind the reader that in the opinion of the alchemists themselves the transformation was a miracle that could take place only with God's help.

From: 'The Psychology of the Transference' (1946) (*CW* 16)

383   Once an unconscious content is constellated, it tends to break down the relationship of conscious trust between doctor and patient by creating, through projection, an atmosphere of illusion which either leads to continual misinterpretations and misunderstandings, or else produces a most disconcerting impression of harmony. The latter is even more trying than the former, which at worst (though it is sometimes for the best!) can only hamper the treatment; whereas in the other case a tremendous effort is needed to discover the points of difference. But in either case the constellation of the unconscious is a troublesome factor. The situation is enveloped in a kind of fog, and this fully accords with the nature of the unconscious content: it is a 'black blacker than black' (*nigrum nigrius nigro*),[32] as the alchemists rightly say, and in addition is charged with dangerous polar tensions, with the *inimicitia elementorum*. One finds oneself in an impenetrable chaos, which is indeed one of the synonyms for the mysterious *prima materia*. The latter corresponds to the nature of the unconscious content in every respect, with one exception: this time it does not appear in the alchemical substance, but in man himself. In the case of alchemy it is quite evident that the unconscious content is of human origin, as I have shown in *Psychology and Alchemy*.[33] Hunted for centuries and never found, the *prima materia* or *lapis philosophorum* is, as a few alchemists rightly suspected, to be discovered in man himself. But it seems that this content can never be found and integrated directly, but only by the circuitous route of projection. For as a rule the unconscious first

appears in projected form. Whenever it appears to obtrude itself directly, as in visions, dreams, illuminations, psychoses, etc., these are always preceded by psychic conditions which give clear proof of projection. A classic example of this is Saul's fanatical persecution of the Christians before Christ appeared to him in a vision.

384   The elusive, deceptive, ever-changing content that possesses the patient like a demon now flits about from patient to doctor and, as the third party in the alliance, continues its game, sometimes impish and teasing, sometimes really diabolical. The alchemists aptly personified it as the wily god of revelation, Hermes or Mercurius; and though they lament over the way he hoodwinks them, they still give him the highest names, which bring him very near to deity.[34] But for all that, they deem themselves good Christians whose faithfulness of heart is never in doubt, and they begin and end their treatises with pious invocations.[35] Yet it would be an altogether unjustifiable suppression of the truth were I to confine myself to the negative description of Mercurius' impish drolleries, his inexhaustible invention, his insinuations, his intriguing ideas and schemes, his ambivalence and – often – his unmistakable malice. He is also capable of the exact opposite, and I can well understand why the alchemists endowed their Mercurius with the highest spiritual qualities, although these stand in flagrant contrast to his exceedingly shady character. The contents of the unconscious are indeed of the greatest importance, for the unconscious is after all the matrix of the human mind and its inventions. Wonderful and ingenious as this other side of the unconscious is, it can be most dangerously deceptive on account of its numinous nature. Involuntarily one thinks of the devils mentioned by St Athanasius in his life of St Anthony, who talk very piously, sing psalms, read the holy books, and – worst of all – speak the truth. The difficulties of our psychotherapeutic work teach us to take truth, goodness and beauty where we find them. They are not always found where we look for them: often they are hidden in the dirt or are in the keeping of the dragon. 'In stercore invenitur' (it is found in filth)[36] runs an alchemical dictum – nor is it any the less valuable on that account. But, it does not transfigure the dirt and does not diminish the evil, any more than these lessen God's gifts. The contrast is painful and the paradox bewildering. Sayings like

ουρανο ανω	(Heaven above
ουρανο κατω	Heaven below
αστρα ανω	Stars above
αστρα κατω	Stars below
παν ο ανω	All that is above
τουτο κατω	Also is below
ταυτα λαβε	Grasp this
κε ευτυχε	And rejoice)[37]

are too optimistic and superficial; they forget the moral torment occasioned by the opposites, and the importance of ethical values.

385   The refining of the *prima materia*, the unconscious content, demands endless patience, perseverance,[38] equanimity, knowledge and ability on the part of the doctor; and, on the part of the patient, the putting forth of his best powers and a capacity for suffering which does not leave the doctor altogether unaffected. The deep meaning of the Christian virtues, especially the greatest among these, will become clear even to the unbeliever; for there are times when he needs them all if he is to rescue his consciousness, and his very life, from this pocket of chaos, whose final subjugation, without violence, is no ordinary task. If the work succeeds, it often works like a miracle, and one can understand what it was that prompted the alchemists to insert a heartfelt *Deo concedente* in their recipes, or to allow that only if God wrought a miracle could their procedure be brought to a successful conclusion.

420   The conventional meeting is followed by an unconscious 'familiarization' of one's partner, brought about by the projection of archaic, infantile fantasies which were originally vested in members of the patient's own family and which, because of their positive or negative fascination, attach him to parents, brothers and sisters.[39] The transference of these fantasies to the doctor draws him into the atmosphere of family intimacy, and although this is the last thing he wants, it nevertheless provides a workable *prima materia*. Once the transference has appeared, the doctor must accept it as part of the treatment and try to understand it, otherwise it will be just another piece of neurotic stupidity. The transference itself is a perfectly natural phenomenon which does not by any means happen only in the consulting-room – it can be seen everywhere and may lead to all sorts of nonsense, like all unrecognized projections. Medical treatment of the transference gives the patient a priceless opportunity to withdraw his projections, to make good his losses and to integrate his personality. The impulses underlying it certainly show their dark side to begin with, however much one may try to whitewash them; for an integral part of the work is the *umbra solis* or *solis niger* of the alchemists, the black shadow which everybody carries with him, the inferior and therefore hidden aspect of the personality, the weakness that goes with every strength, the night that follows every day, the evil in the good.[40] The realization of this fact is naturally coupled with the danger of falling victim to the shadow, but the danger also brings with it the possibility of consciously deciding not to become its victim. A visible enemy is always better than an invisible one.

From: 'Paracelsus as a Spiritual Phenomenon'(1942) (*CW* 13)

157   The alchemical operation consisted essentially in separating the *prima materia*, the so-called chaos, into the active principle, the soul, and the

passive principle, the body, which were then reunited in personified form in the *coniunctio* or 'chymical marriage'. In other words, the *coniunctio* was allegorized as the *hieros gamos*, the ritual cohabitation of Sol and Luna. From this union sprang the *filius sapientiae* or *filius philosophorum*, the transformed Mercurius, who was thought of as hermaphroditic in token of his rounded perfection.

From: 'The Psychology of the Transference'(1946) (*CW* 16)

519   I would like to draw attention to the curious pictures of the *arbor philosophica* in the fourteenth-century Codex Ashburnham.[41] One picture shows Adam struck by an arrow,[42] and the tree growing out of his genitals; in the other pictures the tree grows out of Eve's head. Her right hand covers her genitals, her left points to a skull. Plainly this is a hint that the man's *opus* is concerned with the erotic aspect of the *anima*, while the woman's is concerned with the *animus*, which is a 'function of the head'.[43] The *prima materia*, i.e. the unconscious, is represented in man by the 'unconscious' *anima*, and in woman by the 'unconscious' *animus*. Out of the *prima materia* grows the philosophical tree, the unfolding *opus*. In their symbolical sense, too, the pictures are in accord with the findings of psychology, since Adam would then stand for the woman's *animus* who generates 'philosophical' ideas with his member, and Eve for the man's *anima* who, as Sapientia or Sophia, produces out of her head the intellectual content of the work.

From: 'The Components of the Coniunctio', *Mysterium coniunctionis* (1955–6) (*CW* 14)

14   The terms 'son of the widow' and 'children of the widow' appear to be of Manichaean origin. The Manichaeans themselves were called 'children of the widow'.[44] The 'orphan' referred to by Hermes must therefore have for his counterpart a *vidua* (widow) as the *prima materia*. For this there are synonyms such as *mater, matrix*, Venus, *regina, femina, virgo, puella praegnans*, 'virgin in the centre of the earth',[45] Luna,[46] *meretrix* (whore), *vetula* (old woman), more specifically *vetula extenuata* (enfeebled, exhausted),[47] Mater Alchimia, 'who is dropsical in the lower limbs and paralysed from the knees down',[48] and finally virago. All these synonyms allude to the virginal or maternal quality of the *prima materia*, which exists without a man[49] and yet is the 'matter of all things'.[50] Above all, the *prima materia* is the mother of the *lapis*, the *filius philosophorum*. Michael Maier[51] mentions the treatise of an anonymous author Delphinas, which

he dates to some time before 1447.[52] He stresses that this author insisted particularly on the mother–son incest. Maier even constructs a genealogical tree showing the origin of the seven metals. At the top of the tree is the *lapis*. Its father is 'Gabritius', who in turn was born of Isis and Osiris. After the death of Osiris Isis married their son Gabritius;[53] she is identified with Beya – 'the widow marries her son'. The widow appears here as the classical figure of the mourning Isis. To this event Maier devotes a special 'Epithalamium in Honour of the Nuptials of the Mother Beya and Her Son Gabritius'.[54] 'But this marriage, which was begun with the expression of great joyfulness, ended in the bitterness of mourning', says Maier, adding the verses:

> Within the flower itself there grows the gnawing canker:
> Where honey is, there gall, where swelling breast, the chancre.[55]

For, 'when the son sleeps with the mother, she kills him with the stroke of a viper' (*viperino conatu*). This viciousness recalls the murderous role of Isis,[56] who laid the 'noble worm' in the path of the heavenly Father, Ra.[57] Isis, however, is also the healer, for she not only cured Ra of the poisoning but put together the dismembered body of Osiris.

From: 'Rex and Regina', *Mysterium coniunctionis* (1955–6) (*CW* 14)

422   Like the rose, the figure of the mother–beloved shines in all the hues of heavenly and earthly love. She is the chaste bride and whore who symbolizes the *prima materia*, which 'nature left imperfected'. It is clear from the material we have cited that this refers to the *anima*. She is that piece of chaos which is everywhere and yet hidden, she is that vessel of contradictions and many colours – a totality in the form of a *massa confusa*, yet a substance endowed with every quality in which the splendour of the hidden deity can be revealed.

From: 'The Spirit Mercurius' (1943/8) (*CW* 13)

282   Mercurius, it is generally affirmed, is the arcanum,[58] the *prima materia*,[59] the 'father of all metals',[60] the primeval chaos, the earth of paradise, the 'material upon which nature worked a little, but nevertheless left imperfect'.[61] He is also the *ultima materia*, the goal of his own transformation, the stone,[62] the tincture, the philosophic gold, the carbuncle, the philosophic man, the second Adam, the analogue of Christ, the king, the light of lights, the *deus terrestris*, indeed the divinity itself or its perfect counterpart. Since I have already discussed the synonyms and

meanings of the stone elsewhere there is no need for me to go into further details now.

274   But the most important of all for an interpretation of Mercurius is his relation to Saturn. Mercurius *senex* is identical with Saturn and, to the earlier alchemists especially, it is not quicksilver, but the lead associated with Saturn, which usually represents the *prima materia*. In the Arabic text of the *Turba*[63] quicksilver is identical with the 'water of the moon and of Saturn'. In the 'Dicta Belini' Saturn says: 'My spirit is the water that loosens the rigid limbs of my brothers.'[64] This refers to the 'eternal water', which is just what Mercurius is. Raymond Lully remarks that 'a certain oil of a golden colour is extracted from the philosophic lead'.[65] In Khunrath Mercurius is the 'salt of Saturn',[66] or Saturn is simply Mercurius. Saturn 'draws the eternal water'.[67] Like Mercurius, Saturn is hermaphroditic.[68] Saturn is 'an old man on a mountain, and in him the natures are bound with their complement [i.e. the four elements], and all this is in Saturn'.[69]

From: 'Rex and Regina', *Mysterium coniunctionis* (1955–6) (*CW* 14)

In the age-old image of the *uroboros* lies the thought of devouring oneself and turning oneself into a circulatory process, for it was clear to the more astute alchemists that the *prima materia* of the art was man himself.[70] The *uroboros* is a dramatic symbol for the integration and assimilation of the opposite, i.e. of the shadow. This 'feed-back' process is at the same time a symbol of immortality, since it is said of the *uroboros* that he slays himself and brings himself to life, fertilizes himself and gives birth to himself. He symbolizes the One, who proceeds from the clash of opposites, and he therefore constitutes the secret of the *prima materia* which, as a projection, unquestionably stems from man's unconscious. Accordingly, there must be some psychic datum in it which gives rise to such assertions, and these assertions must somehow characterize that datum even if they are not to be taken literally. What the ultimate reason is for these assertions or manifestations must remain a mystery, but a mystery whose inner kinship with the mystery of faith was sensed by the adepts, so that for them the two were identical.

NOTES

1 Berthelot, *Alch. grecs*, IV, xx, 8.
2 Dorn, 'Congeries Paracelsicae chemicae', *Theatr. chem.*, I, p. 578. In the same place Dorn explains: 'Mercurium istum componi corpore, spiritu et anima, eumque naturam elementorum omnium et proprietatem assumpsisse. Qua propter ingenio et intellectu validissimis adseverarunt suum lapidem esse animalem, quem etiam vocaverunt suum Adamum, qui suam invisibilem Evam occultam in suo corpore gestaret.' ('This Mercurius is composed of body, spirit, and soul, and has

assumed the nature and quality of all the elements. Wherefore they affirmed with
most powerful genius and understanding that their stone was a living thing, which
they also called their Adam, who bore his invisible Eve hidden in his body.')
Hoghelande ('De alch, diff.', *Theatr. chem.*, I, pp. 178f.) says: 'They have
compared the *prima materia* to everything, to male and female, to the hermaphroditic monster, to heaven and earth, to body and spirit, chaos, microcosm,
and the confused mass [*massa confusa*]: it contains in itself all colours and
potentially all metals: there is nothing more wonderful in the world, for it begets
itself, conceives itself and gives birth to itself.'

3   'Tractatus aureus', *Mus. herm.*, p. 10, and many other passages.
4   Dee, 'Monas hieroglyphica', *Theatr. chem.*, II, p. 218. In Aegidius de Vadis
('Dialogus', *Theatr. chem.*, *II*, p. 110) the monad is the effective *forma* in matter.
Khunrath (*Amphitheatrum*, p. 203) writes: 'In Cabala est hominis ad monadis
simplicitatem reducti, cum Deo, Unio: id in Physico-Chemia ad Lapidis nostri . . .
cum Macrocosmo Fermentatio.' ('In the Cabala is the Union of man, reduced to
the simplicity of the monad, with God: in Physio-Chemistry it is the Fermentation
[of] man reduced to [the simplicity of] our stone, with the Macrocosm.') There is
a similar passage in his *Von hyleal. Chaos* (pp. 33, 204), where the monad is more
a symbol of the perfected *lapis*. Dorn ('De spagirico artificio Trithemii sententia',
Theatr. chem., I, p. 441) says: 'In uno est enim unum et non est unum, est simplex
et in quaternario componitur' ('For in the One there is and there is not the One;
it is simple and it is composed in the quaternity'). In his doctrine of the *res simplex*
Dorn is very much influenced by the 'Liber Platonis quartorum'. (On one occasion
he even mentions magic.) In the same passage he also uses the term *monad* for
the goal: 'A ternario et quaternario fit ad monadem progressus' ('The progression
is from the ternary and the quaternary to the Monad'). The term *lapis* is used all
through the literature for the beginning and the goal.
5   *Theatr. chem.*, V, p. 130.
6   Mylius, *Philosphia reformata*, p. 174.
7   *Art. aurif.*, I, p. 66. Eximindus (Eximindius or Eximenus in the first version) is
a corruption of Anaximenes or Anaximander.
8   *Turba* (ed. Ruska), p. 116.
9   'Practica', *Mus herm.*, pp. 403f.
10 Sudhoff Matthiessen edn, XIII, p. 390: 'Thus the supreme artist has prepared a
great uncreated mystery and no mystery will ever be the same nor will it ever
return, for, just as cheese will never again become milk, so generation will never
return to its first state.' Dorn ('Physica genesis', *Theatr. chem.*, I, p. 380)
translates: 'Increatum igitur mysterium hoc fuit ab altissimo opifice Deo praeparatum, ut ei simile nunquam futurum sit, nec ipsum unquam rediturum, ut fuit.'
11 Paracelsus continues (XIII, pp. 390f.): 'This *mysterium magnum* was a mother to
all the elements, and in them likewise a grandmother to all stars, trees, and
creatures of the flesh; for all sentient and insentient creatures, and all others of a
like form, are born from the *mysterium magnum*, just as children are born from a
mother. And it is a *mysterium magnum*, one unique mother of all mortal things,
and they have all originated in her', and so on. 'Now, whereas all other mortal
beings grew out of and originated in the *mysterium increatum*, it is to be
understood that no creature was created earlier, later, or in particular, but all were
created together. For the highest arcanum and great treasure of the creator has
fashioned all things in the *increatum*, not in form, not in essence, not in quality,
but they were in the *increatum*, as an image is in the wood, although this same is
not to be seen until the other wood is cut away: this is the image recognized. Nor
is the *mysterium increatum* to be understood in any other manner, save that
through its separation the corporeal and the insentient severally took on the form
and shape that are their own.'

12 Cf. Grenfell *et al.*, *New Sayings of Jesus,* pp. 15f.: 'Jesus saith, (Ye ask? who are those that draw us to the kingdom, if) the kingdom is in Heaven? . . . the fowls of the air and all beasts that are under the earth or upon the earth, and the fishes of the sea.'

13 Ripley, *Opera omnia chemica*, p. 10.

14 Ibid., p. 130.

15 Ibid., p. 369.

16 Ibid., p. 427.

17 Ibid., p. 9.

18 In the 'Ripley Scrowle' (British Museum, MS. Add. 5025), the sphere of water is represented with dragon's wings. In the 'Verses belonging to an emblematical scrowle' (*Theatr. chem. Brit.*, p. 376) the 'spiritus Mercurii' says:

> Of my blood and water I wis.
> Plenty in all the world there is.
> It runneth in every place;
> Who it findeth he hath grace:
> In the world it runneth over all,
> And goeth round as a ball.

19 Ripley, *Opera omnia chemica*, p. 197.

20 *Mus. herm.*, p. 606.

21 'Hortulani commentarius', in *De alchemia*, p. 366.

22 Cf. Aegidius de Vadis ('Dialogus', *Theatr. chem.*, II, p. 101): 'The chaos is the *materia confusa*. This *materia prima* is necessary to the art. Four elements are mixed in a state of disorder in the *materia prima*, because earth and water, which are heavier than the other elements, reached the sphere of the moon, while fire and air, which are lighter than the others, descended as far as the centre of the earth: for which reason such a *materia* is rightly called disordered. Only a part of this disordered material remained in the world, and this is known to everyone and is sold publicly.'

23 Hortulanus, 'Commentarius', *De alchemia*, p. 371.

24 Zeller, *Die Philosophie der Griechen*, III, p. 120.

25 Ibid., p. 102; also p. 154.

26 Ibid., p. 687.

27 Also defined as 'the round fish in the sea' ('Allegoriae super librum Turbae', *Art. aurif.*, I, p. 141).

28 Maier, *Symbola aureae mensae*, pp. 379f.

29 'They fall into madness through ignorance', Berthelot, *Alch. grecs*, II, iv, 46.

30 *Isis*, XVIII, p. 237. On p. 238 Wei Po-yang describes the madness that attacks the adept. Cf. 'The Philosophical Tree', paras 423ff.

31 Berthelot, II, iv, 52. An alchemist would say that he knew the secret of gold-making. Psychologically it would mean that he knew about the transformation of consciousness, but that it was abortive, so that instead of being illuminated he fell into deeper darkness.

32 Cf. Lully, 'Testamentum', *Bibliotheca chemica curiosa*, I, pp. 790ff., and Maier, *Symbola aureae mensae*, pp. 379f.

33 Pars. 342f.

34 Cf. 'The Spirit Mercurius', Part II, sec. 6.

35 Thus *Aurora consurgens*, II (*Art. aurif.*, I, pp. 185–246) closes with the words: 'Et sic probata est medicina Philosophorum, quam omni [investiganti] fideli et pio praestare dignetur Deus omnipotens, unigenitusque filius Dei Dominus noster Jesus Christus, qui cum Patre et Spiritu sancto vivit et regnat, unus Deus per infinita saeculorum. Amen' ('And this is the approved medicine of the philosophers, which may our Lord Jesus Christ, who liveth and reigneth with the Father

and the Holy Ghost, one God for ever and ever, deign to give to every searcher who is faithful, pious, and of good will, Amen'). This conclusion no doubt comes from the Offertorium (prayer during the *commixtio*), where it says: 'qui humanitatis nostrae fieri dignatus est particeps, Jesus Christus, Filius tuus, Dominus noster: qui tecum vivit et regnat in unitate Spiritus Sancti Deus per omnia saecula saeculorum. Amen.' ('who vouchsafed to become partaker of our humanity, Jesus Christ, Thy Son, our Lord: who liveth and reigneth with Thee in the unity of the Holy Ghost, one God, world without end. Amen').

36 Cf. 'Tractatus aureus', *Ars chemica*, p. 21.

37 Kircher, 'Oedipus Aegyptiacus', II, Class X, Ch. V, p. 414. There is a connection between this text and the 'Tabula smaragdina'; cf. Ruska, *Tabula smaragdina*, p. 217.

38 The *Rosarium* (*Art. aurif.*, II, p. 230) says: 'Et scias, quod haec est longissima via, ergo patientia et mora sunt necessariae in nostro magisterio' ('And you must know that this is a very long road; therefore patience and deliberation are needful in our magistery'). Cf. *Aurora consurgens*, I, Ch. 10: 'Tria sunt necessaria videlicet patientia mora et aptitudo instrumentorum' ('Three things are necessary, namely: patience, deliberation, and skill with the instruments').

39 According to Freud, these projections are infantile wish-fantasies. But a more thorough examination of neuroses in childhood shows that such fantasies are largely dependent on the psychology of the parents, that is, are caused by the parents' wrong attitude to the child. Cf. 'Analytical Psychology and Education', paras 216ff.

40 Hence *Aurora consurgens*, I, Ch. VI, says: 'and all my bones are troubled before the face of my iniquity'. Cf. Ps. 37:4 (D.V.): 'there is no peace for my bones because of my sins'.

41 Florence, Ashburnham 1166, 14th cent. They are reproduced as figs 131 and 135 in *Psychology and Alchemy*.

42 The arrow refers to the *telum passionis* of Mercurius. Cf. 'Cantilena Riplaei', ibid., para. 491, and *Mysterium coniunctionis*, pp. 285ff. Cf. also 'The Spirit Mercurius', Part II, sec. 8, and St Bernard of Clairvaux, *Sermones in Cantica*, XXX, 8 (Migne, *P.L.*, vol. 183, cols. 932–3): 'Est et sagitta sermo Dei vivus et efficax et penetrabilior omni gladio ancipiti. . . . Est etiam sagitta electa amor Christi, quae Mariae animam non modo confixit, sed etiam pertransivit, ut nullam in pectore virginali particulam vacuam amore relinqueret' ('God's word is an arrow; it is lively and effective and more penetrating than a double-edged sword. . . . And the love of Christ is a choice arrow too, which not only entered, but transfixed, the soul of Mary, so that it left no particle of her virgin heart free of love'). Trans. by a priest of Mount Melleray, I, p. 346.

43 Cf. the Alaskan Eskimo tale 'The Woman Who Became a Spider', in Rasmussen, *Die Gabe des Adlers,* pp. 121ff., and the Siberian tale 'The Girl and the Skull', in Kunike (ed.), *Märchen aus Sibirien*, no. 31, where a woman marries a skull.

44 It is said that in the Book of Secrets Mani spoke of 'the son of the widow', Jesus (Schaeder, *Urform und Fortbildungen des manichäischen Systems*, p. 75 n.). Bousset (*The Antichrist Legend*, p. 70) mentions the reign of a widow who will precede the Antichrist (according to a Greek and Armenian Apocalypse of Daniel, p. 68). Freemasons are also reckoned among the 'children of the widow' (Eckert, *Die Mysterien der Heidenkirche, erhalten und fortgebildet im Bunde der alten und neuen Kinder der Wittwe*). 'Widow' in the Cabala is a designation for Malchuth. Knorr von Rosenroth, *Kabbala denudata*, I, p. 118.

45 Mylius, *Phil. ref.*, p. 173.

46 Gratarolus, *Verae alch.*, II, p. 265.

47 This expression appears for the first time in *Aurora consurgens*, Part II, *Art. aurif.*, I, p. 201. Mylius (*Phil. ref.*) copies it. The 'vieille exténuée' mentioned in Pernety

(*Dictionnaire mytho-hermétique*, p. 280) goes back to the same source. Cf. also 'a mistress of about a hundred years of age' in 'Aureum saeculum redivivum', *Mus. herm.*, p. 64 (Waite, I, p. 59).

48 *Aurora consurgens* II, *Art. aurif.*, I, p. 196.
49 In *Aurora Consurgens,* p. 77, seven women seek one husband.
50 Cf. the 'matrices of all things' in Rulandus, *Lexicon of Alchemy*, p. 226.
51 *Symb. aur. mensae*, p. 344.
52 Printed in *Theatr. chem.*, III, pp. 871ff. under the title 'Antiqui Philosophi Galli Delphinati anonymi Liber Secreti Maximi totius mundanae gloriae'.
53 Gabritius therefore corresponds to Horus. In ancient Egypt Horus had long been equated with Osiris. Cf. Brugsch, *Religion und Mythologie der alten Ägypter*, p. 406. The Papyrus Mimaut has: 'Do the terrible deed to me, the orphan of the honoured widow.' Preisendanz relates the 'widow' to Isis and the 'orphan' to Horus, with whom the magician identifies himself (*Papyri Graecae magicae*, I, pp. 54f.). We find the 'medicine of the widow' in the treatise 'Isis to Horus', Berthelot, *Alch. grecs*, I, xiii, 16.
54 *Symb. aur. mensae*, p. 515. The epithalamium begins with the words: 'When the mother is joined with the son in the covenant of marriage, count it not as incest. For so doth nature ordain, so doth the holy law of fate require, and the thing is not unpleasing to God.'
55 Est quod in ipsis floribus angat,
    Et ubi mel, ibi fel, ubi uber, ibi tuber.
56 In Greco-Roman times Isis was represented as a human-headed snake. Cf. illustration in Erman, *Religion der Ägypter*, p. 391. For Isis as δράκων see Reitzenstein, *Poimandres*, p. 31.
57 Erman, p. 301. The text derives from the time of the New Kingdom.
58 'Tract. aur. cum scholiis', *Theatr. chem.*, IV (1659), p. 608.
59 Mylius, *Phil. ref.*, p. 179; 'Tract. aureus', *Mus. herm.*, p. 25; Trevisanus in *Theatr. chem.*, I (1659), p. 695.
60 Exercit. in Turb.', *Art. aurif.*, I, p. 154.
61 *Rosarium*, ibid., II, p. 231.
62 Ventura, in *Theatr. chem.*, II (1659), p. 232: 'lapis benedictus'; Dorn, in *Theatr. chem.*, I (1659), p. 510: 'fiery and perfect Mercurius'; p. 520: 'The Adamic stone is made out of the Adamic Mercurius in the woman Eve'; Lully, *Codicillus*, pp. 880f.: 'The good that is sought is our stone and Mercurius.'
63 Ed. Ruska, p. 204.
64 *Art. aurif.*, II, p. 379. The same in Dorn, *Theatr. chem.*, I (1659), pp. 560f.
65 Cited in Mylius, *Phil. ref.*, p. 302.
66 *Hyl. Chaos*, p. 197.
67 'Aenigma philosophorum', *Theatr. chem.*, IV (1659), pp. 458ff.
68 *Hyl. Chaos*, p. 195.
69 'Rhasis Epist.', in Maier, *Symb. aur. mens.*, p. 211. Like Saturn, Mercurius combines all metals in himself (ibid., p. 531).
70 Thus Morienus (7th–8th cent.) states: 'This thing is extracted from thee, for thou art its ore; in thee they find it; and, to speak more plainly, from thee they take it; and when thou hast experienced this, the love and desire for it will be increased in thee. And thou shalt know that this thing subsists truly and beyond all doubt' (*Art. aurif.*, II, p. 37).

2 The alchemical mind

From: 'The Paradoxa', *Mysterium coniunctionis* (1955–6) (*CW* 14)

53   Everything psychic is pregnant with the future. The sixteenth and seventeenth centuries were a time of transition from a world founded on metaphysics to an era of immanentist explanatory principles, the motto no longer being *omne animal a Deo* (God is the source of all life) but *omne vivum ex ovo* (in the beginning was life). What was then brewing in the unconscious came to fruition in the tremendous development of the natural sciences, whose youngest sister is empirical psychology. Everything that was naively presumed to be a knowledge of transcendental and divine things, which human beings can never know with certainty, and everything that seemed to be irretrievably lost with the decline of the Middle Ages, rose up again with the discovery of the psyche. This premonition of future discoveries in the psychic sphere expressed itself in the phantasmagoric speculations of philosophers who, until then, had appeared to be the arch-pedlars of sterile verbiage.

From: 'Religious Ideas in Alchemy' (1937) (*CW* 12)

421   The substance that harbours the divine secret is everywhere, including the human body.[1] It can be had for the asking and can be found anywhere, even in the most loathsome filth.[2] In these circumstances the *opus* is no longer a ritualistic *officium*, but the same work of redemption which God himself accomplished upon mankind through the example of Christ, and which is now recognized by the philosopher who has received the *donum spiritus sancti*, the divine art, as his own individual *opus*. The alchemists emphasize this point: 'He who works through the spirit of another and by a hired hand will behold results that are far from the truth: and conversely he who gives his services to another as assistant in the laboratory will never be admitted to the Queen's mysteries.'[3] One might quote the words of Kabasilas: 'As kings, when they bring a gift to God, they bear it themselves and do not permit it to be borne by others.'

422   Alchemists are, in fact, decided solitaries:[4] each has his say in his own way.[5] They rarely have pupils, and of direct tradition there seems to have

been very little, nor is there much evidence of any secret societies or the like.[6] Each worked in the laboratory for himself and suffered from loneliness. On the other hand, quarrels were rare. Their writings are relatively free of polemic, and the way they quote each other shows a remarkable agreement on first principles, even if one cannot understand what they are really agreeing about.[7] There is little of that disputatiousness and splitting of hairs that so often mar theology and philosophy. The reason for this is probably the fact that 'true' alchemy was never a business or a career, but a genuine *opus* to be achieved by quiet, self-sacrificing work. One has the impression that each individual tried to express his own particular experiences, quoting the dicta of the masters only when they seemed to offer analogies.

423 All, from the very earliest times, are agreed that their art is sacred and divine,[8] and likewise that their work can be completed only with the help of God. This science of theirs is given only to the few, and none understands it unless God or a master has opened his understanding.[9] The knowledge acquired may not be passed on to others unless they are worthy of it.[10] Since all the essentials are expressed in metaphors they can be communicated only to the intelligent who possess the gift of comprehension.[11] The foolish allow themselves to be infatuated by literal interpretations and recipes, and fall into error.[12] When reading the literature, one must not be content with just *one* book but must possess many books,[13] for 'one book opens another'.[14] Moreover one must read carefully, paragraph by paragraph: then one will make discoveries.[15] The terminology is admitted to be quite unreliable.[16] Sometimes the nature of the coveted substance will be revealed in a dream.[17]

From: 'Rex and Regina', *Mysterium coniunctionis* (1955–6) (*CW* 14)

446   One must bear in mind that the alchemists, guided by their keenness for research, were in fact on a hopeful path since the fruit that alchemy bore after centuries of endeavour was chemistry and its staggering discoveries. The emotional dynamism of alchemy is largely explained by a premonition of these then unheard-of possibilities. However barren of useful or even enlightening results its labours were, these efforts, notwithstanding their chronic failure, seem to have had a psychic effect of a positive nature, something akin to satisfaction or even a perceptible increase in wisdom. Otherwise it would be impossible to explain why the alchemists did not turn away in disgust from their almost invariably futile projects. Not that such disillusionments never came to them; indeed the futility of alchemy brought it into increasing disrepute. There remain, nevertheless, a number of witnesses who make it quite clear that their hopeless fumbling, inept as it was from the chemical standpoint, presents a very different appearance

when seen from a psychological angle. As I have shown in *Psychology and Alchemy*, there occurred during the chemical procedure psychic projections which brought unconscious contents to light, often in the form of vivid visions. The medical psychologist knows today that such projections may be of the greatest therapeutic value. It was not for nothing that the old Masters identified their *nigredo* with melancholia and extolled the *opus* as the sovereign remedy for all 'afflictions of the soul'; for they had discovered, as was only to be expected, that though their purses shrank their soul gained in stature – provided of course that they survived certain by no means inconsiderable psychic dangers. The projections of the alchemists were nothing other than unconscious contents appearing in matter, the same contents that modern psychotherapy makes conscious by the method of active imagination before they unconsciously change into projections. Making them conscious and giving form to what is unformed has a specific effect in cases where the conscious attitude offers an overcrowded unconscious no possible means of expressing itself. In these circumstances the unconscious has, as it were, no alternative but to generate projections and neurotic symptoms. The conscious milieu of the Middle Ages provided no adequate outlet for these things. The immense world of natural science lay folded in the bud, as also did that questing religious spirit which we meet in many of the alchemical treatises and which, we may well conjecture, was closely akin to the empiricism of scientific research.

From: 'The Personification of the Opposites', *Mysterium coniunctionis* (1955–6) (*CW* 14)

345   Revelation conveys general truths which often do not illuminate the individual's actual situation in the slightest, nor was it traditional revelation that gave us the microscope and the machine. And since human life is not enacted exclusively, or even to a noticeable degree, on the plane of the higher verities, the source of knowledge unlocked by the old alchemists and physicians has done humanity a great and welcome service – so great that for many people the light of revelation has been extinguished altogether. Within the confines of civilization man's wilful rationality apparently suffices. Outside of this shines, or should shine, the light of faith. But where the darkness comprehendeth it not (this being the prerogative of darkness!) those labouring in the darkness must try to accomplish an opus that will cause the 'fishes' eyes' to shine in the depths of the sea, or to catch the 'refracted rays of the divine majesty' even though this produces a light which the darkness, as usual, does not comprehend. But when there is a light in the darkness which comprehends the darkness, darkness no longer prevails. The longing of the darkness for light is fulfilled only when the light can no longer be rationally explained by the

darkness. For the darkness has its own peculiar intellect and its own logic, which should be taken very seriously. Only the 'light which the darkness comprehendeth not' can illuminate the darkness. Everything that the darkness thinks, grasps and comprehends by itself is dark; therefore it is illuminated only by what, to it, is unexpected, unwanted and incomprehensible. The psychotherapeutic method of active imagination offers excellent examples of this; sometimes a numinous dream or some external event will have the same effect.

346   Alchemy announced a source of knowledge, parallel if not equivalent to revelation, which yields a 'bitter' water by no means acceptable to our human judgment. It is harsh and bitter or like vinegar,[18] for it is a bitter thing to accept the darkness and blackness of the *umbra solis* and to pass through this valley of the shadow. It is bitter indeed to discover behind one's lofty ideals narrow, fanatical convictions, all the more cherished for that, and behind one's heroic pretensions nothing but crude egotism, infantile greed, and complacency. This painful corrective is an unavoidable stage in every psychotherapeutic process. As the alchemists said, it begins with the *nigredo*, or generates it as the indispensable prerequisite for synthesis, for unless the opposites are constellated and brought to consciousness they can never be united. Freud halted the process at the reduction to the inferior half of the personality and tended to overlook the demonic dangerousness of the dark side, which by no means consists only of relatively harmless infantilisms. Man is neither so reasonable nor so good that he can cope *eo ipso* with evil. The darkness can quite well engulf him, especially when he finds himself with those of like mind. Mass-mindedness increases unconsciousness and then the evil swells like an avalanche, as contemporary events have shown. Even so, society can also work for good; it is even necessary because of the moral weakness of most human beings, who, to maintain themselves at all, must have some external good to cling on to. The great religions are psychotherapeutic systems that give a foothold to all those who cannot stand by themselves, and they are in the overwhelming majority.

347   In spite of their undoubtedly 'heretical methods' the alchemists showed by their positive attitude to the Church that they were cleverer than certain modern apostles of enlightenment. Also – very much in contrast to the rationalistic tendencies of today – they displayed, despite its 'tortuousness', a remarkable understanding of the imagery upon which the Christian cosmos is built. This world of images, in its historical form, is irretrievably lost to modern man; its loss has spiritually impoverished the masses and compelled them to find pitiful substitutes, as poisonous as they are worthless. No one can be held responsible for this development. It is due rather to the restless tempo of spiritual growth and change, whose motive forces go far beyond the horizon of the individual. He can only hope to keep pace with it and try to understand it so far that he is not blindly

swallowed up by it. For that is the alarming thing about mass movements, even if they are good, that they demand and must demand blind faith. The Church can never explain the truth of her images because she acknowledges no point of view but her own. She moves solely within the framework of her images, and her arguments must always beg the question. The flock of harmless sheep was ever the symbolic prototype of the credulous crowd, though the Church is quick to recognize the wolves in sheep's clothing who lead the faith of the multitude astray in order to destroy them. The tragedy is that the blind trust which leads to perdition is practised just as much inside the Church and is praised as the highest virtue. Yet our Lord says: 'Be ye therefore wise as serpents',[19] and the Bible itself stresses the cleverness and cunning of the serpent. But where are these necessary if not altogether praiseworthy qualities developed and given their due? The serpent has become a by-word for everything morally abhorrent, and yet anyone who is not as smart as a snake is liable to land himself in trouble through blind faith.

348   The alchemists knew about the snake and the 'cold' half of nature,[20] and they said enough to make it clear to their successors that they endeavoured by their art to lead that serpentine Nous of the darkness, the *serpens mercurialis*, through the stages of transformation to the goal of perfection (*telesmus*).[21] The more or less symbolical or projected integration of the unconscious that went hand in hand with this evidently had so many favourable effects that the alchemists felt encouraged to express a tempered optimism.

From: 'The Conjunction', *Mysterium coniunctionis* (1955–6) (*CW* 14)

665   The adepts strove to realize their speculative ideas in the form of a chemical substance which they thought was endowed with all kinds of magical powers. This is the literal meaning of their uniting the *unio mentalis* with the body. For us it is certainly not easy to include moral and philosophical reflections in this amalgamation, as the alchemists obviously did. For one thing we know too much about the real nature of chemical combination, and for another we have a much too abstract conception of the mind to be able to understand how a 'truth' can be hidden in matter or what an effective 'balsam' must be like. Owing to medieval ignorance both of chemistry and of psychology, and the lack of any epistemological criticism, the two concepts could easily mix, so that things that for us have no recognizable connection with one another could enter into mutual relationship.

From: 'The Personification of the Opposites', *Mysterium coniunctionis* (1955–6) (*CW* 14)

336   But the greatest of all riddles, of course, is the ever-recurring question of what the alchemists really meant by their substances. What, for instance, is the meaning of a 'sal spirituale'? The only possible answer seems to be this: chemical matter was so completely unknown to them that it instantly became a carrier for projections. Its darkness was so loaded with unconscious contents that a state of *participation mystique*,[22] or unconscious identity, arose between them and the chemical substance, which caused this substance to behave, at any rate in part, like an unconscious content. Of this relationship the alchemists had a dim presentiment – enough, anyway, to enable them to make statements which can only be understood as psychological.

From: 'Religious Ideas in Alchemy' (1937) (*CW* 12)

380   It should now be sufficiently clear that from its earliest days alchemy had a double face: on the one hand the practical chemical work in the laboratory, on the other a psychological process, in part consciously psychic, in part unconsciously projected and seen in the various transformations of matter.

381   Not much effort is needed at the beginning of the work; it is sufficient to approach it with 'a free and empty mind', as one text says.[23] But one important rule must be observed: 'the mind [*mens*] must be in harmony with the work'[24] and the work must be above all else. Another text says that in order to acquire the 'golden understanding' (*aurea apprehensio*) one must keep the eyes of the mind and soul well open, observing and contemplating by means of that inner light which God has lit in nature and in our hearts from the beginning.[25]

382   Since the investigator's psyche was so closely bound up with the work—not only as its necessary medium but also as its cause and point of departure – it is easy to understand why so much emphasis was laid on the psychic condition and mental attitude of the laboratory worker. Alphidius says: 'Know that thou canst not have this science unless thou shalt purify thy mind before God, that is, wipe away all corruption from thy heart.'[26] According to *Aurora*, the treasure-house of Hermetic wisdom rests on a firm foundation of fourteen principal virtues: health, humility, holiness, chastity, virtue,[27] victory, faith, hope, charity, goodness (*benignitas*), patience, temperance, a spiritual discipline or understanding,[28] and obedience.

383   The Pseudo-Thomas who is author of this same treatise quotes the saying 'Purge the horrible darknesses of our mind',[29] and gives as a parallel Senior's 'he maketh all that is black white.'[30] Here the 'darknesses of our mind' coincide unmistakably with the *nigredo*; i.e. the author feels

or experiences the initial stage of the alchemical process as identical with his own psychic condition.

384   Another old authority is Geber. The *Rosarium* says that in his *Liber perfecti magisterii* Geber requires the following psychological and characterological qualities of the artifex: he must have a most subtle mind and an adequate knowledge of metals and minerals. But he must not have a coarse or rigid mind, nor should he be greedy and avaricious, nor irresolute and vacillating. Further, he must not be hasty or vain. On the contrary, he must be firm in purpose, persevering, patient, mild, long-suffering and good tempered.[31]

385   The author of the *Rosarium* goes on to say that he who wishes to be initiated into this art and wisdom must not be arrogant, but devout, upright, of profound understanding, humane, of a cheerful countenance and a happy nature. He continues: 'My son, above all I admonish thee to fear God, who knoweth what manner of man thou art and in whom is help for the solitary, whosoever he may be.'[32]

386   Particularly instructive is the introduction to the art given by Morienus to Kalid.[33]

> This thing for which you have sought so long is not to be acquired or accomplished by force or passion. It is to be won only by patience and humility and by a determined and most perfect love. For God bestows this divine and immaculate science on his faithful servants, namely those on whom he resolved to bestow it from the original nature of things.[34] . . . [Some remarks follow concerning the handing-down of the art to pupils.] Nor were they [the elect] able to hold anything back save through the strength granted to them by God, and they themselves could no longer direct their minds save towards the goal[35] appointed for them by God. For God charges those of his servants whom he has purposely chosen [Figure 2.1] that they seek this divine science which is hidden from men, and that they keep it to themselves. This is the science that draws its master away from the suffering of this world and leads to the knowledge of future good.
>
> When Morienus was asked by the kind why he lived in mountains and deserts rather than in hermitages, he answered: 'I do not doubt that in hermitages and brotherhoods I would find greater repose, and fatiguing work in the deserts and in the mountains; but no one reaps who does not sow. . . . Exceeding narrow is the gateway to peace, and none may enter save through affliction of the soul.'[36]

387   We must not forget, in considering this last sentence, that Morienus is not speaking for the general edification but is referring to the divine art and its work. Michael Maier expresses himself in similar vein when he says:

> There is in our chemistry a certain noble substance, in the beginning whereof is wretchedness with vinegar, but in its ending joy with

Figure 2.1 God enlightening the artifex.
Source: From Barchusen, *Elementa chemiae* (1718); reproduced in Jung's *Collected Works*, Vol. 12.

gladness. Therefore I have supposed that the same will happen to me, namely that I shall suffer difficulty, grief, and weariness at first, but in the end shall come to glimpse pleasanter and easier things.[37]

388   The same author also affirms that 'our chemistry stirs up the artifex to a meditation of the heavenly good',[38] and that whoso is initiated by God into these mysteries 'casts aside all insignificant cares like food and clothing, and feels himself as it were new-born.'[39]

From: 'The Conjunction', *Mysterium coniunctionis* (1955–6) (*CW* 14)

764   Although the alchemist thought he knew better than anyone else that, at the Creation, at least a little bit of the divinity, the *anima mundi*, entered into material things and was caught there, he nevertheless believed in the possibility of a one-sided spiritualization, without considering that the precondition for this is a materialization of the spirit in the form of the blue quintessence. In reality his labours elevated the body into proximity with the spirit while at the same time drawing the spirit down into matter. By sublimating matter he concretized spirit.

765   This self-evident truth was still strange to medieval man and it has been

only partially digested even by the man of today. But if a union is to take place between opposites like spirit and matter, conscious and unconscious, bright and dark, and so on, it will happen in a third thing, which represents not a compromise but something new, just as for the alchemists the cosmic strife of the elements was composed by the λίθος οὐ λίθος (stone that is no stone), by a transcendental entity that could be described only in paradoxes.[40] Dorn's *caelum*, which corresponded to the stone, was on the one hand a liquid that could be poured out of a bottle and on the other the Microcosm itself. For the psychologist it is the self – man as he is, and the indescribable and super-empirical totality of that same man. This totality is a mere postulate, but a necessary one, because no one can assert that he has complete knowledge of man as he is. Not only in the psychic man is there something unknown, but also in the physical. We should be able to include this unknown quantity in a total picture of man, but we cannot. Man himself is partly empirical, partly transcendental; he too is a λίθος οὐ λίθος. Also, we do not know whether what we on the empirical plane regard as physical may not, in the Unknown beyond our experience, be identical with what on this side of the border we distinguish from the physical as psychic. Though we know from experience that psychic processes are related to material ones, we are not in a position to say in what this relationship consists or how it is possible at all. Precisely because the psychic and the physical are mutually dependent it has often been conjectured that they may be identical somewhere beyond our present experience, though this certainly does not justify the arbitrary hypothesis of either materialism of spiritualism.

766   With this conjecture of the identity of the psychic and the physical we approach the alchemical view of the *unus mundus*, the potential world of the first day of creation, when there was as yet 'no second'. Before the time of Paracelsus the alchemists believed in *creatio ex nihilo*. For them, therefore, God himself was the principle of matter. But Paracelsus and his school assumed that matter was an 'increatum', and hence coexistent and coeternal with God. Whether they considered this view monistic or dualistic I am unable to discover. The only certain thing is that for all the alchemists matter had a divine aspect, whether on the ground that God was imprisoned in it in the form of the *anima mundi* or *anima media natura*, or that matter represented God's 'reality'. In no case was matter de-deified, and certainly not the potential matter of the first day of Creation. It seems that only the Paracelsists were influenced by the dualistic words of Genesis.

From: 'The Psychology of the Transference' (1946) (*CW* 16)

497   It is difficult to tell whether the alchemists were so hopelessly muddled that they did not notice flat contradictions, or whether their paradoxes were

sublimely deliberate. I suspect it was a bit of both, since the *ignorantes, stulti, fatui* would take the texts at their face value and get bogged in the welter of analogies, while the more astute reader, realizing the necessity for symbolism, would handle it like a virtuoso with no trouble at all. Intellectual responsibility seems always to have been the alchemists' weak spot, though a few of them tell us plainly enough how we are to regard their peculiar language.[41] The less respect they showed for the bowed shoulders of the sweating reader, the greater was their debt, willing or unwilling, to the unconscious, for it is just the infinite variety of their images and paradoxes that points to a psychological fact of prime importance: the indefiniteness of the archetype with its multitude of meanings, all presenting different facets of a single, simple truth. The alchemists were so steeped in their inner experiences that their sole concern was to devise fitting images and expressions regardless of whether these were intelligible or not. Although in this respect they remained behind the times, they nevertheless performed the inestimable service of having constructed a phenomenology of the unconscious long before the advent of psychology. We, as heirs to these riches, do not find our heritage at all easy to enjoy. Yet we can comfort ourselves with the reflection that the old masters were equally at a loss to understand one another, or that they did so only with difficulty. Thus the author of the *Rosarium* says that the 'antiqui Philosophi tam obscure quam confuse scripserunt', so that they only baffled the reader or put him off altogether. For his part, he says, he would make the 'experimentum verissimum' plain for all eyes to see and reveal it 'in the most certain and human manner' – and then proceeds to write exactly like all the others before him. This was inevitable, as the alchemists did not really know what they were writing about. Whether we know today seems to me not altogether sure. At any rate we no longer believe that the secret lies in chemical substances, but that it is rather to be found in one of the darker and deeper layers of the psyche, although we do not know the nature of this layer. Perhaps in another century or so we shall discover a new darkness from which there will emerge something we do not understand either, but whose presence we sense with the utmost certainty.

498   The alchemist saw no contradiction in comparing the diadem with a 'foul deposit' and then, in the next breath, saying that it is of heavenly origin. He follows the rule laid down in the 'Tabula smaragdina': 'Quod est inferius, est sicut quod est superius. Et quod est superius, est sicut quod est inferius.'[42] His faculty for conscious discrimination was not as acute as modern man's, and was distinctly blunter than the scholastic thought of his contemporaries. This apparent regression cannot be explained by any mental backwardness on the part of the alchemist; it is more the case that his main interest is focussed on the unconscious itself and not at all on the powers of discrimination and formulation which mark the concise conceptual thinking of the schoolmen. He is content if he succeeds in finding

expressions to delineate afresh the secret he feels. How these expressions relate to and differ from one another is of the smallest account to him, for he never supposes that anybody could reconstruct the art from his ideas about it, but that those who approach the art at all are already fascinated by its secret and are guided by sure intuition, or are actually elected and predestined thereto by God. Thus the *Rosarium*[43] says, quoting Hortulanus:[44] 'Solus ille, qui scit facere lapidem Philosophorum, intelligit verba eorum de lapide' (Only he who knows how to make the philosophers' stone can understand their words concerning it). The darkness of the symbolism scatters before the eyes of the enlightened philosopher. Hortulanus says again: 'Nihil enim prodest occultatio philosophorum in sermonibus, ubi doctrina Spiritus sancti operatur'[45] (The mystification in the sayings of the philosophers is of no avail where the teaching of the Holy Ghost is at work).

499   The alchemist's failure to distinguish between *corpus* and *spiritus* is in our case assisted by the assumption that, owing to the preceding *mortificatio* and *sublimatio*, the body has taken on 'quintessential' or spiritual form and consequently, as a *corpus mundum* (pure substance), is not so very different from spirit. It may shelter spirit or even draw it down to itself.[46] All these ideas lead one to conclude that not only the *coniunctio* but the reanimation of the 'body' is an altogether transmundane event, a process occurring in the psychic non-ego. This would explain why the process is so easily projected, for if it were of a personal nature its liability to projection would be considerably reduced, because it could then be made conscious without too much difficulty. At any rate this liability would not have been sufficient to cause a projection upon inanimate matter, which is the polar opposite of the living psyche. Experience shows that the carrier of the projection is not just *any* object but is always one that proves adequate to the nature of the content projected – that is to say, it must offer the content a 'hook' to hang on.[47]

From: 'The Personification of the Opposites', (1955–6) (*CW* 14)

147   As investigators of nature the alchemists showed their Christian attitude by their *pistis* [faith] in the object of their science, and it was not their fault if in many cases the psyche proved stronger than the chemical substance and its well-guarded secrets by distorting the results. It was only the acuter powers of observation in modern man which showed that weighing and measuring provided the key to the locked doors of chemical combination, after the intuition of the alchemists had stressed for centuries the importance of 'measure, number, and weight'.[48] The prime and most immediate experience of matter was that it is animated, which for medieval man was self-evident; indeed every Mass, every rite of the Church, and

the miraculous effect of relics all demonstrated for him this natural and obvious fact. The French Enlightenment and the shattering of the metaphysical view of the world were needed before a scientist like Lavoisier had the courage finally to reach out for the scales. To begin with, however, the alchemists were fascinated by the soul of matter, which, unknown to them, it had received from the human psyche by way of projection. For all their intensive preoccupation with matter as a concrete fact they followed this psychic trail, which was to lead them into a region that, to our way of thinking, had not the remotest connection with chemistry. Their mental labours consisted in a predominantly intuitive apprehension of psychic facts, the intellect playing only the modest role of a *famulus*. The results of this curious method of research proved, however, to be beyond the grasp of any psychology for several centuries. If one does not understand a person, one tends to regard him as a fool. The misfortune of the alchemists was that they themselves did not know what they were talking about. Nevertheless, we possess witnesses enough to the high esteem in which they held their science and to the wonderment which the mystery of matter instilled into them. For they discovered – to keep to sulphur as our example – in this substance, which was one of the customary attributes of hell and the devil, as well as in the poisonous, crafty and treacherous Mercurius, an analogy with the most sacrosanct figure of their religion. They therefore imbued this arcanum with symbols intended to characterize its malicious, dangerous and uncanny nature, choosing precisely those which in the positive sense were used for Christ in the patristic literature. These were the snake, the lion, the eagle, fire, cloud, shadow, fish, stone, the unicorn and the rhinoceros, the dragon, the night-raven, the man encompassed by a woman, the hen, water, and many others. This strange usage is explained by the fact that the majority of the patristic allegories have in addition to their positive meaning a negative one. Thus in St Eucherius[49] the rapacious wolf 'in its good part' signifies the apostle Paul, but 'in its bad part' the devil.

148   From this we would have to conclude that the alchemists had discovered the psychological existence of a shadow which opposes and compensates the conscious, positive figure. For them the shadow was in no sense a *privatio lucis*; it was so real that they even thought they could discern its material density, and this concretism led them to attribute to it the dignity of being the matrix of an incorruptible and eternal substance. In the religious sphere this psychological discovery is reflected in the historical fact that only with the rise of Christianity did the devil, the 'eternal counterpart of Christ', assume his true form, and that the figure of Antichrist appears on the scene already in the New Testament. It would have been natural for the alchemists to suppose that they had lured the devil out of the darkness of matter.

From: 'Religious Ideas in Alchemy' (1937) (*CW* 12)

366   The importance or necessity of understanding and intelligence is insisted upon all through the literature, not only because intelligence above the ordinary is needed in the performance of so difficult a work, but because it is assumed that a species of magical power capable of transforming even brute matter dwells in the human mind.

From: 'Rex and Regina', *Mysterium coniunctionis* (1955–6) (*CW* 14)

456   In the latter category we must distinguish two kinds of alchemists: those who believed that the revealed truth represented by the Church could derive nothing but gain if it were combined with a knowledge of the God in nature; and those for whom the projection of the Christian mystery of faith into the physical world invested nature with a mystical significance, whose mysterious light outshone the splendid incomprehensibilities of Church ceremonial. The first group hoped for a rebirth of dogma, the second for a new incarnation of it and its transformation into a natural revelation.

457   I lay particular stress on the phenomena of assimilation in alchemy because they are, in a sense, a prelude to the modern approximation between empirical psychology and Christian dogma – an approximation which Nietzsche clearly foresaw. Psychology, as a science, observes religious ideas from the standpoint of their psychic phenomenology without intruding on their theological content. It puts the dogmatic images into the category of psychic contents, because this constitutes its field of research. It is compelled to do so by the nature of the psyche itself; it does not, like alchemy, try to explain psychic processes in theological terms, but rather to illuminate the darkness of religious images by relating them to similar images in the psyche. The result is a kind of amalgamation of ideas of – so it would seem – the most varied provenience, and this sometimes leads to parallels with and comparisons which to an uncritical mind unacquainted with the epistemological method may seem like a devaluation or a false interpretation. If this were to be construed as an objection to psychology one could easily say the same thing about the hermeneutics of the Church Fathers, which are often very risky indeed, or about the dubious nature of textual criticism. The psychologist has to investigate religious symbols because his empirical material, of which the theologian usually knows nothing, compels him to do so. Presumably no one would wish to hand over the chemistry of albuminous bodies to some other department of science on the ground that they are organic and that the investigation of life is a matter for the biologist. A *rapprochement* between empirical science and religious experience would in my opinion

be fruitful for both. Harm can result only if one side or the other remains unconscious of the limitations of its claim to validity. Alchemy, certainly, cannot be defended against the charge of unconsciousness. It is and remains a puzzle whether Ripley ever reflected on his theological enormities and what he thought about them. From a scientific point of view, his mentality resembles that of a dream-state.

From: 'The Conjunction', *Mysterium coniunctionis* (1955–6) (*CW* 14)

772   What, then, do the statements of the alchemists concerning their arcanum mean, looked at psychologically? In order to answer this question we must remember the working hypothesis we have used for the interpretation of dreams: the images in dreams and spontaneous fantasies are symbols, that is, the best possible formulation for still unknown or unconscious facts, which generally compensate the content of consciousness or the conscious attitude. If we apply this basic rule to the alchemical arcanum, we come to the conclusion that its most conspicuous quality, namely, *its unity and uniqueness* – one is the stone, one the medicine, one the vessel, one the procedure, and one the disposition[50] – presupposes a *dissociated consciousness*. For no one who is one himself needs oneness as a medicine – nor, we might add, does anyone who is unconscious of his dissociation, for a *conscious* situation of distress is needed in order to activate the archetype of unity. From this we may conclude that the more philosophically minded alchemists were people who did not feel satisfied with the then prevailing view of the world, that is, with the Christian faith, although they were convinced of its truth. In this latter respect we find in the classical Latin and Greek literature of alchemy no evidences to the contrary, but rather, so far as Christian treatises are concerned, abundant testimony to the firmness of their Christian convictions. Since Christianity is expressly a system of 'salvation', founded moreover on God's 'plan of redemption', and God is unity *par excellence*, one must ask oneself why the alchemists still felt a disunity in themselves, or not at one with themselves, when their faith, so it would appear, gave them every opportunity for unity and unison. (This question has lost nothing of its topicality today, on the contrary!) The question answers itself when we examine more closely the other attributes that are predicated of the arcanum.

773   The next quality, therefore, which we have to consider is its *physical* nature. Although the alchemists attached the greatest importance to this, and the 'stone' was the whole *raison d'être* of their art, yet it cannot be regarded as merely physical since it is stressed that the stone was alive and possessed a soul and spirit, or even that it was a man or some creature like a man. And although it was also said of God that the world is his physical manifestation, this pantheistic view was rejected by the Church,

for 'God is Spirit' and the very reverse of matter. In that case the Christian standpoint would correspond to the '*unio mentalis* in the overcoming of the body'. So far as the alchemist professed the Christian faith, he knew that according to his own lights he was still at the second stage of conjunction, and that the Christian 'truth' was not yet 'realized'. The soul was drawn up by the spirit to the lofty regions of abstraction; but the body was de-souled, and since it also had claims to live, the unsatisfactoriness of the situation could not remain hidden from him. He was unable to feel himself a whole, and whatever the spiritualization of his existence may have meant to him he could not get beyond the Here and Now of his bodily life in the physical world. The spirit precluded his orientation to Physis, and vice versa. Despite all assurances to the contrary Christ is not a unifying factor but a dividing 'sword' which sunders the spiritual man from the physical. The alchemists, who, unlike certain moderns, were clever enough to see the necessity and fitness of a further development of consciousness, held fast to their Christian convictions and did not slip back to a more unconscious level. They could not and would not deny the truth of Christianity, and for this reason it would be wrong to accuse them of heresy. On the contrary, they wanted to 'realize' the unity foreshadowed in the idea of God by struggling to unite the *unio mentalis* with the body.

774   The mainspring of this endeavour was the conviction that this world was in a morbid condition and that everything was corrupted by Original Sin. They saw that the soul could be redeemed only if it was freed by the spirit from its natural attachment to the body, though this neither altered nor in any way improved the status of physical life. The Microcosm, i.e. the inner man, was capable of redemption, but not the corrupt body. This insight was reason enough for a dissociation of consciousness into a spiritual and a physical personality. They could all declare with St Paul: 'O wretched man that I am, who shall deliver me from the body of this death?'[51] They therefore strove to find the medicine that would heal all the sufferings of the body and the disunion of the soul, the φάρμακον ἀθανασίας which frees the body of its corruptibility, and the *elixir vitae* which grants the long life of the Biblical aforetime, or even immortality. Since most of them were physicians, they had plenty of opportunities to form an overwhelming impression of the transitoriness of human existence, and to develop that kind of impatience which refuses to wait till Kingdom come for more endurable conditions better in accord with the message of salvation. It is precisely the claims of the physical man and the unendurability of his dissociation that are expressed in this gnawing discontent. The alchemists, consequently, saw themselves faced with the extremely difficult task of uniting the wayward physical man with his spiritual truth. As they were neither unbelievers nor heretics, they could not and would not alter this truth in order to make it more favourably disposed to the body. Besides, the body was in the wrong anyway since it had succumbed to Original Sin by its moral weakness. It was therefore the body with its darkness that had

to be 'prepared'. This, as we have seen, was done by extracting a quintessence which was the physical equivalent of heaven, of the potential world, and on that account was named 'caelum'. It was the very essence of the body, an incorruptible and therefore pure and eternal substance, a *corpus glorificatum*, capable and worthy of being united with the *unio mentalis*. What was left over from the body was a 'terra damnata', a dross that had to be abandoned to its fate. The quintessence, the *caelum*, on the other hand, corresponded to the pure, incorrupt, original stuff of the world, God's adequate and perfectly obedient instrument, whose production, therefore, permitted the alchemist to 'hope and expect' the conjunction with the *unus mundus*.

775   This solution was a compromise to the disadvantage of Physis, but it was nevertheless a noteworthy attempt to bridge the dissociation between spirit and matter. It was not a solution of principle, for the very reason that the procedure did not take place in the real object at all but was a fruitless projection, since the *caelum* could never be fabricated in reality. It was a hope that was extinguished with alchemy and then, it seems, was struck off the agenda for ever. But the dissociation remained, and, in quite the contrary sense, brought about a far better knowledge of nature and a sounder medicine, while on the other hand it deposed the spirit in a manner that would paralyse Dorn with horror could he see it today. The *elixir vitae* of modern science has already increased the expectation of life very considerably and hopes for still better results in the future. The *unio mentalis*, on the other hand, has become a pale phantom, and the *veritas christiana* feels itself on the defensive. As for a truth that is hidden in the human body, there is no longer any talk of that. History has remorselessly made good what the alchemical compromise left unfinished: the physical man has been unexpectedly thrust into the foreground and has conquered nature in an undreamed-of way. At the same time he has become conscious of his *empirical* psyche, which has loosened itself from the embrace of the spirit and begun to take on so concrete a form that its individual features are now the object of clinical observation. It has long ceased to be a life-principle or some kind of philosophical abstraction; on the contrary, it is suspected of being a mere epiphenomenon of the chemistry of the brain. Nor does the spirit any longer give it life; rather is it conjectured that the spirit owes its existence to psychic activity. Today psychology can call itself a science, and this is a big concession on the part of the spirit. What demands psychology will make on the other natural sciences, and on physics in particular, only the future can tell.

NOTES

1   Morienus says to King Kalid (*Art. aurif.*, II, p. 37): 'Haec enim res a te extrahitur: cuius etiam minera tu existis, apud te namque illam inveniunt, et ut verius confitear, a te accipiunt: quod cum probaveris, amor eius et dilectio in te augebitur.

Et scias hoc verum et indubitabile permanere' ('For this thing is extracted from thee, and thou art its ore [raw material]: in thee they find it, and that I may speak more plainly, from thee they take it: and when thou hast experienced this, the love and desire for it will be increased in thee. And know that this remains true and indubitable').

2 'In stercore invenitur.'

3 Maier, *Symbola aureae mensae*, p. 336.

4 Khunrath (*Von hyleal. Chaos*, p. 410), for instance, says: 'So work even in the laboratory by thyself alone, without collaborators or assistants, in order that God, the Jealous, may not withdraw the art from thee, on account of thy assistants to whom He may not wish to impart it.'

5 Geber, 'Summa perfectionis', *Bibl. chem.*, I, p. 557b: 'Quia nobis solis artem per nos solos investigatam tradimus et non aliis' ('Because we hand down the art which we alone have investigated, to ourselves alone and to no one else').

6 I am setting aside the later Rosicrucians and the early 'Poimandres' community, of which Zosimos speaks. Between these two widely separated epochs I have found only one questionable passage, in the 'Practica Mariae Prophetissae' (*Art. aurif.*, I, p. 323), where the 'interlocutor' Aros (Horus) asks Maria: 'O domina, obedisti in societate Scoyari: O prophetissa, an invenisti in secretis Philosophorum'. ('O lady, did you obey in the society of Scoyarus: O Prophetess, did you find the secrets of the philosophers?'). The name *Scoyaris* or *Scoyarus* recalls the mysterious *Scayolus* in the writings of Paracelsus (*De vita longa*), where it means the adept. (*Scayolae* are the higher spiritual forces or principles. See 'Paracelsus as a Spiritual Phenomenon', paras 206ff.) Is there perhaps a connection here? At any rate there seems to be an allusion to a *societas*. The treatise of Maria may go back to very early times and thus to the Gnostic societies. Agrippa (*De incertitudine scientiarum*, ch. XC) mentions an alchemical initiation vow which may possibly refer to the existence of secret societies. Waite (*The Secret Tradition in Alchemy*) comes to a negative conclusion in this respect.

7 The *Turba philosophorum* is an instructive example in this respect.

8 Morienus, 'De transmut. metall.'. *Art. aurif.*, II, p. 37: 'Magisterium est arcanum Dei gloriosi', 'Consil. coniug.', *Ars chemica*, p. 56: 'Donum et secretorum secretum Dei', *Rosarium, Art. aurif.*, II, p. 280: 'Divinam mysterium a Deo datum et in mundo non est res sublimior post animam rationalem' ('The divine mystery was given by God and there is in the world no thing more sublime except the rational soul').

9 Ibid., pp. 212, 228.

10 Ibid., pp. 219, 269.

11 Ibid., p. 230. Alchemy is superior to all other sciences in the opinion of Djabir or Geber (8th cent.): 'Indeed, any man who is learned in any science whatever, who has not given part of his time to the study of one of the principles of the Work, in theory or in practice, his intellectual culture is utterly insufficient' (Berthelot, *Chimie au moyen àge*, III, p. 214). Diabir is said to have been a Christian or Sabaean. See also Ruska, 'Die siebzig Bücher des Gabir ibn Haijan', p. 38. Synesius also appeals to the intelligence (Berthelot, *Alch. grecs*, II, iii, 16). Olympiodorus even compares the art to the divine intelligence (ibid., II, iv, 45) and appeals to the intelligence of his public (ibid., II, iv, 55). Christianos, too, lays stress on intelligence (ibid., VI, i, 4, and iii, 2). Likewise *Aurora* II, in *Art. aurif.*, I, 'Prologus': 'oportet intellectum valde subtiliter et ingeniose acuere' ('one must sharpen the intellect very subtly and ingeniously').

12 *Rosarium, Art. aurif.*, II, p. 210.

13 Hoghelande, 'De alchem. difficultatibus', *Bibl. chem. curiosa*, I, p. 342: 'Librorum magnam habeat copiam.'

14 'Rhasis dixit: liber enim librum aperit.' (Quoted by Bonus, 'Pret. marg. nov.', *Bibl. chem.*, II, ch. VIII).

15 *Rosarium, Art. aurif.*, II, p. 230.

16 Ibid., pp. 211, 243, 269.

17 Sendivogius, 'Parabola', *Bibl. chem. curiosa*, II, p. 475: 'Aqua Philosophica tibi in somno aliquoties manifestata' ('The philosophic water that was shown to you a number of times in a dream').

18 Maier (*Symb. aur. mensae*, p. 568): 'There is in our chemistry a certain noble substance . . . in the beginning whereof is wretchedness with vinegar, but in its ending joy with gladness. And so I have supposed it will fare with me, that at first I shall taste, suffer, and experience much difficulty, bitterness, grief, and weariness, but in the end shall come to glimpse pleasanter and easier things.'

19 Matthew 10: 16.

20 Hippolytus reports the following saying of the Peratics: 'The universal serpent is the wise word of Eve.' This was the mystery and the river of Paradise, and the sign that protected Cain so that no one should kill him, for the God of this world (ὁ θεὸς τοῦδε του κόσμου) had not accepted his offering. This God reminds us very much of the 'prince of this world' in St John. Among the Peratics it was naturally the demiurge, the 'father below' (πατὴρ κάτωθεν). See *Elenchos*, V, 16, 8f. (Legge, I, p. 155f.).

21 'This is the father of all perfection.' Ruska, *Tabula smaragdina*, p. 2.

22 I take the concept of *participation mystique*, in the sense defined above, from the works of Lévy-Bruhl. Recently this idea has been repudiated by ethnologists, partly for the reason that primitives know very well how to differentiate between things. There is no doubt about that; but it cannot be denied, either, that incommensurable things can have, for them, an equally incommensurable *tertium comparationis*. One has only to think of the ubiquitous application of 'mana', the werewolf motif, etc. Furthermore, 'unconscious identity' is a psychic phenomenon which the psychotherapist has to deal with every day. Certain ethnologists have also rejected Lévy-Bruhl's concept of the *état prélogique*, which is closely connected with that of *participation*. The term is not a very happy one, for in his own way the primitive thinks just as logically as we do. Lévy-Bruhl was aware of this, as I know from personal conversation with him. By 'prelogical' he meant the primitive presuppositions that contradict only our rationalistic logic. These presuppositions are often exceedingly strange, and though they may not deserve to be called 'prelogical' they certain merit the term 'irrational'. Astonishingly enough Lévy-Bruhl, in his posthumously published diary, recanted both these concepts. This is the more remarkable in that they had a thoroughly sound psychological basis.

23 Mehung, 'Demonstratio naturae', *Mus. herm.*, p. 157: 'liberi et vacui anima'. (Jean de Meung born between 1250 and 1280.)

24 Norton, 'Ordinale', *Mus. herm.*, p. 519: 'nam mens eius cum opere consentiat'.

25 'Aquarium sapientum', *Mus. herm.*, p. 107.

26 *Aurora consurgens*, I, ch. X, parab. V: 'Alfidius: Scito quod hanc scientiam habere non poteris, quousque mentem tuam deo purifices, hoc est in corde omnem corruptionem deleas.'

27 The text has 'virtus, de qua dicitur: virtus ornat animam. Et Hermes: et recipit virtutem superiorum et inferiorum planetarum et sua virtute penetrat omnem rem solidam' ('virtue of which it is said: virtue adorneth the soul. And Hermes: and it receiveth the virtue of the upper and lower planets and by its virtue penetrateth every solid thing'). Cf. 'Tabula smaragdina', ed. Ruska, p. 2: 'et recipit vim superiorum et inferiorum'.

28 The text explains by quoting the Vulgate, Eph. 4: 23, 24: 'Renovamini [autem] spiritu mentis vestrae, et induite novum hominem', (D.V.: 'And be renewed in

the spirit of your mind: and put on the new man') and adds: 'hoc est intellectum subtilem'.

29 *Aurora*, I, ch. IV, parab. IV: 'horridas nostrae mentis purga tenebras'.

30 Ibid., 'Senior: et facit omne nigrum album.'

31 *Art. aurif.*, II, p. 228. The text in Geber's *Summa perfectionis* is much more detailed. It occupies the whole of ch. V of Lib. I, under the title 'De impedimentis ex parte animae artificis'. See Darmstaedter, *Die Alchemie des Geber*, pp. 20ff.

32 *Art. aurif.*, II, p. 227: 'Deum timere, in quo dispositionis tuae visus est, et adjuvatio cuiuslibet sequestrati.' This quotation dervies from the 'Tractatus aureus' in what was probably the first edition (*Ars chemica*). But there the passage (which comes at the beginning of ch. II) runs: 'Fili mi, ante omnia moneo te Deum timere, in quo est nisus tuae dispositionis et adunatio cuiuslibet sequestrati' ('My son, above all I admonish thee to fear God in whom is the strength of thy disposition, and companionship for the solitary, whosoever he may be'). Concerning the alteration of the Hermes quotations in *Rosarium*, see para. 140, n. 17.

33 Cf. Reitzenstein, 'Alchemistische Lehrschriften', Morienus (Morienes or Marianus) is said to have been the teacher of the Omayyad prince Kalid or Khalid ibn-Jazid ibn-Muawivah (635–704). Cf. Lippmann, *Entstehung und Ausbreitung der Alchemie*, I, p. 357. The passage is to be found in Morienus, 'De transmutatione metallorum', *Art. aurif.*, II, pp. 22f.

34 'Quibus eam a primaeva rerum natura conferre disposuit' (ibid., p. 22).

35 'Animos suos etiam ipsi regere non possunt diutius, nisi usque ad terminum', etc. (ibid., p. 23).

36 '. . . nisi per animae afflictionem' (ibid., pp. 17f.).

37 Maier, *Symbola aureae mensae*, p. 568.

38 Ibid., p. 144.

39 Ibid., p. 143.

40 The antiquity of the stone symbolism is shown by the fact that it occurs not only among primitives living today but in the documents of ancient cultures as well, as for instance in the Hurrian texts of Boghazköy, where the son of the father-god Kumarbi is the stone Ullikummi, a 'terrible' diorite stone that 'grew in the water'. This stone parallels the Greek myth of the stone which Kronos swallowed and spat out again when Zeus compelled him to yield up the children he had devoured. Zeus then set it up as a cult-object in Pytho. Ullikummi is a Titanic being and, interestingly enough, an implacable enemy of the gods. (Cf. Güterbock, 'Kumarbi', *Istanbuler Schriften*, no. 16; Gurney, *The Hittites*, pp. 190ff.)

41 Norton's 'Ordinall' (*Theatr. chem. britannicum*, p. 40) says:

> For greatly doubted evermore all suche,
> That of this Scyence they may write too muche:
> Every each of them tought but one pointe or twayne,
> Whereby his fellowes were made certayne:
> How that he was to them a Brother,
> For every one of them understoode each other;
> Alsoe they wrote not every man to teache,
> But to shew themselves by a secret speache:
> Trust not therefore to reading of one Boke,
> But in many Auctors works ye may looke;
> Liber librum apperit saith Arnolde the great Clerke.

'The Book of Krates' (Berthelot, *Moyen âge*, III, p. 52) says: 'Your intentions are excellent, but your soul will never bring itself to divulge the truth, because of the diversities of opinion and of wretched pride.' Hoghelande ('De alch. diff.', *Theatr. chem.*, I, p. 155) says: 'At haec [scientia] . . . tradit opus suum immiscendo falsa veris et vera falsis, nunc diminute nimium, nunc superabundanter, et sine ordine, et saepius praepostero ordine, et nititur obscure tradere et occultare quantum potest' ('This [science] transmits its work by mixing the false with the true and the true with the false, sometimes very briefly, at other times in a most prolix manner, without order and quite often in the reverse order; and it endeavours to transmit [the work] obscurely, and to hide it as much as possible'. Senior (*De chemia*, p. 55) says: 'Verum dixerunt per omnia, Homines vero non intelligunt verba eorum . . . unde falsificant veridicos, et verificant falsificos opinionibus suis. . . . Error enim eorum est ex ignorantia intentionis eorum, quando audiunt diversa verba, sed ignota intellectui eorum, cum sint in intellectu occulto' ('They told the truth in regard to all things, but men do not understand their words . . . whence through their assumptions they falsify the verities and verify the falsities. . . . The error springs from ignorance of their [the writers'] meaning, when they hear diver words unknown to their understanding, since these have a hidden meaning') Of the secret hidden in the words of the wise, Senior says: 'Est enim illud interius subtiliter perspicientis et cognoscentis' ('For this belongs to him who subtly perceives and is cognizant of the inner meaning'). The *Rosarium* (p. 230) explains: 'Ego non dixi omnia apparentia et necessaria in hoc opere, quia sunt aliqua quae non licet homini loqui' ('So I have not declared all that appears and is necessary in this work, because there are things of which a man may not speak'). Again (p. 274): 'Talis materia debet tradi mystice, sicut poësis fabulose et parabolice' ('Such matters must be transmitted in mystical terms, like poetry employing fables and parables'). Khunrath (*Von hyleal Chaos*, p. 21) mentions the saying: 'Arcana publicata vilescunt' ('secrets that are published become cheap') – words which Andreae used as a motto for his *Chymical Wedding*. Abū'l Qāsim Muhammad ibn Ahmad al-Simāwī, known as al-Irāqī, says in his 'Book of the Seven Climes' (see Holmyard, 'Abū'l-Qāsim', p. 410) regarding Jābir ibn Hayyān's method of instruction: 'Then he spoke enigmatically concerning the composition of the External and the Internal. . . . Then he spoke darkly . . . that in the External there is no complete tincture and that the complete tincture is to be found only in the Internal. Then he spoke darkly . . . saying, Verily we have made the External nothing more than a veil over the Internal . . . that the Internal is like this and like that and he did not cease from this kind of behaviour until he had completely confused all except the most quick-witted of his pupils.' Wei Po-yang (*c.* 142 AD) says: 'It would be a great sin on my part not to transmit the Tao which would otherwise be lost to the world forever. I shall not write on silk lest the divine secret be unwittingly spread abroad. In hesitation I sigh' ('An Ancient Chinese Treatise', p. 243).

42 The parallel to this is the paradoxical relation of Malchuth to Kether, the lowest to the highest.

43 P. 270.

44 He is thought to be indentical with Joannes de Garlandia, who lived in the second half of the 12th cent. and wrote the 'Commentarius in Tabulam smaragdinam', in *De alchemia* (1541).

45 Ibid., p. 365. Since the alchemists were, as 'philosophers', the empiricists of the psyche, their terminology is of secondary importance compared with their experience, as is the case with empiricism generally. The discoverer is seldom a good classifier.

46 Thus Dorn ('Physica Trismegisti', *Theatr. chem.*, I, p. 409) says: 'Spagirica foetura terrestris caelicam naturam induat per ascensum, et deinceps suo descensu centri naturam terreni recipiat' ('This earthly, spagyric birth clothes itself with heavenly nature by its ascent, and then by its descent visibly puts on the nature of the centre of the earth').

47 This explains why the projection usually has some influence on the carrier, which

is why the alchemists in their turn expected the 'projection' of the stone to bring about a transmutation of base metals.

48 'Mensura, numerus et pondus.' Cf. von Franz, *Aurora consurgens*, Parable 4 (p. 83).
49 *Liber formularum spiritalis intelligentiae*, V (Migne, *P.L.*, vol. 50, col. 751).
50 *Ros. phil., Art. aurif.*, II, p. 206.
51 Romans 7:24.

3   Projection and imagination in alchemy

From: 'Individual Dream Symbolism in Relation to Alchemy' (1936) (*CW* 12)

346   Strictly speaking, projection is never made; it happens, it is simply there. In the darkness of anything external to me I find, without recognizing it as such, an interior or psychic life that is my own. It would therefore be a mistake in my opinion to explain the formula *tam ethice quam physice* [ethically as well as physically] by the theory of correspondences, and to say that this is its 'cause'. On the contrary, this theory is more likely to be a rationalization of the experience of projection. The alchemist did not practise his art because he believed on theoretical grounds in correspondence; the point is that he had a theory of correspondence because he experienced the presence of pre-existing ideas in physical matter. I am therefore inclined to assume that the real root of alchemy is to be sought less in philosophical doctrines than in the projections of individual investigators. I mean by this that while working on his chemical experiments the operator had certain psychic experiences which appeared to him as the particular behaviour of the chemical process. Since it was a question of projection, he was naturally unconscious of the fact experience had nothing to do with matter itself (that is, with matter as we know it today). He experienced his projection as a property of matter; but what he was in reality experiencing was his own unconscious. In this way he recapitulated the whole history of man's knowledge of nature. As we all know, science began with the stars, and mankind discovered in them the dominants of the unconscious, the 'gods', as well as the curious psychological qualities of the zodiac: a complete projected theory of human character. Astrology is a primordial experience similar to alchemy. Such projections repeat themselves whenever man tries to explore an empty darkness and involuntarily fills it with living form.

From: *Nietzsche's Zarathustra* (1988), 2: 1494–8

My point of view concerning projections, then, is that they are unavoidable. You are simply confronted with them; they are there and nobody is without them. For at any time a new projection may creep into your system – you don't know from where, but you suddenly discover that it looks almost as if you had a projection. You are not even sure at first; you think you are alright and it is really the other fellow, until somebody calls your attention to it, tells you that you are talking a bit too much of that fellow – and what is your relation to him anyhow? Then it appears that there is a sort of fascination. He may be a particularly bad character, and that is in a way fascinating and makes you talk of him day and night; you are fascinated just by that which you revile in him. Now, from that you can conclude as to your own condition: your attention is particularly attracted; that evil fascinates you. Because you have it, it is your own evil. You may not know how much is your own but you can grant that there is quite a lot; and inasmuch as you have it, you add to it, because as Christ says, 'Unto everyone which hath shall be given', so that he has it in abundance.[1] Where there is the possibility of making a projection, even a slight one, you are tempted to add to it. If an ass walks past carrying a sack on its back, you say, 'Oh, he can carry my umbrella as well, because he is already carrying something.' If a camel passed you, anything which you don't want to carry just jumps out of your pocket on to the back of that camel.

There are people who even attract projections, as if they were meant to carry burdens. And others who are always losing their own contents by projecting them, so they either have a particularly good conscience or they are particularly empty people, because their surroundings have to carry all their loads. Empty people, or people who have an excellent opinion of themselves and cherish amazing virtues, have always somebody in their surroundings who carries all their evil. That is literally true. For instance, it may happen that parents are unaware of their contents and then their children have to live them. I remember a case, a man, who had no dreams at all. I told him that that was abnormal, his condition was such that he must have dreams, otherwise somebody in his surroundings must have them. At first I thought it was his wife, but she had no undue amount and they cast no light on his problems. But his oldest son, who was eight years old, had most amazing dreams which did not belong to his age at all. So I told him to ask his son for his dreams and bring them to me, and I analysed them as if they were his own. And they were his own dreams, and finally by that procedure they got into him and the son was exonerated.[2]

Such things can happen: a projection is a very tangible thing, a sort of semisubstantial thing which forms a load as if it had real weight. It is exactly as the primitives understand it, a subtle body. Primitives – also the Tibetans and many other peoples – inasmuch as they are aware of such things at all, understand projections as sort of projectiles, and of course they play a role chiefly in their magic. Primitive sorcerers throw out such projectiles. There are three monasteries in Tibet mentioned by name by Lama Kagi Dawa-Sandup, the famous Tibetan scholar who worked with John Woodroffe and Evans-Wentz, where they train people in the art of making projections.[3] And that term was used by the alchemists for the final performance in the making of the gold. It was supposed that they projected the red matter – or the tinctura or the eternal water – upon lead or silver or quicksilver, and by that act transformed it into gold or into the philosopher's stone. It is interesting that they themselves explained the making of the stone as a projection. That is to say, it is something that is detached from one; you detach something and establish it as an independent existence, put it outside yourself. Now, that may be quite legitimate inasmuch as it is a matter of objectifying contents; or it may be most illegitimate if it is used for magical purposes, or if it is a simple projection where you get rid of something. But people are not to be blamed directly for making other people suffer under such projections because they are not conscious of them.

You see, our whole mental life, our consciousness, began with projections. Our mind under primitive conditions was entirely projected, and it is interesting that those internal contents, which made the foundation of real consciousness, were projected the farthest into space – into the stars. So the first science was astrology. That was an attempt of man to establish a line or communication between the remotest objects and himself. Then he slowly fetched back all those projections out of space into himself. Primitive man – well, even up to modern times – lives in a world of animated objects. Therefore that term of Tylor's, *animism*, which is simply the state of projection where man experiences his psychical contents as parts of the objects of the world. Stones, trees, human beings, families are all alive along with my own psyche and therefore I have a *participation mystique* with them.[4] I influence them and I am influenced by them in a magical way, which is only possible because there is that bond of sameness. What appears in the animal, say, is identical with myself because it *is* myself – it is a projection. So our psychology has really been a sort of coming-together, a confluence of projections. The old gods, for instance, were very clearly psychical functions, or events, or certain emotions; some are thoughts and some are definite emotions. A wrathful god is your own wrathfulness. A goddess like Venus or Aphrodite is very much your own sexuality, but projected. Now, inasmuch as these figures have been deflated, inasmuch as they do not exist any longer, you gradually become conscious of having those qualities or concepts; you speak of *your* sexuality. That was no concept in the early centuries, but was the god, Aphrodite or Cupid or Kama or whatever name it was called by. Then slowly we sucked in those projections and that accumulation made up psychological consciousness.

Now, inasmuch as our world is still animated to a certain extent, or inasmuch as we are still in *participation mystique*, our contents are still projected; we have not yet gathered them in. The future of mankind will probably be that we shall have gathered in all our projections, though I don't know whether that is possible. It is more probable that a fair amount of projections will still go on and that they will still be perfectly unconscious to ourselves. But we have not made them; they are a part of our condition, part of the original world in which we were born, and it is only our moral and intellectual progress that makes us aware of them. So the projection in a neurosis is merely one case among many; one would hardly call it abnormal even, but it is more visible – too obvious. Nowadays, one might assume that a person would be conscious of his sexuality and not think that all other people were abnormal perverts; because one is unconscious of it, one thinks that other people are therefore wrong. Of course that is an abnormal condition, and to any normal, balanced individual, it seems absurd. It is an exaggeration, but we are always inclined to function like that to a certain extent: again and again it happens that something is impressive and obvious in another individual which has not been impressive at all in ourselves. The thought that we might be like that never comes anywhere near us, but we emphatically insist upon that other fellow having such-and-such a peculiarity. Whenever this happens we should always ask ourselves: now have I that peculiarity perhaps because I make such a fuss about it?

You see, whenever you make an emotional statement, there is a fair suspicion that you are talking of your own case; in other words, that there is a projection because of your emotion. And you always have emotions where you are not adapted. If you are adapted you need no emotion; an emotion is only an instinctive explosion which denotes that you have not been up to your task. When you don't know how to deal with a situation or with people, you get emotional. Since you were not adapted, you had a wrong idea of the situation, or at all events you did not use the right means, and there was as a consequence a certain projection. For instance, you perhaps project the notion that a certain person is particularly sensitive and if you should say something disagreeable to him he would reply in such-and-such a way. Therefore you say nothing, though he would not have shown such a reaction because that was a projection. You wait instead until you get an emotion, and then you blurt it out nevertheless, and of course it is then far more offensive. You waited too long. If you had spoken at the time, there would have been no emotion. And usually the worst consequences of all are not in that individual but in yourself, because you don't like to hurt your own feelings, don't want to hear your own voice sounding disagreeable and harsh and rasping. You want to maintain the idea that you are very nice and kind, which naturally is not true. So sure enough, any projection adds to the weight which you have to carry.

From: 'Religious Ideas in Alchemy' (1937) (*CW* 12)

375   Because of the intimate connection between man and the secret of matter, both Dorn and the much earlier *Liber Platonis quartorum* demand that the operator should rise to the height of his task: he must accomplish in his own self the same process that he attributes to matter, 'for things are perfected by their like'. Therefore the operator must himself participate in the work ('oportet operatorem interesse operi'), 'for if the investigator

does not remotely possess the likeness [i.e. to the work] he will not climb the height I have described, nor reach the road that leads to the goal'.[5]

376 As a result of the projection there is an unconscious identity between the psyche of the alchemist and the arcane substance, i.e. the spirit imprisoned in matter. The *Liber Platonis quartorum* accordingly recommends the use of the *occiput* as the vessel of transformation,[6] because it is the container of thought and intellect.[7] For we need the brain as the seat of the 'divine part'. The text continues:

> Through time and exact definition things are converted into intellect, inasmuch as the parts are assimilated [to one another] in composition and in form. But on account of its proximity to the *anima rationalis* the brain had to be assimilated to the amalgam, and the *anima rationalis* is simple, as we have said.[8]

377 The assumption underlying this train of thought is the causative effect of analogy. In other words, just as in the psyche the multiplicity of sense perceptions produces the unity and simplicity of an idea, so the primal water finally produces fire, i.e. the ethereal substance – not (and this is the decisive point) as a mere analogy but as the result of the mind's working on matter. Consequently Dorn says: 'Within the human body is concealed a certain metaphysical substance, known to very few, which needs no medicament, being itself an incorrupt medicament.' This medicine is 'of threefold nature: metaphysical, physical, and moral' ('moral' is what we would call 'psychological'). 'From this', Dorn goes on, 'the attentive reader will conclude that one must pass from the metaphysical to the physical by a philosophic procedure'.[9] This medicine is clearly the arcane substance which he defines elsewhere as *veritas*:

> There is in natural things a certain truth which cannot be seen with the outward eye, but is perceived by the mind alone [*sola mente*], and of this the Philosophers have had experience, and have ascertained that its virtue is such as to work miracles.[10]
>
> In this [truth] lies the whole art of freeing the spirit [*spiritus*] from its fetters, in the same way that, as we have said, the mind [*mens*] can be freed [i.e. morally] from the body.[11]
>
> As faith works miracles in man, so this power, the *veritas efficaciae*, brings them about in matter. This truth is the highest power and an impregnable fortress wherein the stone of the philosophers lies hid.[12]

378 By studying the philosophers man acquires the skill to attain this stone. But again, the stone is man. Thus Dorn exclaims: 'Transform yourselves from dead stones into living philosophical stones!'[13] Here he is expressing in the clearest possible way the identity of something in man with something concealed in matter.

411 In such visionary images as the Anthropos glimpsing his own reflection there is expressed the whole phenomenon of the unconscious projection

of autonomous contents. These myth-pictures are like dreams, telling us that a projection has taken place and also what has been projected. This, as the contemporary evidence shows, was Nous, the divine daemon, the god–man, *pneuma*, etc. In so far as the standpoint of analytical psychology is realistic, i.e. based on the assumption that the contents of the psyche are realities, all these figures stand for an unconscious component of the personality which might well be endowed with a higher form of consciousness transcending that of the ordinary human being. Experience shows that such figures always express superior insight or qualities that are not yet conscious: indeed, it is extremely doubtful whether they can be attributed to the ego at all in the proper sense of the word. This problem of attribution may appear a captious one to the layman, but in practical work it is of great importance. A wrong attribution may bring about dangerous inflations, which seem unimportant to the layman only because he has no idea of the inward and outward disasters that may result.[14]

412　　As a matter of fact, we are dealing here with a content that up to the present has only very rarely been attributed to any human personality. The one great exception is Christ. As υἱός τοῦ ἀνθρωπου (the Son of Man), and as θεοῦ υἱός (the Son of God), he embodies the god–man; and as an incarnation of the Logos by 'pneumatic' impregnation, he is an avatar of the divine Nous.

413　　Thus the Christian projection acts upon the unknown in man, or upon the unknown man, who becomes the bearer of the 'terrible and unheard-of secret'.[15] The pagan projection, on the other hand, goes beyond man and acts upon the unknown in the material world, the unknown substance which, like the chosen man, is somehow filled with God. And just as, in Christianity, the Godhead conceals itself in the man of low degree, so in the 'philosophy' it hides in the uncomely stone. In the Christian projection the *descensus spiritus sancti* stops at the *living body* of the Chosen One, who is at once very man and very God, whereas in alchemy the descent goes right down into the darkness of inanimate matter whose nether regions, according to the Neopythagoreans, are ruled by evil.[16] Evil and matter together form the Dyad, the duality. This is feminine in nature, an *anima mundi*, the feminine Physis who longs for the embrace of the One, the Monad, the good and perfect.[17]

From: 'Epilogue' to *Psychology and Alchemy* (1944) (*CW* 12)

557　　The alchemy of the classical epoch (from antiquity to about the middle of the seventeenth century) was, in essence, chemical research work into which there entered, by way of projection, an admixture of unconscious psychic material. For this reason the psychological conditions necessary for the work are frequently stressed in the texts. The contents under consideration were those that lent themselves to projection upon the unknown chemical substance. Owing to the impersonal, purely objective nature of matter, it was the impersonal, collective archetypes that were projected: first and foremost, as a parallel to the collective spiritual life of the times, the image of the spirit imprisoned in the darkness of the world. In other words, the state of relative consciousness in which man found himself, and which he felt to be painful and in need of redemption, was reflected in matter and accordingly dealt with in matter. Since the psychological condition of any unconscious content is one of potential reality, characterized by the polar opposites 'being' and 'not-being', it follows that the union of opposites must play a decisive role in the alchemical process. The result is something in the nature of a 'uniting symbol', and this usually has a numinous character.[18] The projection of the redeemer-image, i.e. the correspondence between Christ and the *lapis*, is therefore almost a psychological necessity, as is the parallelism between the redeeming *opus* or *officium divinum* and the magistery – with the essential difference that the Christian *opus* is an *operari* in honour of God the Redeemer undertaken by man who stands in need of redemption, while the alchemical *opus* is the labour of Man the Redeemer in the cause of the divine world-soul slumbering and awaiting redemption in matter. The Christian earns the fruits of grace *ex opere operato*, but the alchemist creates for himself – *ex opere operantis* in the most literal sense – a 'panacea of life' which he regards either as a substitute for the Church's means of grace or as the complement and parallel of the divine work of redemption that is continued in man. The two opposed points of view meet in the ecclesiastical formula of the *opus operatum* and the *opus operantis*[19] – but in the last analysis they are irreconcilable. Fundamentally it is a question of polar opposites: the collective or the individual, society or personality. This is a modern problem in so far as it needed the hypertrophy of collective life and the herding-together of incredible masses of people in our own day to make the individual aware that he was being suffocated in the toils of the organized mob. The collectivism of the medieval Church seldom or never exerted sufficient pressure on the individual to turn his relations with society into a general problem. So this question, too, remained on the level of projection, and it was reserved for our own day to tackle it with at least an embryonic degree of consciousness under the mask of neurotic individualism.

From: 'The Personification of the Opposites', *Mysterium coniunctionis* (1955–6) (*CW* 14)

125   Once again, therefore, it is the medical investigators of nature who, equipped with new means of knowledge, have rescued these tangled problems from projection by making them the proper subject of psychol-

ogy. This could never have happened before, for the simple reason that there was no psychology of the unconscious. But the medical investigator, thanks to his knowledge of archetypal processes, is in the fortunate position of being able to recognize in the abstruse and grotesque-looking symbolisms of alchemy the nearest relatives of those serial fantasies which underlie the delusions of paranoid schizophrenia as well as the healing processes at work in the psychogenic neuroses.

From: 'Rex and Regina', *Mysterium coniunctionis* (1955–6) (*CW* 14)

410   It may well be a prejudice to restrict the psyche to being 'inside the body'. In so far as the psyche has a non-spatial aspect, there may be a psychic 'outside-the-body', a region so utterly different from 'my' psychic space that one has to get outside oneself or make use of some auxiliary technique in order to get there. If this view is at all correct, the alchemical consummation of the royal marriage in the *cucurbita* could be understood as a synthetic process in the psyche 'outside' the ego.[20]

From: 'The Conjunction', *Mysterium coniunctionis* (1955–6) (*CW* 14)

705   In nature the resolution of opposites is always an energic process: she acts *symbolically* in the truest sense of the word,[21] doing something that expresses both sides, just as a waterfall visibly mediates between above and below. The waterfall itself is then the incommensurable third. In an open and unresolved conflict dreams and fantasies occur which, like the waterfall, illustrate the tension and nature of the opposites, and thus prepare the synthesis.

706   This process can, as I have said, take place spontaneously or be artificially induced. In the latter case you choose a dream, or some other fantasy-image, and concentrate on it by simply catching hold of it and looking at it. You can also use a bad mood as a starting-point, and then try to find out what sort of fantasy-image it will produce, or what image expresses this mood. You then fix this image in the mind by concentrating your attention. Usually it will alter, as the mere fact of contemplating it animates it. The alterations must be carefully noted down all the time, for they reflect the psychic processes in the unconscious background, which appear in the form of images consisting of conscious memory material. In this way conscious and unconscious are united, just as a waterfall connects above and below. A chain of fantasy ideas develops and gradually takes on a dramatic character: the passive process becomes an action. At first it

consists of projected figures, and these images are observed like scenes in the theatre. In other words, you dream with open eyes. As a rule there is a marked tendency simply to enjoy this interior entertainment and to leave it at that. Then, of course, there is no real progress but only endless variations on the same theme, which is not the point of the exercise at all. What is enacted on the stage still remains a background process; it does not move the observer in any way, and the less it moves him the smaller will be the cathartic effect of this private theatre. The piece that is being played does not want merely to be watched impartially, it wants to compel his participation. If the observer understands that his own drama is being performed on this inner stage, he cannot remain indifferent to the plot and its denouement. He will notice, as the actors appear one by one and the plot thickens, that they all have some purposeful relationship to his conscious situation, that he is being addressed by the unconscious, and that *it* causes these fantasy-images to appear before him. He therefore feels compelled, or is encouraged by his analyst, to take part in the play and, instead of just sitting in a theatre, really have it out with his *alter ego*. For nothing in us ever remains quite uncontradicted, and consciousness can take up no position which will not call up, somewhere in the dark corners of the psyche, a negation or a compensatory effect, approval or resentment. This process of coming to terms with the Other in us is well worthwhile, because in this way we get to know aspects of our nature which we would not allow anybody else to show us and which we ourselves would never have admitted.[22] It is very important to fix this whole procedure in writing at the time of its occurrence, for you then have ocular evidence that will effectively counteract the ever-ready tendency to self-deception. A running commentary is absolutely necessary in dealing with the shadow, because otherwise its actuality cannot be fixed. Only in this painful way is it possible to gain a positive insight into the complex nature of one's own personality.

749   What the alchemist sought, then, to help him out of his dilemma was a chemical operation which we today would describe as a symbol. The procedure he followed was obviously an allegory of his postulated *substantia coelestis* and its chemical equivalent. To that extent the operation was not symbolical for him but purposive and rational. For us, who know that no amount of incineration, sublimation and centrifuging of the vinous residue can ever produce an 'air-coloured' quintessence, the entire procedure is fantastic if taken literally. We can hardly suppose that Dorn, either, meant a real wine but, after the manner of the alchemists, *vinum ardens*, *acetum*, *spiritualis sanguis*, etc., in other words *Mercurius non vulgi*, who embodied the *anima mundi*. Just as the air encompasses the earth, so in the old view the soul is wrapped round the world. As I have shown, we can most easily equate the concept of Mercurius with that of the unconscious. If we add this term to the recipe, it would run: take the unconscious in one of its handiest forms, say a spontaneous fantasy, a

dream, an irrational mood, an affect, or something of the kind, and operate with it. Give it your special attention, concentrate on it, and observe its alterations objectively. Spare no effort to devote yourself to this task, follow the subsequent transformation of the spontaneous fantasy attentively and carefully. Above all, don't let anything from outside, that does not belong, get into it, for the fantasy-image has 'everything it needs'. In this way one is certain of not interfering by conscious caprice and of giving the unconscious a free hand. In short, the alchemical operation seems to us the equivalent of the psychological process of active imagination.

From: 'Individual Dream Symbolism in Relation to Alchemy' (1936) (*CW* 12)

218   The squaring of the circle was one of the methods for producing the *lapis*; another was the use of *imaginatio*, as the following text unmistakably proves:

> And take care that thy door be well and firmly closed, so that he who is within cannot escape, and – God willing – thou wilt reach the goal. Nature performeth her operations gradually; and indeed I would have thee do the same: let thy imagination be guided wholly by nature. And observe according to nature, through whom the substances regenerate themselves in the bowels of the earth. And imagine this with true and not with fantastic imagination.[23]

219   The *vas bene clausum* (well-sealed vessel) is a precautionary measure very frequently mentioned in alchemy, and is the equivalent of the magic circle. In both cases the idea is to protect what is within from the intrusion and admixture of what is without, as well as to prevent it from escaping.[24] The *imaginatio* is to be understood here as the real and literal power to create images (*Einbildungskraft* = imagination) – the classical use of the word in contrast to *phantasia*, which means a mere 'conceit' in the sense of insubstantial thought. In the *Satyricon* this connotation is more pointed still: *phantasia* means something ridiculous.[25] *Imaginatio* is the active evocation of (inner) images *secundum naturam*, an authentic feat of thought or ideation, which does not spin aimless and groundless fantasies 'into the blue' – does not, that is to say, just play with its objects, but tries to grasp the inner facts and portray them in images true to their nature. This activity is an *opus*, a work.

From: 'Religious Ideas in Alchemy' (1937) (*CW* 12)

360   The anonymous author of the *Rosarium* says in another place that the work must be performed 'with the true and not with the fantastic

Figure 3.1 Adam as *prima materia*, pierced by the arrow of Mercurius. The *arbor philosophica* is growing out of him.
Source: From the *Miscellanea d'alchimia* (fourteenth century); reproduced from Jung's *Collected Works*, Vol. 12.

imagination',[26] and again that the stone will be found 'when the search lies heavy on the searcher'.[27] This remark can only be understood as meaning that a certain psychological condition is indispensable for the discovery of the miraculous stone.

350   Hoghelande quotes Senior as saying that the 'vision' of the Hermetic vessel 'is more to be sought than the scripture'.[28] The authors speak of seeing with the eyes of the spirit, but it is not always clear whether they mean vision in a real or a figurative sense. Thus the *Novum lumen* says:

> To cause things hidden in the shadow to appear, and to take away the shadow from them, this is permitted to the intelligent philosopher by God through nature. . . . All these things happen, and the eyes of the common men do not see them, but the eyes of the understanding [*intellectus*] and of the imagination perceive them [*percipiunt*] with true and truest vision [*visu*].[29]

351   Raymond Lully writes:

> You should know, dear son, that the course of nature is turned about, so that without invocation [e.g. of the *familiaris*] and without spiritual exaltation you can see certain fugitive spirits condensed in the air in the shape of divers monsters, beasts and men, which move like the clouds hither and thither.[30]

352   Dorn says much the same:

> Thus he will come to see with his mental eyes [*oculis mentalibus*] an indefinite number of sparks shining through day by day and more and more and growing into a great light.[31]

353   The psychologist will find nothing strange in a figure of speech becoming concretized and turning into an hallucination. Thus in his biographical notes (1594), Hoghelande describes how, on the third day of the *decoctio*, he saw the surface of the substance cover itself with colours, 'chiefly green, red, grey, and for the rest irridescent'. Whenever he remembered that day a verse of Virgil's came into his mind: 'Ut vidi, ut perii, ut me malus abstulit error' ('When I saw, how utterly I perished and evil delusion took me off'). This error or optical illusion (*ludibrium oculis oblatum*), he said, was the cause of much subsequent trouble and expense, for he had believed that he was on the point of attaining the *nigredo*. But a few days later his fire went out in the night, which led to an *irreparabile damnum*; in other words, he never succeeded in repeating the phenomenon.[32] Not that the iridescent skin on molten metal is necessarily an hallucination; but the text shows a remarkable willingness on the part of the author to suspect something of the sort.

390   Ruland's *Lexicon alchemiae* defines *meditatio* as follows: 'The word *meditatio* is used when a man has an inner dialogue with someone unseen. It may be with God, when He is invoked, or with himself, or with his good

angel'[33] (Figure 3.2). The psychologist is familiar with this 'inner dialogue'; it is an essential part of the technique for coming to terms with the unconscious.[34] Ruland's definition proves beyond all doubt that when the alchemists speak of *meditari* they do not mean mere cogitation, but explicitly an inner dialogue and hence a living relationship to the answering voice of the 'Other' in ourselves, i.e. of the unconscious. The use of the term 'meditation' in the Hermetic dictum 'And as all things proceed from the One through the meditation of the One' must therefore be understood in this alchemical sense as a creative dialogue, by means of which things pass from an unconscious potential state to a manifest one. Thus we read in a treatise of Philalethes:[35] 'Above all it is marvellous that our stone, although already perfect and able to impart a perfect tincture, does voluntarily humble itself again and will meditate a new volatility, apart from all manipulation.'[36] What is meant by a 'meditated volatility' we discover a few lines lower down, where it says: 'Of its own accord it will liquefy . . . and by God's command become endowed with spirit, which will fly up and take the stone with it.'[37] Again, therefore, to 'meditate' means that through a dialogue with God yet more spirit will be infused into the stone, i.e. it will become still more spiritualized, volatilized or sublimated. Khunrath says much the same thing:

Figure 3.2 Alchemist in the initial *nigredo* state, meditating.
Source: From Jamsthaler, *Viatorium spagyricum* (1625); reproduced from Jung's *Collected Works*, Vol. 12.

Therefore study, meditate, sweat, work, cook ... so will a healthful
flood be opened to you which comes from the Heart of the Son of the
great World, a Water which the Son of the Great World pours forth from
his Body and Heart, to be for us a True and Natural Aqua Vitae.[38]

391   Likewise the 'meditation of the heavenly good', mentioned earlier,
must be taken in the sense of a living dialectical relationship to certain
dominants of the unconscious. We have excellent confirmation of this in
a treatise by a French alchemist living in the seventeenth and eighteenth
centuries.[39] He says:

How often did I see them [*the Sacerdotes Aegyptiorum*] overcome with
joy at my understanding, how affectionately they kissed me, for the true
grasp of the ambiguities of their paradoxical teaching came easily to my
mind. How often did their pleasure in the wonderful discoveries I made
concerning the abstruse doctrines of the ancients move them to reveal
unto my eyes and fingers the Hermetic vessel, the salamander [Figure
3.3], the full moon and the rising sun.

Figure 3.3 The Mercurial spirit of the *prima materia*, in the shape of a
salamander, frolicking in the fire.
Source: From Maier, *Scrutinium chymicum* (1687); reproduced from Jung's *Collected
Works*, Vol. 12.

392   This treatise, although it is not so much a personal confession as a description of the golden age of alchemy, nevertheless tells us how the alchemist imagined the psychological structure of his *opus*. Its association with the invisible forces of the psyche was the real secret of the *magisterium*. In order to express this secret the old masters readily resorted to allegory. One of the oldest records of this kind, which had a considerable influence on the later literature, is the *Visio Arislei*,[40] and its whole character relates it very closely to those visions known to us from the psychology of the unconscious.

393   As I have already said, the term *imaginatio*, like *meditatio*, is of particular importance in the alchemical *opus*. Earlier on we came across that remarkable passage in the *Rosarium* telling us that the work must be done with the true *imaginatio*, and we saw elsewhere how the philosophical tree can be made to grow through contemplation. Ruland's *Lexicon* once more helps us to understand what the alchemist meant by *imaginatio*.

394   Ruland says: 'Imagination is the star in man, the celestial or supercelestial body.'[41] This astounding definition throws a quite special light on the fantasy processes connected with the *opus*. We have to conceive of these processes not as the immaterial phantoms we readily take fantasy-pictures to be but as something corporeal, a 'subtle body', semi-spiritual in nature. In an age when there was as yet no empirical psychology such a concretization was bound to be made, because everything unconscious, once it was activated, was projected into matter – that is to say, it approached people from outside. It was a hybrid phenomenon, as it were, half spiritual, half physical: a concretization such as we frequently encounter in the psychology of primitives. The *imaginatio*, or the act of imagining, was thus a physical activity that could be fitted into the cycle of material changes, that brought these about and was brought about by them in turn. In this way the alchemist related himself not only to the unconscious but directly to the very substance which he hoped to transform through the power of imagination. The singular expression *astrum* (star) is a Paracelsan term, whch in this context means something like 'quintessence'.[42] Imagination is therefore a concentrated extract of the life forces, both physical and psychic. So the demand that the artifex must have a sound physical constitution is quite intelligible, since he works with and through his own quintessence and is himself the indispensable condition of his own experiment. But, just because of this intermingling of the physical and the psychic, it always remains an obscure point whether the ultimate transformations in the alchemical process are to be sought more in the material or more in the spiritual realm. Actually, however, the question is wrongly put: there was no 'either–or' for that age, but there did exist an intermediate realm between mind and matter, i.e. a psychic realm of subtle bodies[43] whose characteristic it is to manifest themselves in a mental as well as a material form. This is the only view that makes

sense of alchemical ways of thought, which must otherwise appear
nonsensical. Obviously, the existence of this intermediate realm comes to
a sudden stop the moment we try to investigate the matter in and for itself,
apart from all projection; and it remains non-existent so long as we believe
we know anything conclusive about the matter or the psyche. But the
moment when physics touches on the 'untrodden, untreadable regions', and
when psychology has at the same time to admit that there are other forms
of psychic life besides the acquisitions of personal consciousness – in other
words, when psychology too touches on an impenetrable darkness – then
the intermediate realm of subtle bodies comes to life again, and the
physical and the psychic are once more blended in an indissoluble unity.
We have come very near to this turning-point today.

395   Such reflections are unavoidable if we want to gain any understanding
of alchemy's peculiar terminology. The earlier talk of the 'aberration' of
alchemy sounds rather old-fashioned today, when the psychological
aspects of it have faced science with new tasks. There are very modern
problems in alchemy, though they lie outside the province of chemistry.

396   The concept of *imaginatio* is perhaps the most important key to the
understanding of the *opus*. The author of the treatise *De sulphure*[44] speaks
of the 'imaginative faculty' of the soul in that passage where he is trying
to do just what the ancients had failed to do, that is, give a clear indication
of the secret of the art. The soul, he says, is the vice-regent of God (*sui
locum tenens seu vice Rex est*) and dwells in the life-spirit of the pure
blood. It rules the mind (*illa gubernat mentem*) and this rules the body.
The soul functions (*operatur*) in the body, but has the greater part of its
function (*operatio*) outside the body (or, we might add by way of
explanation, in projection). This peculiarity is divine, since divine wisdom
is only partly enclosed in the body of the world: the greater part of it is
'outside, and it imagines far higher things than the body of the world can
conceive [*concipere*]'. And these things are outside nature: God's own
secrets. The soul is an example of this: it too imagines many things of the
utmost profundity (*profundissima*) outside the body, just as God does.
True, what the soul imagines happens only in the mind (*non exequitur nisi
in mente*), but what God imagines happens in reality. 'The soul, however,
has absolute and independent power [*absolutam et separatam potestatem*]
to do other things [*alia facere*] than those the body can grasp. But, when
it so desires, it has the greatest power over the body [*potestatem in corpus*],
for otherwise our philosophy would be in vain. Thou canst conceive the
greater, for we have opened the gates unto thee.'

NOTES

1 Matthew 15:19–20.
2 In mentioning this case (*CW* 17, para. 106), Jung identifies the father's problems
as erotic and religious.

3 Lama Kazi Dawa-Sandup was the translator of *The Bardo Thodol* or *Liberation by Hearing on the After Death Plane*, which W. Evans Wentz compiled and edited as *The Tibetan Book of the Dead*; John Woodroffe (Avalon), *The Serpent Power* (Madras, 3rd rev., 11th edn, 1931), is an interpretation of *kundalini* yoga.

4 Edward Burnett Tylor (1832–1917) English evolutionary anthropologist, invented the concept 'animism' to explain how 'the notion of a ghost-soul as the animating principle of man' can be readily extended to 'souls of lower animals, and even lifeless objects' (*Primitive Culture,* 2 vols (Gloucester, Mass., 1958; orig. 1917), vol. I, p. 145).

5 Ibid., p. 137.

6 Ibid., p. 124: 'Si utaris opere exteriori, non utaris nisi occipitio capitis et invenies' ('If you use an exterior operation you should use only the occiput and then you will find [the goal]'). The conjecture 'goal' is subject to the reservation that I have not yet been able to obtain the Arabic text.

7 Ibid., p. 124: 'Os capitis est mundum et est . . . minus os, quod sit in [h]omine [text: nomine], et vas mansionis cogitationis et intellectus' ('The skull is pure and . . . moreover it is a comparatively small bone in [man], and it is the vessel of cogitation and intellect').

8 'Res convertuntur per tempus ad intellectum per certitudinem, quantum partes assimulantur in compositione et in forma. Cerebrum vero propter vicinitatem cum anima rationali [the 'et' here should be deleted] permixtioni oportuit assimulari, et anima rationalis est simplex sicut diximus.'

9 Speculativa philosophia', *Theatr. chem.*, I, p. 265.

10 Ibid., p. 298.

11 Ibid., p. 264.

12 Ibid., p. 266.

13 Ibid., p. 267: 'Transmutemini de lapidibus mortuis in vivos lapides philosophicos.'

14 The effect of inflation is that one is not only 'puffed up' but too 'high up'. This may lead to attacks of giddiness, or to a tendency to fall downstairs, to twist one's ankle, to stumble over steps and chairs, and so on.

15 Berthelot, *Alch. grecs*, IV, xx, 8: τὸ μυστήριον τὸ φρικτὸν καὶ παράδοξον.

16 Zeller, *Philosophie der Griechen*, II, p. 152.

17 Ibid., III, pp. 99, 151.

18 Cf. Jung, *Psychological Types*, paras 318ff.

19 [These Latin phrases may be translated: *ex opere operato* (by the performed work); *ex opere operantis* (by the work of the operator); *opus operatum* (the performed work); *opus operantis* (the work of the operator) – EDITORS.]

20 Cf. my 'Synchronicity: An Acausal Connecting Principle', paras 949ff.

21 A σύμβολον is a 'throwing together.'

22 Cf. 'Relations between the Ego and the Unconscious', paras 341ff.

23 *Rosarium, Art. aurif.*, II, p. 214.

24 Ibid., p. 213: 'Nec intrat in eum [lapidem], quod non sit ortum ex eo, quoniam si aliquid extranei sibi apponatur, statim corrumpitur' ('Nothing enters into it [the stone] that did not come from it; since, if anything extraneous were to be added to it, it would at once be spoilt').

25 Petronius, *Satyricon*, para. 38. 'Phantasia non homo' ('He's a fantasy, not a man').

26 *Art. aurif.* II, p, 214: 'Et vide secundum naturam, de qua regenerantur corpora in visceribus terrae. Et hoc imaginare per veram imaginationem et non phantasticam' ('And look according to nature, by which the bodies are regenerated in the bowels of the earth. And imagine this with the true and not with the fantastic imagination').

27 Ibid., p. 243: 'Et invenitur in omni loco et in quolibet tempore et apud omnem rem, cam inquisitio aggravat inquirentem' ('And it is found in every place and at

any time and in every circumstance, when the search lies heavy on the searcher').

28 'De alch. diff.', *Theatr. chem.*, I, p. 199. It is not clear whether by 'scripture' he means the traditional description of the vessel in the treatises of the masters, or the Holy Scripture.

29 Sendivogius, 'Novum lumen', *Mus. herm.*, p. 574.

30 'Compendium', *Bibl. chem. curiosa*, I, p. 875.

31 'Speculativa philosophia', *Theatr. chem.*, I, p. 275.

32 Hoghelande, 'De alch. diff.', *Theatr. chem.*, I, p. 150.

33 P. 327: 'Meditatio (s.v.) dicitur, quoties cum aliquo alio colloquium habetur internum, qui tamen non videtur. Ut cum Deo ipsum invocando, vel cum se ipso, vel proprio angelo bono.' 'This description is very similar to the *colloquium* in the *Exercitia spiritualia* of Ignatius of Loyola. All the authors are unanimous in emphasizing the importance of meditation. Examples are unnecessary.

34 Cf. Jung, 'The Relations between the Ego and the Unconscious', paras 341ff.

35 'Introitus apertus', *Mus. herm.*, p. 693.

36 '. . . novam volatilitatem citra ullam manuum impositionem meditabitur'.

37 Cf. the Mohammedan legend of the rock in the mosque of Omar, at Jerusalem, which wanted to fly up with Mohammed when he ascended to heaven.

38 *Von hyleal, Chaos*, pp. 274f.

39 I take this text from a manuscript in my possession entitled 'Figurarum Aegyptiorum secretarum . . .', *incipit*: 'Ab omni aevo aegyptiorum sacerdotes'; colophon: 'laus jesu in saecula', (vol. 47, parchment, 18th cent.). The pictures in this manuscript are identical with those in MS No. 973 (18th cent.), Bibliothèque de l'Arsenal, Paris. They come from the 'Pratique' of Nicolas Flamel (1330–1418). The origin of the Latin text in my manuscript is at present unknown.

40 *Art. aurif.*, I. Cf. Ruska's version in *Historische Studien und Skizzen* (ed. Sudhoff), pp. 22ff. A still older series of visions is that of Zosimos in περὶ ἀρετῆς (Berthelot, *Alch. grecs*, III) and also of Krates (Berthelot, *Chimie au moyen âge*, III).

41 'Astrum in homine, coeleste sive supracoeleste corpus.' Since Ruland joins forces with Paracelsus here, I refer the reader to my 'Paracelsus as a Spiritual Phenomenon' [especially para. 173].

42 Ruland, *Lexicon*, s.v. 'astrum': 'virtus et potentia rerum, ex praeparationibus acquisita' ('the virtue and power of things, that is acquired through the preparations'). Hence also extract or Quinta Essentia.

43 Figulus (*Rosarium novum olympicum*, p. 109) says: '[*Anima*] is a subtle imperceptible smoke.'

44 Senivogius, in *Mus. herm.*, pp. 601ff.

4 Alchemy and individuation

From: 'The Psychology of the Child Archetype' (1940) (*CW* 9i)

289   The urge and compulsion to self-realization is a law of nature and thus of invincible power, even though its effect, at the start, is insignificant and improbable. Its power is revealed in the miraculous deeds of the child hero, and later in the *athla* (works) of the bondsman or thrall (of the Heracles type), where, although the hero has outgrown the impotence of the 'child', he is still in a menial position. The figure of the thrall generally leads up to the real epiphany of the semi-divine hero. Oddly enough, we have a similar modulation of themes in alchemy – in the synonyms for the *lapis*. As the *materia prima*, it is the *lapis exilis et vilis*. As a substance in process of transmutation, it is *servus rubeus* or *fugitivus*; and finally, in its true apotheosis, it attains the dignity of a *filius sapientiae* or *deus terrenus*, a 'light above all lights', a power that contains in itself all the powers of the upper and nether regions. It becomes a *corpus glorificatum* which enjoys everlasting incorruptibility and is therefore a *panacea* (bringer of healing).[1] The size and invincibility of the 'child' are bound up in Hindu speculation with the nature of the *atman*, which corresponds to the 'smaller than small yet bigger than big' motif. As an individual phenomenon, the self is 'smaller than small'; as the equivalent of the cosmos, it is 'bigger than big'. The self, regarded as the counter-pole of the world, its 'absolutely other', is the *sine qua non* of all empirical knowledge and consciousness of subject and object. Only because of this psychic 'otherness' is consciousness possible at all. Identity does not make consciousness possible; it is only separation, detachment and agonizing confrontation through opposition that produce consciousness and insight.

From: 'The Conjunction', *Mysterium coniunctionis* (1955–6) (*CW* 14)

778   The ego never lacks moral and rational counterarguments, which one cannot and should not set aside so long as it is possible to hold on to them. For you only feel yourself on the right road when the conflicts of duty

seem to have resolved themselves, and you have become the victim of a decision made over your head or in defiance of the heart. From this we can see the numinous power of the self, which can hardly be experienced in any other way. For this reason *the experience of the self is always a defeat for the ego.* The extraordinary difficulty in this experience is that the self can be distinguished only conceptually from what has always been referred to as 'God', but not practically. Both concepts apparently rest on an identical numinous factor which is a condition of reality. The ego enters into the picture only so far as it can offer resistance, defend itself, and in the event of defeat still affirm its existence. The prototype of this situation is Job's encounter with Yahweh. This hint is intended only to give some indication of the nature of the problems involved. From this general statement one should not draw the over-hasty conclusion that in every case there is a hybris of ego-consciousness which fully deserves to be over-powered by the unconscious. That is not so at all, because it very often happens that ego-consciousness and the ego's sense of responsibility are too weak and need, if anything, strengthening. But these are questions of practical psychotherapy, and I mention them here only because I have been accused of underestimating the importance of the ego and giving undue prominence to the unconscious. This strange insinuation emanates from a theological quarter. Obviously my critic has failed to realize that the mystical experiences of the saints are no different from other effects of the unconscious.

779   In contrast to the ideal of alchemy, which consisted in the production of a mysterious substance, a man, an *anima mundi* or a *deus terrenus* who was expected to be a saviour from all human ills, the psychological interpretation (foreshadowed by the alchemists) points to the concept of human wholeness. This concept has primarily a therapeutic significance in that it attempts to portray the psychic state which results from bridging over a dissociation between conscious and unconscious. The alchemical compensation corresponds to the integration of the unconscious with consciousness, whereby both are altered. Above all, consciousness experiences a widening of its horizon. This certainly brings about a considerable improvement of the whole psychic situation, since the disturbance of consciousness by the counteraction of the unconscious is eliminated. But, because all good things must be paid for dearly, the previously unconscious conflict is brought to the surface instead and imposes on consciousness a heavy responsibility, as *it* is now expected to solve the conflict. But it seems as badly equipped and prepared for this as was the consciousness of the medieval alchemist. Like him, the modern man needs a special method for investigating and giving shape to the unconscious contents in order to get consciousness out of its fix. As I have shown elsewhere, an experience of the self may be expected as a result of these psychotherapeutic endeavours, and quite often these experiences are numinous. It is not worth the effort to try to describe their totality

character. Anyone who has experienced anything of the sort will know what I mean, and anyone who has not had the experience will not be satisfied by any amount of descriptions. Moreover there are countless descriptions of it in world literature. But I know of no case in which the bare description conveyed the experience.

780   It is not the least astonishing that numinous experiences should occur in the course of psychological treatment and that they may even be expected with some regularity, for they also occur very frequently in exceptional psychic states that are not treated and may even cause them. They do not belong exclusively to the domain of psychopathology but can be observed in normal people as well. Naturally, modern ignorance of and prejudice against intimate psychic experiences dismiss them as psychic anomalies and put them in psychiatric pigeon-holes without making the least attempt to understand them. But that neither gets rid of the fact of their occurrence nor explains it.

From: 'The Paradoxa', *Mysterium coniunctionis* (1955–6) (*CW* 14)

47   The eye, like the sun, is a symbol as well as an allegory of conscious-ness.[2] In alchemy the *scintillulae* are put together to form the gold (Sol); in the Gnostic systems the atoms of light are reintegrated. Psychologically, this doctrine testifies to the personality- or ego-character of psychic complexes: just as the distinguishing mark of the ego-complex is con-sciousness, so it is possible that other, 'unconscious' complexes may possess, as splinter psyches, a certain luminosity of their own.[3] From these atoms is produced the Monad (and the lapis in its various significations), in agreement with the teachings of Epicurus, who held that the concourse of atoms even produced God.[4]

48   In his chapter on knowledge,[5] Dorn uses the concept of the *scintillae* in moral form: 'Let every man consider diligently in his heart what has been said above, and thus little by little he will come to see with his mental eyes a number of sparks shining day by day and more and more and growing into such a great light that thereafter all things needful to him will be made known.' This light is the 'light of nature'. As Dorn says in his *Philosophia meditativa*:

What madness deludes you? For in you, and not proceeding from you, he wills all this to be found, which you seek outside you and not within yourselves. Such is the vice of the common man, to despise everything his own, and always to lust after the strange . . .. The life, the light of men, shineth in us, albeit dimly, and as though in darkness.[6] It is not to be sought as proceeding from us, though it is in us and not of us,[7] but of Him to Whom it belongeth, Who hath deigned to make us his dwelling place. . . . He hath implanted that light in us that we may see in its light the light of Him who dwelleth in light inaccessible, and that we may excel his other creatures. In this especially we are made like unto Him, that He hath given us a spark of His light. Thus the truth is to be sought not in ourselves, but in the image of God[8] which is within us.[9]

49   In Dorn's view there is in man an 'invisible sun', which he identifies with the Archeus.[10] This sun is identical with the 'sun in the earth'. The invisible sun enkindles an elemental fire which consumes man's substance[11] and reduces his body to the *prima materia*. It is also compared with 'salt' or 'natural balsam', 'which has in itself corruption and protection against corruption'. This paradoxical aspect is borne out by a curious saying: 'Man is the bait, wherein the sparks struck by the flint, i.e. Mercurius, and by the steel,[12] i.e. heaven, seize upon the tinder and show their power.'[13] Mercurius as the 'flint' is evidently thought of here in his feminine, chthonic form, and 'heaven' stands for his masculine, spiritual quintessence. From the (nuptial) impact between the two the spark is struck, the Archeus, which is a 'corrupter of the body', just as the 'chemist' is a 'corrupter of metals'. This negative aspect of the *scintilla* is remarkable, but it agrees very well with the alchemists' less optimistic, medico-scientific view of the world.[14] For them the dark side of the world and of life had not been conquered, and this was the task they set themselves in their work. In their eyes the fire-point, the divine centre in man, was something dangerous, a powerful poison which required very careful handling if it was to be changed into the panacea. The process of individuation, likewise, has its own specific dangers. Dorn expresses the standpoint of the alchemists in his fine saying: 'There is nothing in nature that does not contain as much evil as good.'[15]

From: 'The Personification of the Opposites', *Mysterium coniunctionis* (1955–6) (*CW* 14)

283   It is worth noting that the animal is the symbolic carrier of the self. This hint in Maier is borne out by modern individuals who have no notion of alchemy.[16] It expresses the fact that the structure of wholeness was always present but was buried in profound unconsciousness, where it can always be found again if one is willing to risk one's skin to attain the greatest possible range of consciousness through the greatest possible self-knowledge – a 'harsh and bitter drink' usually reserved for hell. The throne of God seems to be no unworthy reward for such trials. For self-knowledge – in the total meaning of the word – is not a one-sided intellectual pastime but a journey through the four continents, where one is exposed to all the dangers of land, sea, air and fire. Any total act of recognition worthy of the name embraces the four – or 360! – aspects of

existence. Nothing may be 'disregarded'. When Ignatius Loyola recommended 'imagination through the five senses'[17] to the meditant, and told
him to imitate Christ 'by use of his senses',[18] what he had in mind was the
fullest possible 'realization' of the object of contemplation. Quite apart
from the moral or other effects of this kind of meditation, its chief effect
is the training of consciousness, of the capacity for concentration, and of
attention and clarity of thought. The corresponding forms of yoga have
similar effects. But in contrast to these traditional modes of realization,
where the meditant projects himself into some prescribed form, the self-
knowledge alluded to by Maier is a projection into the empirical self as it
actually is. It is not the 'self' we like to imagine ourselves to be after
carefully removing all the blemishes, but the empirical ego just as it is,
with everything that it does and everything that happens to it. Everybody
would like to be quit of this odious adjunct, which is precisely why in the
East the ego is explained as illusion and why in the West it is offered up
in sacrifice to the Christ figure.

284   By contrast, the aim of the mystical peregrination is to understand all
parts of the world, to achieve the greatest possible extension of consciousness, as though its guiding principle were the Carpocratic[19] idea that one
is delivered from no sin which one has not committed. Not a turning-away
from its empirical 'so-ness', but the fullest possible experience of the ego
as reflected in the 'ten thousand things' – that is the goal of the
peregrination.[20] This follows logically from the psychological recognition
that God cannot be experienced at all unless this futile and ridiculous ego
offers a modest vessel in which to catch the effluence of the Most High
and name it with his name. The significance of the *vas*-symbol in alchemy
shows how concerned the artifex was to have the right vessel for the right
content: 'One is the *lapis*, one the medicament, one the vessel, one the
procedure, and one the disposition.' The *aqua nostra*, the transformative
substance, is even its own vessel.[21] From this it is but a step to the
paradoxical statement of Angelus Silesius:

> God is my centre when I close him in,
> And my circumference when I melt in him.[22]

From: 'Religious Ideas in Alchemy' (1937) (*CW* 12)

333   Alchemy, as is well known, describes a process of chemical transformation and gives numberless directions for its accomplishment. Although
hardly two authors are of the same opinion regarding the exact course of
the process and the sequence of its stages, the majority are agreed on the
principal points at issue, and have been so from the earliest times, i.e.
since the beginning of the Christian era. Four stages are distinguished
(Figure 4.1), characterized by the original colours mentioned in Heraclitus:

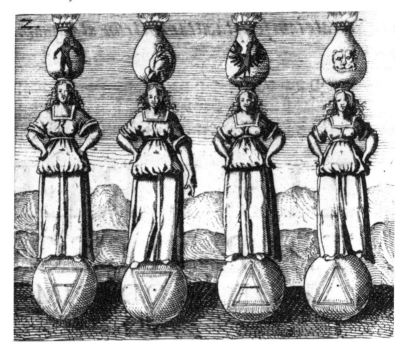

Figure 4.1 The four stages of the alchemical process. The four elements are indicated on the balls.
Source: From Mylius, *Philosophia reformata* (1622); reproduced from Jung's *Collected Works*, Vol. 12.

melanosis (blackening), *leukosis* (whitening), *xanthosis* (yellowing) and *iosis* (reddening).[23] This division of the process into four was called the τετραμερειν τὴν φιλοσοφίαν, the quartering of the philosophy. Later, about the fifteenth or sixteenth century, the colours were reduced to three, and the *xanthosis*, otherwise called the *citrinitas*, gradually fell into disuse or was but seldom mentioned. Instead, the *viriditas* (greenness) sometimes appears after the *melanosis* or *nigredo* in exceptional cases, though it was never generally recognized. Whereas the original *tetrameria* corresponded exactly to the quaternity of elements, it was now frequently stressed that although there were four elements (earth, water, fire and air) and four qualities (hot, cold, dry and moist), there were only three colours: black, white and red.

From: 'The Personification of the Opposites', *Mysterium coniunctionis* (1955–6) (*CW* 14)

274   The process of transformation does not come to an end with the production of the quaternity symbol. The continuation of the opus leads

to the dangerous crossing of the Red Sea, signifying death and rebirth. It is very remarkable that our author, by his paradox 'running without running, moving without motion', introduces a coincidence of opposites just at this point, and that the Hippolytus text speaks, equally paradoxically, of the 'gods of destruction and the god of salvation' being together. The quaternity, as we have seen, is a *quaternio* of opposites, a synthesis of the four originally divergent functions. Their synthesis is here achieved in an image, but in psychic reality becoming conscious of the whole psyche[24] faces us with a highly problematical situation. We can indicate its scope in a single question: What am I to do with the unconscious?

275   For this, unfortunately, there are no recipes or general rules. I have tried to present the main outlines of what the psychotherapist can observe of this wearisome and all too familiar process in my study 'The Relations between the Ego and the Unconscious'. For the layman these experiences are a *terra incognita* which is not made any more accessible by broad generalizations. Even the imagination of the alchemists, otherwise so fertile, fails us completely here. Only a thorough investigation of the texts could shed a little light on this question. The same task challenges our endeavours in the field of psychotherapy. Here too are thousands of images, symbols, dreams, fantasies and visions that still await comparative research. The only thing that can be said with some certainty at present is that there is a gradual process of approximation whereby the two positions, the conscious and the unconscious, are both modified. Differences in individual cases, however, are just as great as they were among the alchemists.

296   Ascent and descent, above and below, up and down, represent an emotional realization of opposites, and this realization gradually leads, or should lead, to their equilibrium. This motif occurs very frequently in dreams, in the form of going up- and downhill, climbing stairs, going up or down in a lift, balloon, aeroplane, etc.[25] It corresponds to the struggle between the winged and the wingless dragon, i.e. the *uroboros*. Dorn describes it also as the 'circular distillation'[26] and as the 'spagyric vessel' which has to be constructed after the likeness of the natural vessel, i.e. in the form of a sphere. As Dorn interprets it, this vacillating between the opposites and being tossed back and forth means being contained *in* the opposites. They become a vessel in which what was previously now one thing and now another floats vibrating, so that the painful suspension between opposites gradually changes into the bilateral activity of the point in the centre.[27] This is the 'liberation from opposites', the *nirdvandva* of Hindu philosophy, though it is not really a philosophical but rather a psychological development. The *Aurelia occulta* puts this thought in the words of the dragon: 'Many from one and one from many, issue of a famous line, I rise from the lowest to the highest. The nethermost power of the whole earth is united with the highest. I therefore am the One and

the Many within me.'[28] In these words the dragon makes it clear that he is the chthonic forerunner of the self.

342   The psychological equivalent of the chaotic water of the beginning[29] is the unconscious, which the old writers could grasp only in projected form, just as today most people cannot see the beam in their own eye but are all too well aware of the mote in their brother's. Political propaganda exploits this primitivity and conquers the naive with their own defect. The only defence against this overwhelming danger is recognition of the shadow. The sight of its darkness is itself an illumination, a widening of consciousness through integration of the hitherto unconscious components of the personality. Freud's efforts to bring the shadow to consciousness are the logical and salutary answer to the almost universal unconsciousness and projection-proneness of the general public. It is as though Freud, with sure instinct, had sought to avert the danger of nationwide psychic epidemics that threatened Europe. What he did not see was that the confrontation with the shadow is not just a harmless affair that can be settled by 'reason'. The shadow is the primitive who is still alive and active in civilized man, and our civilized reason means nothing to him. He needs to be ruled by a higher authority, such as is found in the great religions. Even when Reason triumphed at the beginning of the French Revolution it was quickly turned into a goddess and enthroned in Notre-Dame.

343   The shadow exerts a dangerous fascination which can be countered only by another *fascinosum*. It cannot be got at by reason, even in the most rational person, but only by illumination, of a degree and kind that are equal to the darkness but are the exact opposite of 'enlightenment'. For what we call 'rational' is everything that seems 'fitting' to the man in the street, and the question then arises whether this 'fitness' may not in the end prove to be 'irrational' in the bad sense of the word. Sometimes, even with the best intentions this dilemma cannot be solved. This is the moment when the primitive trusts himself to a higher authority and to a decision beyond his comprehension. The civilized man in his closed-in environment functions in a fitting and appropriate manner, that is, rationally. But if, because of some apparently insoluble dilemma, he gets outside the confines of civilization, he becomes a primitive again; then he has irrational ideas and acts on hunches; then he no longer thinks but 'it' thinks in him; then he needs 'magical' practices in order to gain a feeling of security; then the latent autonomy of the unconscious becomes active and begins to manifest itself as it has always done in the past.

344   The good tidings announced by alchemy are that, as once a fountain sprang up in Judaea, so now there is a secret Judaea the way to which is not easily found, and a hidden spring whose waters seem so worthless[30] and so bitter that they are deemed of no use at all. We know from numerous hints[31] that man's inner life is the 'secret place' where the *aqua solvens et coagulans*, the *medicina catholica* or *panacea*, the spark of the light of nature,[32] are to be found. Our text shows us how much the alchemists put

their art on the level of divine revelation and regarded it as at least an essential complement to the work of redemption. True, only a few of them were the elect who formed the golden chain linking earth to heaven, but still they were the fathers of natural science today. They were the unwitting instigators of the schism between faith and knowledge, and it was they who made the world conscious that the revelation was neither complete nor final. 'Since these things are so', says an ecclesiastic of the seventeenth century, 'it will suffice, after the light of faith, for human ingenuity to recognize, as it were, the refracted rays of the Divine majesty in the world and in created things.'[33] The 'refracted rays' correspond to the 'certain luminosity' which the alchemists said was inherent in the material world.

345 Revelation conveys general truths which often do not illuminate the individual's actual situation in the slightest, nor was it traditional revelation that gave us the microscope and the machine. And since human life is not enacted exclusively, or even to a noticeable degree, on the plane of the higher verities, the source of knowledge unlocked by the old alchemists and physicians has done humanity a great and welcome service – so great that for many people the light of revelation has been extinguished altogether. Within the confines of civilization man's wilful rationality apparently suffices. Outside of this shines, or should shine, the light of faith. But where the darkness comprehendeth it not (this being the prerogative of darkness!) those labouring in the darkness must try to accomplish an *opus* that will cause the 'fishes' eyes' to shine in the depths of the sea, or to catch the 'refracted rays of the divine majesty' even though this produces a light which the darkness, as usual, does not comprehend. But when there is a light in the darkness which comprehends the darkness, darkness no longer prevails. The longing of the darkness for light is fulfilled only when the light can no longer be rationally explained by the darkness. For the darkness has its own peculiar intellect and its own logic, which should be taken very seriously. Only the 'light which the darkness comprehendeth not' can illuminate the darkness. Everything that the darkness thinks, grasps and comprehends by itself is dark; therefore it is illuminated only by what, to it, is unexpected, unwanted and incomprehensible. The psychotherapeutic method of active imagination offers excellent examples of this; sometimes a numinous dream or some external event will have the same effect.

307 The illumination comes to a certain extent from the unconscious, since it is mainly dreams that put us on the track of enlightenment. This dawning light corresponds to the *albedo*, the moonlight which in the opinion of some alchemists heralds the rising sun. The growing redness (*rubedo*) which now follows denotes an increase of warmth and light coming from the sun, consciousness. This corresponds to the increasing participation of consciousness, which now begins to react emotionally to the contents produced by the unconscious. At first the process of integration is a 'fiery' conflict, but gradually it leads over to the 'melting' or synthesis of the

opposites. The alchemists termed this the *rubedo*, in which the marriage of the red man and the white woman, Sol and Luna, is consummated. Although the opposites flee from one another they nevertheless strive for balance, since a state of conflict is too inimical to life to be endured indefinitely. They do this by wearing each other out: the one eats the other, like the two dragons or the other ravenous beasts of alchemical symbolism.

304   In alchemy the fire purifies, but it also melts the opposites into a unity. He who ascends unites the powers of Above and Below and shows his full power when he returns again to earth.[34] By this is to be understood the production on the one hand of the *panacea* or *medicina catholica*, and on the other of a living being with a human form, the *filius philosophorum*, who is often depicted as a youth or hermaphrodite or child. He is a parallel of the Gnostic Anthropos, but he also appear as an Anthroparion, a kind of goblin, a familiar who stands by the adept in his work and helps the physician to heal.[35] This being ascends and descends and unites Below with Above, gaining a new power which carries its effect over into everyday life. His mistress gives Hermas this advice: 'Therefore do not cease to speak to the ears of the saints'[36] – in other words, work among your fellow-men by spreading the news of the Risen.

From: 'The Conjunction', *Mysterium coniunctionis* (1955–6) (*CW* 14)

669   Already in the sixteenth century, Gerard Dorn had recognized the psychological aspect of the chymical marriage and clearly understood it as what we today would call the individuation process. This is a step beyond the bounds which were set to the *coniunctio*, both in ecclesiastical doctrine and in alchemy, by its archetypal symbolism. It seems to me that Dorn's view represents a logical understanding of it in two respects: first because the discrepancy between the chemical operation and the psychic events associated with it could not remain permanently hidden from an attentive and critical observer; and second because the marriage symbolism obviously never quite satisfied the alchemical thinkers themselves, since they constantly felt obliged to make use of other 'uniting symbols', besides the numerous variants of the *hieros gamos*, to express the all but incomprehensible nature of the mystery. Thus the *coniunctio* is represented by the dragon embracing the woman in the grave,[37] or by two animals fighting,[38] or by the king dissolving in water,[39] and so on. Similarly, in Chinese philosophy the meaning of *yang* is far from exhausted with its masculine connotation. It also means dry, bright, and the south side of the mountain, just as the feminine *yin* means damp, dark, and the north side of the mountain.

675   If the demand for self-knowledge is willed by fate and is refused, this

negative attitude may end in real death. The demand would not have come to this person had he still been able to strike out on some promising by-path. But he is caught in a blind alley from which only self-knowledge can extricate him. If he refuses this then no other way is open to him. Usually he is not conscious of his situation, either, and the more unconscious he is the more he is at the mercy of unforeseen dangers: he cannot get out of the way of a car quickly enough; in climbing a mountain he misses his foothold somewhere; out skiing he thinks he can just negotiate a tricky slope; and in an illness he suddenly loses the courage to live. The unconscious has a thousand ways of snuffing out a meaningless existence with surprising swiftness. The connection of the *unio mentalis* with the death-motif is therefore obvious, even when death consists only in the cessation of spiritual progress.

676   The alchemists rightly regarded 'mental union in the overcoming of the body' as only the first stage of conjunction or individuation, in the same way that Khunrath understood Christ as the 'Saviour of the Microcosm' but not of the Macrocosm, whose saviour was the *lapis*. In general, the alchemists strove for a *total* union of opposites in symbolic form, and this they regarded as the indispensable condition for the healing of all ills. Hence they sought to find ways and means to produce that substance in which all opposites were united. It had to be material as well as spiritual, living as well as inert, masculine as well as feminine, old as well as young, and – presumably – morally neutral. It had to be created by man, and at the same time, since it was an 'increatum', by God himself, the *Deus terrestris*.

677   The second step on the way to the production of this substance was the reunion of the spirit with the body. For this procedure there were many symbols. One of the most important was the chymical marriage, which took place in the retort. The older alchemists were still so unconscious of the psychological implications of the *opus* that they understood their own symbols as mere allegories or – semiotically – as secret names for chemical combinations, thus stripping mythology, of which they made such copious use, of its true meaning and using only its terminology. Later this was to change, and already in the fourteenth century it began to dawn on them that the *lapis* was more than a chemical compound. This realization expressed itself mainly in the Christ-parallel.[40] Dorn was probably the first to recognize the psychological implications for what they were, so far as this was intellectually possible for a man of that age. Proof of this is his demand that the pupil must have a good physical and, more particularly, a good moral constitution.[41] A religious attitude was essential.[42] For in the individual was hidden that 'substance of celestial nature known to very few', the 'incorrupt medicament' which 'can be freed from its fetters, not by its contrary but by its like'.

686   Thus Dorn describes the secret of the second stage of conjunction. To the modern mind such contrivances of thought will seem like nebulous

products of a dreaming fancy. So, in a sense, they are, and for this reason they lend themselves to decipherment by the method of complex psychology. In his attempt to make the obviously confused situation clearer, Dorn involved himself in a discussion of the ways and means for producing the quintessence, which was evidently needed for uniting the *unio mentalis* with the body. One naturally asks oneself how this alchemical procedure enters into it at all. The *unio mentalis* is so patently a spiritual and moral attitude that one cannot doubt its psychological nature. To our way of thinking, this immediately sets up a dividing wall between the psychic and the chemical process. For us the two things are incommensurable, but they were not so for the medieval mind. It knew nothing of the nature of chemical substances and their combination. It saw only enigmatic substances which, united with one another, inexplicably brought forth equally mysterious new substances. In this profound darkness the alchemist's fantasy had free play and could playfully combine the most inconceivable things. It could act without restraint and, in so doing, portray itself without being aware of what was happening.

687   The free-ranging psyche of the adept used chemical substances and processes as a painter uses colours to shape out the images of his fancy. If Dorn, in order to describe the union of the *unio mentalis* with the body, reaches out for his chemical substances and implements, this only means that he was illustrating his fantasies by chemical procedures. For this purpose he chose the most suitable substances, just as the painter chooses the right colours. Honey, for instance, had to go into the mixture because of its purifying quality. As a Paracelsist, Dorn knew from the writings of the Master what high praises he had heaped upon it, calling it the 'sweetness of the earths', the 'resin of the earth' which permeates all growing things, the 'Indian spirit' which is turned by the 'influence of summer' into a 'corporeal spirit'.[43] Thereby the mixture acquired the property not only of eliminating impurities but of changing spirit into body, and in view of the proposed conjunction of the spirit and the body this seemed a particularly promising sign. To be sure, the 'sweetness of the earths' was not without its dangers, for the honey could change into a deadly poison. According to Paracelsus it contains 'Tartarum', which as its name implies has to do with Hades. Further, Tartarum is a 'calcined Saturn' and consequently has affinities with this malefic planet. For another ingredient Dorn takes Chelidonia (*Chelidonium maius*, celandine), which cures eye diseases and is particularly good for night-blindness, and even heals the spiritual 'benightedness' (affliction of the soul, melancholy-madness) so much feared by the adepts. It protects against 'thunderstorms', i.e. outbursts of affect. It is a precious ingredient, because its yellow flowers symbolize the philosophical gold, the highest treasure. What is more important here, it draws the humidity, the 'soul',[44] out of Mercurius. It therefore assists the 'spiritualization' of the body and makes visible the essence of Mercurius, the supreme chthonic spirit. But Mercurius is also

the devil.[45] Perhaps that is why the section in which Lagneus defines the nature of Mercurius is entitled 'Dominus vobiscum'.[46]

688   In addition, the plant Mercurialis (dog's mercury) is indicated. Like the Homeric magic herb Moly, it was found by Hermes himself and must therefore have magical effects. It is particularly favourable to the *coniunctio* because it occurs in male and female form and thus can determine the sex of a child about to be conceived. Mercurius himself was said to be generated from an extract of it – that spirit which acts as a mediator (because he is *utriusque capax*, 'capable of either') and saviour of the Macrocosm, and is therefore best able to unite the above with the below. In his ithyphallic form as Hermes Kyllenios, he contributes the attractive power of sexuality, which plays a great role in the *coniunctio* symbolism.[47] Like honey, he is dangerous because of his possibly poisonous effect, for which reason it naturally seemed advisable to our author to add rosemary to the mixture as an alexipharmic (antidote) and a synonym for Mercurius (*aqua permanens*), perhaps on the principle that 'like cures like'. Dorn could hardly resist the temptation to exploit the alchemical allusion to *ros marinus* (sea-dew). In agreement with ecclesiastical symbolism there was in alchemy, too, a 'dew of grace', the *aqua vitae*, the perpetual, permanent and two-meaninged ὕδωρ θεῖον, divine water or sulphur water. The water was also called *aqua pontica* (sea-water) or simply 'sea'. This was the great sea over which the alchemist sailed in his mystic peregrination, guided by the 'heart' of Mercurius in the heavenly North Pole, to which nature herself points with the magnetic compass.[48] It was also the bath of regeneration, the spring rain which brings forth the vegetation, and the *aqua doctrinae*.

689   Another alexipharmic is the lily. But it is much more than that: its juice is 'mercurial' and even 'incombustible', a sure sign of its incorruptible and 'eternal' nature. This is confirmed by the fact that the lily was conceived to be Mercurius and the quintessence itself – the noblest thing that human meditation can reach. The red lily stands for the male and the white for the female in the *coniunctio*, the divine pair that unite in the hierosgamos. The lily is therefore a true 'gamonymus' in the Paracelsan sense.

690   Finally, the mixture must not lack the thing that really keeps body and soul together: human blood, which was regarded as the seat of the soul.[49] It was a synonym for the red tincture, a preliminary stage of the *lapis*; moreover, it was an old-established magic charm, a 'ligament' for binding the soul to either God or the devil, and hence a powerful medicine for uniting the *unio mentalis* with the body. The admixture of human blood seems to me unusual if one assumes that the recipe was meant literally. We move here on uncertain ground. Although the vegetable ingredients are obviously indicated because of their symbolic value, we still do not know exactly how far the symbolism had a magical quality. If it had, then the recipe must be taken literally. In the case of blood, increased doubts

arise because either it was simply a synonym for the *aqua permanens* and could then be practically any liquid, or else real blood was meant, and then we must ask where this blood came from. Could it have been the adept's? This problem seems to me not entirely irrelevant, since Dorn, in his *Philosophia meditativa*, was greatly influenced, as we shall see, by the Sabaean *Liber quartorum*, which he obviously knew although he did not mention it. The Sabaeans were reputed to have sacrificed human victims for magical purposes,[50] and even today human blood is used for signing pacts with the devil. It is also not so long since tramps were made drunk and quickly immured on a building-site in order to make the foundations safe. A magical recipe of the sixteenth century, therefore, might easily have used human blood as a *pars pro toto*.

691   This whole mixture was then joined 'with the heaven of the red or white wine or of Tartarus'. The *caelum*, as we have seen, was the product of the alchemical procedure, which in this case consisted in first distilling the 'philosophic wine'. Thereby the soul and spirit were separated from the body and repeatedly sublimated until they were free from all 'phlegm', i.e. from all liquid that contained no more 'spirit'.[51] The residue, called the *corpus* (body), was reduced to ashes in the 'most vehement fire' and, hot water being added, was changed into a *lixivium asperrimum* (very sharp lye), which was then carefully poured off the ashes by tilting the vessel. The residue was treated in the same way again, until in the end no *asperitas* remained in the ashes. The lye was filtered and then evaporated in a glass vessel. What was left over was *tartarum nostrum* ('our winestone', *calculus vini*), the natural 'salt of all things'. This salt 'can be dissolved into tartaric water, in a damp and cool place on a slab of marble'.[52] The tartaric water was the quintessence of the philosophic and even of ordinary wine, and was then subjected to the above-mentioned rotation. As in a centrifuge, the pure was separated from the impure, and a liquid 'of the colour of the air' floated to the top. This was the *caelum*.

692   I have detailed this process in order to give the reader a direct impression of the alchemical procedure. One can hardly suppose that all this is mere poppycock, for Dorn was a man who obviously took things seriously. So far as one can judge he meant what he said, and he himself worked in the laboratory. Of course we do not know what success he had chemically, but we are sufficiently informed about the results of his meditative exertions.

693   The *caelum*, for Dorn, was the celestial substance hidden in man, the secret 'truth', the 'sum of virtue', the 'treasure which is not eaten by moths nor dug out by thieves'. In the world's eyes it is the cheapest thing, but 'to the wise more worthy of love than precious stones and gold, a good that passeth not away, and is taken hence after death'.[53] The reader will gather from this that the adept was describing nothing less than the Kingdom of Heaven on earth. I think that Dorn was not exaggerating, but that he wanted to communicate to his public something very important to him. He believed in the necessity of the alchemical operation as well as

in its success; he was concinved that the quintessence was needed for the 'preparation' of the body,[54] and that the body was so much improved by this 'universal medicine' that the *coniunctio* with spirit and soul could be consummated. If the production of the *caelum* from wine is a hair-raising chemical fantasy, our understanding ceases altogether when the adept mixes this heaven with his 'gamonymous' and other magical herbs. But if the one consists mainly of fantasies, so does the other. This makes it interesting. Fantasies always mean something when they are spontaneous. The question then arises: what is the psychological meaning of the procedure?

From: 'Epilogue' to *Mysterium coniunctionis* (1955–6) (*CW* 14)

792   We can see today that the entire alchemical procedure for uniting the opposites, which I have described in the foregoing, could just as well represent the individuation process of a single individual, though with the not unimportant difference that no single individual ever attains to the richness and scope of the alchemical symbolism. This has the advantage of having been built up through the centuries, whereas the individual in his short life has at his disposal only a limited amount of experience and limited powers of portrayal. It is therefore a difficult and thankless task to try to describe the nature of the individuation process from case-material. Since one aspect tends to predominate in one case and another in another, and one case begins earlier and another later, and the psychic conditions vary without limit, only one or the other version or phase of the process can be demonstrated in any given instance. No case in my experience is comprehensive enough to show all the aspects in such detail that it could be regarded as paradigmatic. Anyone who attempted to describe the individuation process with the help of case-material would have to remain content with a mosaic of bits and pieces without beginning or end, and if he wanted to be understood he would have to count on a reader whose experience in the same field was equal to his own. Alchemy, therefore, has performed for me the great and invaluable service of providing material in which my experience could find sufficient room, and has thereby made it possible for me to describe the individuation process at least in its essential aspects.

NOTES

1 The material is collected in *Psychology and Alchemy*, Parts II and III. For Mercurius as a servant, see the parable of Eirenaeus Philalethes, *Ripley Reviv'd: or, An Exposition upon Sir George Ripley's Hermetico-Poetical Works* (1678).

2 Cf. Rabanus Maurus, *Allegoriae in Sacram Script.* (Migne, *P.L.*, vol. 112, col. 1009: 'The eye is . . . clarity of intellect').

3 Cf. my 'Complex Theory', paras 203f., and 'Nature of the Psyche', paras 388ff.

4 Hippolytus, *Elenchos*, I, 22, 2 (Legge, I, p. 58): 'And that from the concourse of the atoms both God and all the elements came into being and that in them were all animals and other things.'

5 'Speculativa philosophia', *Theatr. chem.*, I, p. 275.

6 John 1: 4f.: 'In him was life, and the life was the light of men. And the light shineth in the darkness.'

7 'If a man knows how to transmute things in the greater world . . . how much more shall he know how to do in the microcosm, that is, in himself, the same that he is able to do outside himself, if he but know that the greatest treasure of man dwells within him and not outside him.' (Dorn, 'Spec. phil.', *Theatr. chem.*, I, p. 307.)

8 *Imago Dei* is 'God-image' in the sense of both a 'reflection' and an archetype.

9 *Theatr. chem.*, I, p. 460. Cf. *Aion*, pp. 37ff.

10 'The Archeus in man naturally practises the chymic art' ('Spec. phil.', p. 308). This agrees with Paracelsus.

11 'Because man is engendered in corruption, his own substance pursues him with hatred' (ibid., p. 308).

12 Here *chalybs* means 'steel', but as *chalybs Sendivogii* it is an arcane substance which is the 'secret Salmiac'. This is Sal Armoniacus, the 'dissolved stone' (Ruland, *Lexicon*, p. 281). Elsewhere Ruland says: 'Sal ammoniac is the star' (Latin edn, p. 71). Mylius (*Phil. ref.*, p. 314) says of the miraculous *aqua*: 'That is the best, which is extracted by the force of our chalybs which is found in the Ram's belly . . . before it is suitably cooked it is a deadly poison.' The ruler of Aries is Mars (= iron). Cf. 'Ares' in Paracelsus ('Paracelsus as a Spiritual Phenomenon', paras 176f.).

13 'Spec. phil.', p. 308.

14 Cf. the 'crime of the spirit'.

15 'Spec. phil.', p. 307.

16 Namely in the form of symbolic animals which appear in dreams as prefigurations of the self.

17 *Spiritual Exercises* (trans. Rickaby), p. 41.

18 Ibid., p. 215.

19 Cf. 'Psychology and Religion', para. 133.

20 Angelus Silesius says, however:

> Turn inward for your voyage! For all your arts
> You will not find the Stone in foreign parts.
>
> (*Cherubinischer Wandersmann*, III, no. 118).

All the same, no one has yet discovered himself without the world.

21 Mylius, *Phil. ref.*, pp. 33 and 245.

22 *Cher. Wand.*, III, no. 148.

23 This word comes from ἰός (poison). But since it has about the same meaning as the red tincture of later alchemy I have translated *iosis* as 'reddening'.

24 'Whole' is meant here only in a relative sense, implying merely the most important aspects of the individual psyche and of the collective unconscious.

25 Cf. *Psychology and Alchemy*, paras 64ff., 78f.

26 'Phys. Trismeg.', *Theatr. chem.*, I, p. 430.

27 This motif is not uncommon in mandalas drawn by patients, the centre being represented either by a fluttering bird, or a pulsing cyst or heart. (In pathology we speak of an 'auricular flutter'.) The same motif appears in the form of concentric rings (see 'A Study in the Process of Individuation', picture 8), or of waves surrounding a centre (picture 3).

28 *Theatr. chem.*, IV, p. 575.

29 'Darkness there was: at first concealed in darkness this All was undiscriminated

chaos' (*Rig-veda*, X, 129, 2 (*Hymns of the Rig-veda*, trans. Griffith, II, p. 575)).
30 'Vilitas' was also something Christ was reproached with. Cf. John 1: 46: 'Can there any good thing come out of Nazareth?'
31 Cf. *Psychology and Alchemy*, para. 421.
32 Or as Morienus (*Art. aurif.*, II, p. 32) so graphically says: 'Until it begins to shine like fishes' eyes.'
33 Caussin, *Polyhistor symbolicus* (1618), p. 3.
34 'Its power is complete when it is turned towards the earth', *Tabula smaragdina* (*De alchemia* (1541), cap. 6).
35 As, for example, Asklepios and his cabir, Telesphoros. Cf. Kerényi, *Asklepios*, pp. 58, 88, and C.A. Meier, *Antike Inkubation und moderne Psychotherapie*, pp. 47f.
36 *Shepherd of Hermas*, IV, 3, 6 (Lake, p. 67).
37 Cf. Emblema L in Maier's *Scrutinum chymicum*, p. 148. Cf. also *Turba*, Sermo LIX.
38 *Scrut. chymicum*, p. 46, and *Mus. herm.*, pp. 351, 357 (Waite, I, pp. 285, 291).
39 'Merlini allegoria', *Art. aurif.*, I, p. 393.
40 Early references are given in *Psychology and Alchemy*, paras 453f.
41 'It is impossible for a man of evil life to possess the treasure that is concealed from the sons of wisdom, and he is unfit to acquire it or to search it out, much less to find it' ('Phil. medit.', p. 457).
42 'I have thought it right to admonish the disciples to implore the divine aid, and [to remind them] of the need for the most careful diligence in preparing themselves for the reception of this grace' (ibid.).
43 *Lumen apothecariorum* (Huser, VII, pp. 222ff.).
44 The essence.
45 Cf. 'The Spirit of Mercurius', para. 276.
46 'Harmonia chemica', *Theatr. chem.*, IV, p. 820.
47 'The Spirit Mercurius', para. 278.
48 Cf. *Psychology and Alchemy*, para. 265; also *Aion*, para. 206.
49 So, too, in Paracelsus, where the soul, Melusine, lives in the blood. Cf. 'Paracelsus as a Spiritual Phenomenon', para. 180.
50 Cf. the passage from the Fihrist-et U'lum of Muhammad ibn Ishak al-Nadim in Chwolsohn, *Die Ssabier und der Ssabismus*, II, pp. 19f., describing the maceration of a man's body in oil and borax. The head of the corpse was then used as an oracle. See also the report by Laurens van der Post in 'Transformation Symbolism in the Mass', para. 370.
51 Cf. the description of the *caput mortuum* in Christianos: 'black and soulless and dead, and so to speak unbreathing' (Berthelot, *Alch. grecs*, VI, xii, 1). Phlegm has also a moral connotation: 'Sow likewise thy wisdom in our hearts, expel from them the phlegm, the corrupt choler and boiling blood, and lead us in the ways of the blessed' ('Allegoriae sap.', *Theatr. chem.*, V, p. 66). The residue, the 'black earth', is the ash of which the 'Tractatus Micreris' says: 'Despise not the ashes . . . for in them is the diadem, the ash of the things that endure' (*Theatr. chem.*, V, p. 104).
52 There is in man a 'marmoreus tartarus', a 'very hard stone' (Ruland, p. 220). Bowls of marble or serpentine are said to give protection against poison (Hellwig, *Lexikon Medico-Chymicum*, p. 162). 'Know also that the spirit is enclosed in a house of marble; open therefore the passages that the dead spirit may come forth' ('Alleg. sap.', p. 66).
53 Dorn, 'Phil. medit.', pp. 457f. Obviously, therefore, the immortal part of man.
54 'Therefore, for the preparation of a good disposition of the body, we make use of the spagyric medicine' (ibid., p. 457).

5   Alchemy and religion

From: 'Epilogue' to *Mysterium coniunctionis* (1955–6) (*CW* 14)

790   Alchemy, with its wealth of symbols, gives us an insight into an endeavour of the human mind which could be compared with a religious rite, an *opus divinum*. The diffcrence between them is that the alchemical *opus* was not a collective activity rigorously defined as to its form and content, but rather, despite the similarity of their fundamental principles, an individual undertaking on which the adept staked his whole soul for the transcendental purpose of producing a *unity*. It was a work of reconciliation between apparently incompatible opposites, which, characteristically, were understood not merely as the natural hostility of the physical elements but at the same time as a moral conflict. Since the object of this endeavour was seen outside as well as inside, as both physical and psychic, the work extended as it were through the whole of nature, and its goal consisted in a symbol which had an empirical and at the same time a transcendental aspect.

From: 'Transformation Symbolism in the Mass' (1942/54) (*CW* 11)

448   The numinous experience of the individuation process is, on the archaic level, the prerogative of shamans and medicine-men; later, of the physician, prophet and priest; and finally, at the civilized stage, of philosophy and religion. The shaman's experience of sickness, torture, death and regeneration implies, at a higher level, the idea of being made whole through sacrifice, of being changed by transubstantiation and exalted to the pneumatic man – in a word, of apotheosis. The Mass is the summation and quintessence of a development which began many thousands of years ago and, with the progressive broadening and deepening of consciousness, gradually made the isolated experience of specifically gifted individuals the common property of a larger group. The underlying psychic process remained, of course, hidden from view and was dramatized in the form of suitable 'mysteries' and 'sacraments', these being reinforced by religious teachings, exercises, meditations and acts of sacrifice which plunge the

celebrant so deeply into the sphere of the mystery that he is able to become conscious of his intimate connection with the mythic happenings. Thus, in ancient Egypt, we see how the experience of 'Osirification',[1] originally the prerogative of the Pharaohs, gradually passed to the aristocracy and finally, towards the end of the Old Kingdom, to the single individual as well. Similarly, the mystery religions of the Greeks, originally esoteric and not talked about, broadened out into collective experience, and at the time of the Caesars it was considered a regular sport for Roman tourists to get themselves initiated into foreign mysteries. Christianity, after some hesitation, went a step further and made celebration of the mysteries a public institution, for, as we know, it was especially concerned to introduce as many people as possible to the experience of the mystery. So, sooner or later, the individual could not fail to become conscious of his own transformation and of the necessary psychological conditions for this, such as confession and repentance of sin. The ground was prepared for the realization that, in the mystery of transubstantiation, it was not so much a question of magical influence as of psychological processes – a realization for which the alchemists had already paved the way by putting their *opus operatum* at least on a level with the ecclesiastical mystery, and even attributing to it a cosmic significance since, by its means, the divine world-soul could be liberated from imprisonment in matter. As I think I have shown, the 'philosophical' side of alchemy is nothing less than a symbolic anticipation of certain psychological insights, and these – to judge by the example of Gerhard Dorn – were pretty far advanced by the end of the sixteenth century.[2] Only our intellectualized age could have been so deluded as to see in alchemy nothing but an abortive attempt at chemistry, and in the interpretative methods of modern psychology a mere 'psychologizing', i.e. annihilation, of the mystery. Just as the alchemists knew that the production of their stone was a miracle that could only happen *Deo concedente*, so the modern psychologist is aware that he can produce no more than a description, couched in scientific symbols, of a psychic process whose real nature transcends consciousness just as much as does the mystery of life or of matter. At no point has he explained the mystery itself, thereby causing it to fade. He has merely, in accordance with the spirit of Christian tradition, brought it a little nearer to individual consciousness, using the empirical material to set forth the individuation process and show it as an actual and experienceable fact. To treat a metaphysical statement as a psychic process is not to say that it is 'merely psychic', as my critics assert – in the fond belief that the word 'psychic' postulates something known. It does not seem to have occurred to people that when we say 'psyche' we are alluding to the densest darkness it is possible to imagine. The ethics of the researcher require him to admit where his knowledge comes to an end. This end is the beginning of true wisdom.

From: 'Introduction to the Religious and Psychological
Problems of Alchemy' (1944) (*CW* 12)

11   An exclusively religious projection may rob the soul of its values so that
through sheer inanition it becomes incapable of further development and
gets stuck in an unconscious state. At the same time it falls victim to the
delusion that the cause of all misfortune lies outside, and people no longer
stop to ask themselves how far it is their own doing. So insignificant does
the soul seem that it is regarded as hardly capable of evil, much less of
good. But if the soul no longer has any part to play, religious life congeals
into externals and formalities. However we may picture the relationship
between God and soul, one thing is certain: that the soul cannot be 'nothing
but'.[3] On the contrary it has the dignity of an entity endowed with
consciousness of a relationship to deity. Even if it were only the relationship of a drop of water to the sea, that sea would not exist but for the
multitude of drops. The immortality of the soul insisted upon by dogma
exalts it above the transitoriness of mortal man and causes it to partake of
some supernatural quality. It thus infinitely surpasses the perishable,
conscious individual in significance, so that logically the Christian is
forbidden to regard the soul as a 'nothing but'.[4] As the eye to the sun, so
the soul corresponds to God. Since our conscious mind does not comprehend the soul it is ridiculous to speak of the things of the soul in a
patronizing or depreciatory manner. Even the believing Christian does not
know God's hidden ways and must leave him to decide whether he will
work on man from outside or from within, through the soul. So the believer
should not boggle at the fact that there are *somnia a Deo missa* (dreams
sent by God) and illuminations of the soul which cannot be traced back to
any external causes. It would be blasphemy to assert that God can manifest
himself everywhere save only in the human soul. Indeed the very intimacy
of the relationship between God and the soul precludes from the start any
devaluation of the latter.[5] It would be going perhaps too far to speak of an
affinity; but at all events the soul must contain in itself the faculty of
relationship to God, i.e. a correspondence, otherwise a connection could
never come about.[6] *This correspondence is, in psychological terms, the
archetype of the God-image.*

12   Every archetype is capable of endless development and differentiation.
It is therefore possible for it to be more developed or less. In an outward
form of religion where all the emphasis is on the outward figure (hence
where we are dealing with a more or less complete projection), the
archetype is identical with externalized ideas but remains unconscious as
a psychic factor. When an unconscious content is replaced by a projected
image to that extent, it is cut off from all participation in and influence
on the conscious mind. Hence it largely forfeits its own life, because
prevented from exerting the formative influence on consciousness natural

to it; what is more, it remains in its original form – unchanged, for nothing changes in the unconscious. At a certain point it even develops a tendency to regress to lower and more archaic levels. It may easily happen, therefore, that a Christian who believes in all the sacred figures is still undeveloped and unchanged in his inmost soul because he has 'all God outside' and does not experience him in the soul. His deciding motives, his ruling interests and impulses, do not spring from the sphere of Christianity but from the unconscious and undeveloped psyche, which is as pagan and archaic as ever. Not the individual alone but the sum total of individual lives in a nation proves the truth of this contention. The great events of our world as planned and executed by man do not breathe the spirit of Christianity but rather of unadorned paganism. These things originate in a psychic condition that has remained archaic and has not been even remotely touched by Christianity. The Church assumes, not altogether without reason, that the fact of *semel credidisse* (having once believed) leaves certain traces behind it; but of these traces nothing is to be seen in the broad march of events. Christian civilization has proved hollow to a terrifying degree: it is all veneer, but the inner man has remained untouched and therefore unchanged. His soul is out of key with his external beliefs; in his soul the Christian has not kept pace with external developments. Yes, everything is to be found outside – in image and in word, in Church and Bible – but never inside. Inside reign the archaic gods, supreme as of old; that is to say the inner correspondence with the outer God-image is undeveloped for lack of psychological culture and has therefore got stuck in heathenism. Christian education has done all that is humanly possible, but it has not been enough. Too few people have experienced the divine image as the innermost possession of their own souls. Christ only meets them from without, never from within the soul; that is why dark paganism still reigns there, a paganism which, now in a form so blatant that it can no longer be denied and now in all too threadbare disguise, is swamping the world of so-called Christian civilization.

13   With the methods employed hitherto we have not succeeded in Christianizing the soul to the point where even the most elementary demands of Christian ethics can exert any decisive influence on the main concerns of the Christian European. The Christian missionary may preach the gospel to the poor naked heathen, but the spiritual heathen who populate Europe have as yet heard nothing of Christianity. Christianity must indeed begin again from the very beginning if it is to meet its high educative task. So long as religion is only faith and outward form, and the religious function is not experienced in our own souls, nothing of any importance has happened. It has yet to be understood that the *mysterium magnum* is not only an actuality but is first and foremost rooted in the human psyche. The man who does not know this from his own experience may be a most learned theologian, but he has no idea of religion and still less of education.

14   Yet when I point out that the soul possesses by nature a religious

function,[7] and when I stipulate that it is the prime task of all education (of adults) to convey the archetype of the God-image, or its emanations and effects, to the conscious mind, then it is precisely the theologian who seizes me by the arm and accuses me of 'psychologism'. But were it not a fact of experience that supreme values reside in the soul (quite apart from the ἀντίμιμον πνεῦμα [imitative soul] who is also there), psychology would not interest me in the least, for the soul would then be nothing but a miserable vapour. I know, however, from hundredfold experience that it is nothing of the sort, but on the contrary contains the equivalents of everything that has been formulated in dogma and a good deal more, which is just what enables it to be an eye destined to behold the light. This requires limitless range and unfathomable depth of vision. I have been accused of 'deifying the soul'. Not I but God himself has deified it! *I* did not attribute a religious function to the soul. I merely produced the facts which prove that the soul is *naturaliter religiosa*, i.e. possesses a religious function. I did not invent or insinuate this function, it produces itself of its own accord without being prompted thereto by any opinions or suggestions of mine. With a truly tragic delusion these theologians fail to see that it is not a matter of proving the existence of the light, but of blind people who do not know that their eyes could see. It is high time we realized that it is pointless to praise the light and preach it if nobody can see it. It is much more needful to teach people the art of seeing. For it is obvious that far too many people are incapable of establishing a connection between the sacred figures and their own psyche: they cannot see to what extent the equivalent images are lying dormant in their own unconscious. In order to facilitate this inner vision we must first clear the way for the faculty of seeing. How this is to be done without psychology, that is, without making contact with the psyche, is frankly beyond my comprehension.[8]

15   Another equally serious misunderstanding lies in imputing to psychology the wish to be a new and possibly heretical doctrine. If a blind man can gradually be helped to see, it is not to be expected that he will at once discern new truths with an eagle eye. One must be glad if he sees anything at all, and if he begins to understand what he sees. Psychology is concerned with the act of seeing and not with the construction of new religious truths, when even the existing teachings have not yet been perceived and understood. In religious matters it is a well-known fact that we cannot understand a thing until we have experienced it inwardly, for it is in the inward experience that the connection between the psyche and the outward image or creed is first revealed as a relationship or correspondence like that of *sponsus* and *sponsa*. Accordingly when I say as a psychologist that God is an archetype, I mean by that the 'type' in the psyche. The word 'type' is, as we know, derived from τύπος (blow or imprint); thus an archetype presupposes an imprinter. Psychology as the science of the soul has to confine itself to its subject and guard against overstepping its proper

boundaries by metaphysical assertions or other professions of faith. Should it set up a God, even as a hypothetical cause, it would have implicitly claimed the possibility of proving God, thus exceeding its competence in an absolutely illegitimate way. Science can only be science; there are no 'scientific' professions of faith and similar *contradictiones in adiecto* [additional contradictions]. We simply do not know the ultimate derivation of the archetype any more than we know the origin of the psyche. The competence of psychology as an empirical science only goes so far as to establish, on the basis of comparative research, whether for instance the imprint found in the psyche can or cannot reasonably be termed a 'God-image'. Nothing positive or negative has thereby been asserted about the possible existence of God, any more than the archetype of the 'hero' posits the actual existence of a hero.

16   Now if my psychological researches have demonstrated the existence of certain psychic types and their correspondence with well-known religious ideas, then we have opened up a possible approach to those experienceable contents which manifestly and undeniably form the empirical foundations of all religious experience. The religious-minded man is free to accept whatever metaphysical explanations he pleases about the origin of these images; not so the intellect, which must keep strictly to the principles of scientific interpretation and avoid trespassing beyond the bounds of what can be known. Nobody can prevent the believer from accepting God, *Purusha*, the *atman* or Tao as the Prime Cause and thus putting an end to the fundamental disquiet of man. The scientist is a scrupulous worker; he cannot take heaven by storm. Should he allow himself to be seduced into such an extravagance he would be sawing off the branch on which he sits.

17   The fact is that with the knowledge and actual experience of these inner images a way is opened for reason and feeling to gain access to those other images which the teachings of religion offer to mankind. Psychology thus does just the opposite of what it is accused of: it provides possible approaches to a better understanding of these things, it opens people's eyes to the real meaning of dogmas, and, far from destroying, it throws open an empty house to new inhabitants. I can corroborate this from countless experiences: people belonging to creeds of all imaginable kinds, who had played the apostate or cooled off in their faith, have found a new approach to their old truths, not a few Catholics among them. Even a Parsee found the way back to the Zoroastrian fire-temple, which should bear witness to the objectivity of my point of view.

22   The Christ-symbol is of the greatest importance for psychology in so far as it is perhaps the most highly developed and differentiated symbol of the self, apart from the figure of the Buddha. We can see this from the scope and substance of all the pronouncements that have been made about Christ: they agree with the psychological phenomenology of the self in unusually high degree, although they do not include all aspects of this

archetype. The almost limitless range of the self might be deemed a disadvantage as compared with the definiteness of a religious figure, but it is by no means the task of science to pass value judgements. Not only is the self indefinite but – paradoxically enough – it also includes the quality of definiteness and even of uniqueness. This is probably one of the reasons why precisely those religions founded by historical personages have become world religions, such as Christianity, Buddhism and Islam. The inclusion in a religion of a unique human personality– especially when conjoined to an indeterminable divine nature – is consistent with the absolute individuality of the self, which combines uniqueness with eternity and the individual with the universal. The self is a union of opposites *par excellence*, and this is where it differs essentially from the Christ-symbol. The androgyny of Christ is the utmost concession the Church has made to the problem of opposites. The opposition between light and good on the one hand and darkness and evil on the other is left in a state of open conflict, since Christ simply represents good, and his counterpart, the devil, evil. This opposition is the real world problem, which at present is still unsolved. The self, however, is absolutely paradoxical in that it represents in every respect thesis and antithesis, and at the same time synthesis. (Psychological proofs of this assertion abound, though it is impossible for me to quote them here *in extenso*. I would refer the knowledgeable reader to the symbolism of the mandala.)[9]

23   Once the exploration of the unconscious has led the conscious mind to an experience of the archetype, the individual is confronted with the abysmal contradictions of human nature, and this confrontation in turn leads to the possibility of a direct experience of light and darkness, of Christ and the devil. For better or worse there is only a bare possibility of this, and not a guarantee; for experiences of this kind cannot of necessity be induced by any human means. There are factors to be considered which are not under our control. Experience of the opposites has nothing whatever to do with intellectual insight or with empathy. It is more what we would call fate. Such an experience can convince one person of the truth of Christ, another of the truth of the Buddha, to the exclusion of all other evidence.

24   Without the experience of the opposites there is no experience of wholeness and hence no inner approach to the sacred figures. For this reason Christianity rightly insists on sinfulness and Original Sin, with the obvious intent of opening up the abyss of universal opposition in every individual – at least from the outside. But this method is bound to break down in the case of a moderately alert intellect: dogma is then simply no longer believed and on top of that is thought absurd. Such an intellect is merely one-sided and sticks at the *ineptia mysterii*. It is miles from Tertullian's antinomies; in fact, it is quite incapable of enduring the suffering such a tension involves. Cases are not unknown where the rigorous exercises and proselytizings of the Catholics, and a certain type of Protestant education that is

always sniffing out sin, have brought about psychic damage that leads not to the Kingdom of Heaven but to the consulting room of the doctor. Although insight into the problem of opposites is absolutely imperative, there are very few people who can stand it in practice – a fact which has not escaped the notice of the confessional. By way of a reaction to this we have the palliative of 'moral probabilism', a doctrine that has suffered frequent attack from all quarters because it tries to mitigate the crushing effect of sin.[10] Whatever one may think of this phenomenon one thing is certain: that apart from anything else it holds within it a large humanity and an understanding of human weakness which compensates for the world's unbearable antinomies. The tremendous paradox implicit in the insistence on Original Sin on the one hand and the concession made by probabilism on the other is, for the psychologist, a necessary consequence of the Christian problem of opposites outlined above – for in the self good and evil are indeed closer than identical twins! The reality of evil and its incompatibility with good cleave the opposites asunder and lead inexorably to the crucifixion and suspension of everything that lives. Since 'the soul is by nature Christian' this result is bound to come as infallibly as it did in the life of Jesus: we all have to be 'crucified with Christ', i.e. suspended in a moral suffering equivalent to veritable crucifixion. In practice this is only possible up to a point, and apart from that is so unbearable and inimical to life that the ordinary human being can afford to get into such a state only occasionally, in fact as seldom as possible. For how could he remain ordinary in face of such suffering! A more or less probabilistic attitude to the problem of evil is therefore unavoidable. Hence the truth about the self – the unfathomable union of good and evil – comes out concretely in the paradox that although sin is the gravest and most pernicious thing there is, it is still not so serious that it cannot be disposed of with 'probabilist' arguments. Nor is this necessarily a lax or frivolous proceeding, but simply a practical necessity of life. The confessional proceeds like life itself, which successfully struggles against being engulfed in an irreconcilable contradiction. Note that at the same time the conflict remains in full force, as is once more consistent with the antinomial character of the self, which is itself both conflict and unity.

25   Christianity has made the antinomy of good and evil into a world problem and, by formulating the conflict dogmatically, raised it to an absolute principle. Into this as yet unresolved conflict the Christian is cast as a protagonist of good, a fellow-player in the world drama. Understood in its deepest sense, being Christ's follower involves a suffering that is unendurable to the great majority of mankind. Consequently the example of Christ is in reality followed either with reservation or not at all, and the pastoral practice of the Church even finds itself obliged to 'lighten the yoke of Christ'. This means a pretty considerable reduction in the severity and harshness of the conflict and hence, in practice, a relativism of good

and evil. Good is equivalent to the unconditional imitation of Christ, and evil is its hindrance. Man's moral weakness and sloth are what chiefly hinder the imitation, and it is to these that probabilism extends a practical understanding which may sometimes, perhaps, come nearer to Christian tolerance, mildness and love of one's neighbour than the attitude of those who see in probabilism a mere laxity. Although one must concede a number of cardinal Christian virtues to the probabilist endeavour, one must still not overlook the fact that it obviates much of the suffering involved in the imitation of Christ and that the conflict of good and evil is thus robbed of its harshness and toned down to tolerable proportions. This brings about an approach to the psychic archetype of the self, where even these opposites seem to be united – though, as I say, it differs from the Christian symbolism, which leaves the conflict open. For the latter there is a rift running through the world: light wars against night, and the upper against the lower. The two are not one, as they are in the psychic archetype. But, even though religious dogma may condemn the idea of two being one, religious practice does, as we have seen, allow the natural psychological symbol of the self at one with itself an approximate means of expression. On the other hand, dogma insists that three are one, while denying that four are one. Since olden times, not only in the West but also in China, uneven numbers have been regarded as masculine and even numbers as feminine. The Trinity is therefore a decidedly masculine deity, of which the androgyny of Christ and the special position and veneration accorded to the Mother of God are not the real equivalent.

26   With this statement, which may strike the reader as peculiar, we come to one of the central axioms of alchemy, namely the saying of Maria Prophetissa: 'One becomes two, two becomes three, and out of the third comes the one as the fourth.' This book is concerned with the psychological significance of alchemy and thus with a problem which, with very few exceptions, has so far eluded scientific research. Until quite recently science was interested only in the part that alchemy played in the history of chemistry, concerning itself very little with the part it played in the history of philosophy and religion. The importance of alchemy for the historical development of chemistry is obvious, but its cultural importance is still so little known that it seems almost impossible to say in a few words wherein that consisted . . . therefore, I have attempted to outline the religious and psychological problems which are germane to the theme of alchemy. The point is that alchemy is rather like an undercurrent to the Christianity that ruled on the surface. It is to this surface as the dream is to consciousness, and just as the dream compensates the conflicts of the conscious mind, so alchemy endeavours to fill the gaps left open by the Christian tension of opposites. Perhaps the most pregnant expression of this is the axiom of Maria Prophetissa quoted above, which runs like a *leitmotiv* throughout almost the whole of the lifetime of alchemy, extending over more than seventeen centuries. In this aphorism the even numbers

which signify the feminine principle, earth, the regions under the earth, and evil itself are interpolated between the uneven numbers of the Christian dogma. They are personified by the *serpens mercurii*, the dragon that creates and destroys itself and represents the *prima materia*. This fundamental idea of alchemy points back to the תהום (Tehom),[11] to Tiamat with her dragon attribute, and thus to the primordial matriarchal world which, in the theomachy of the Marduk myth,[12] was overthrown by the masculine world of the father. The historical shift in the world's consciousness towards the masculine is compensated at first by the chthonic femininity of the unconscious. In certain pre-Christian religions the differentiation of the masculine principle had taken the form of the father–son specification, a change which was to be of the utmost importance for Christianity. Were the unconscious merely complementary, this shift of consciousness would have been accompanied by the production of a mother and daughter, for which the necessary material lay ready to hand in the myth of Demeter and Persephone. But, as alchemy shows, the unconscious chose rather the Cybelle–Attis type in the form of the *prima materia* and the *filius macrocosmi*, thus proving that it is not complementary but compensatory. This goes to show that the unconscious does not simply act *contrary* to the conscious mind but *modifies* it more in the manner of an opponent or partner. The son-type does not call up a daughter as a complementary image from the depths of the 'chthonic' unconscious – it calls up another son. This remarkable fact would seem to be connected with the incarnation in our earthly human nature of a purely spiritual God, brought about by the Holy Ghost impregnating the womb of the Blessed Virgin. Thus the higher, the spiritual, the masculine inclines to the lower, the earthly, the feminine: and accordingly the mother, who was anterior to the world of the father, accommodates herself to the masculine principle and, with the aid of the human spirit (alchemy or 'the philosophy'), produces a son – not the antithesis of Christ but rather his chthonic counterpart, not a divine man but a fabulous being conforming to the nature of the primordial mother. And just as the redemption of man the microcosm is the task of the 'upper' son, so the 'lower' son has the function of a *salvator macrocosmi*.

27   This, in brief, is the drama that was played out in the obscurities of alchemy. It is superfluous to remark that these two sons were never united, except perhaps in the mind and innermost experience of a few particularly gifted alchemists. But it is not very difficult to see the 'purpose' of this drama: in the Incarnation it looked as though the masculine principle of the father-world were approximating to the feminine principle of the mother-world, with the result that the latter felt impelled to approximate in turn to the father-world. What it evidently amounted to was an attempt to bridge the gulf separating the two worlds as compensation for the open conflict between them.

28   I hope the reader will not be offended if my exposition sounds like a

Gnostic myth. We are moving in those psychological regions where, as a matter of fact, Gnosis is rooted. The message of the Christian symbol is Gnosis, and the compensation effected by the unconscious is Gnosis in even higher degree. Myth is the primordial language natural to these psychic processes, and no intellectual formulation comes anywhere near the richness and expressiveness of mythical imagery. Such processes are concerned with the primordial images, and these are best and most succinctly reproduced by figurative language.

29   The process described above displays all the characteristic features of psychological compensation. We know that the mask of the unconscious is not rigid – it reflects the face we turn towards it. Hostility lends it a threatening aspect, friendliness softens its features. It is not a question of mere optical reflection but of an autonomous answer which reveals the self-sufficing nature of that which answers. Thus the *filius philosophorum* is not just the reflected image, in unsuitable material, of the son of God; on the contrary, this son of Tiamat reflects the features of the primordial maternal figure. Although he is decidedly hermaphroditic he has a masculine name – a sign that the chthonic underworld, having been rejected by the spirit and identified with evil, has a tendency to compromise. There is no mistaking the fact that he is a concession to the spiritual and masculine principle, even though he carries in himself the weight of the earth and the whole fabulous nature of primordial animality.

30   This answer of the mother-world shows that the gulf between it and the father-world is not unbridgeable, seeing that the unconscious holds the seed of the unity of both. The essence of the conscious mind is discrimination; it must, if it is to be aware of things, separate the opposites, and it does this *contra naturam*. In nature the opposites seek one another – *les extrêmes se touchent* – and so it is in the unconscious, and particularly in the archetype of unity, the self. Here, as in the deity, the opposites cancel out. But as soon as the unconscious begins to manifest itself they split asunder, as at the Creation; for every act of dawning consciousness is a creative act, and it is from this psychological experience that all our cosmogonic symbols are derived.

31   Alchemy is pre-eminently concerned with the seed of unity which lies hidden in the chaos of Tiamat and forms the counterpart to the divine unity. Like this, the seed of unity has a trinitarian character in Christian alchemy and a triadic character in pagan alchemy. According to other authorities it corresponds to the unity of the four elements and is therefore a quaternity. The overwhelming majority of modern psychological findings speaks in favour of the latter view. The few cases I have observed which produced the number three were marked by a systematic deficiency in consciousness, that is to say, by an unconsciousness of the 'inferior function'. The number three is not a natural expression of wholeness, since four represents the minimum number of determinants in a whole judgement. It must nevertheless be stressed that side by side with the distinct leanings of alchemy

(and of the unconscious) towards quaternity there is always a vacillation between three and four which comes out over and over again. Even in the axiom of Maria Prophetissa the quaternity is muffled and alembicated. In alchemy there are three as well as four *regimina* or procedures, three as well as four colours. There are always four elements, but often three of them are grouped together, with the fourth in a special position – sometimes earth, sometimes fire. Mercurius[13] is of course *quadratus*, but he is also a three-headed snake or simply a triunity. This uncertainty has a duplex character – in other words, the central ideas are ternary as well as quaternary. The psychologist cannot but mention the fact that a similar puzzle exists in the psychology of the unconscious: the least differentiated or 'inferior' function is so much contaminated with the collective unconscious that, on becoming conscious, it brings up among others the archetype of the self as well – τὸ ἕν τέταρτον, as Maria Prophetissa says. Four signifies the feminine, motherly, physical: three the masculine, fatherly, spiritual. Thus the uncertainty as to three or four amounts to a wavering between the spiritual and the physical – a striking example of how every human truth is a last truth but one.

41   Whereas the Church's great buttress is the imitation of Christ, the alchemist, without realizing it and certainly without wanting it, easily fell victim, in the loneliness and obscure problems of his work, to the promptings and unconscious assumptions of his own mind, since, unlike the Christians, he had no clear and unmistakable models on which to rely. The authors he studied provided him with symbols whose meaning he thought he understood in his own way; but in reality they touched and stimulated his unconscious. Ironical towards themselves, the alchemists coined the phrase *obscurum per obscurius*. But with this method of explaining the obscure by the more obscure they only sank themselves deeper in the very process from which the Church was struggling to redeem them. While the dogmas of the Church offered analogies to the alchemical process, these analogies, in strict contrast to alchemy, had become detached from the world of nature through their connection with the historical figure of the Redeemer. The alchemical four in one, the philosophical gold, the *lapis angularis*, the *aqua divina*, became, in the Church, the four-armed cross on which the Only Begotten had sacrificed himself once in history and at the same time for all eternity. The alchemists ran counter to the Church in preferring to seek through knowledge rather than to find through faith, though as medieval people they never thought of themselves as anything but good Christians. Paracelsus is a classic example in this respect. But in reality they were in much the same position as modern man, who prefers immediate personal experience to belief in traditional ideas, or rather has it forced upon him. Dogma is not arbitrarily invented nor is it a unique miracle, although it is often described as miraculous with the obvious intent of lifting it out of its natural context. The central ideas of Christianity are rooted in Gnostic philosophy, which,

in accordance with psychological laws, simply *had* to grow up at a time when the classical religions had become obsolete. It was founded on the perception of symbols thrown up by the unconscious individuation process which always sets in when the collective dominants of human life fall into decay. At such a time there is bound to be a considerable number of individuals who are possessed by archetypes of a numinous nature that force their way to the surface in order to form new dominants. This state of possession shows itself almost without exception in the fact that the possessed identify themselves with the archetypal contents of their unconscious, and, because they do not realize that the role which is being thrust upon them is the effect of new contents still to be understood, they exemplify these concretely in their own lives, thus becoming prophets and reformers. In so far as the archetypal content of the Christian drama was able to give satisying expression to the uneasy and clamorous unconscious of the many, the *consensus omnium* raised this drama to a universally binding truth – not of course by an act of judgement, but by the irrational fact of possession, which is far more effective. Thus Jesus became the tutelary image or amulet against the archetypal powers that threatened to possess everyone. The glad tidings announced: 'It has happened, but it will not happen to you inasmuch as you believe in Jesus Christ, the Son of God!' Yet it could and it can and it will happen to everyone in whom the Christian dominant has decayed. For this reason there have always been people who, not satisfied with the dominants of conscious life, set forth – under cover and by devious paths, to their destruction or salvation – to seek direct experience of the eternal roots, and, following the lure of the restless unconscious psyche, find themselves in the wilderness where, like Jesus, they come up against the son of darkness, the ἀντίμιμον πνεῦμα [imitative soul]. Thus an old alchemist – and he a cleric!– prays: *Horridas nostrae mentis purga tenebras, accende lumen sensibus!* (Purge the horrible darknesses of our mind, light a light for our senses!) The author of this sentence must have been undergoing the experience of the *nigredo*, the first stage of the work, which was felt as 'melancholia' in alchemy and corresponds to the encounter with the shadow in psychology.

42   When, therefore, modern psychotherapy once more meets with the activated archetypes of the collective unconscious, it is merely the repetition of a phenomenon that has often been observed in moments of great religious crisis, although it can also occur in individuals for whom the ruling ideas have lost their meaning. An example of this is the *descensus ad inferos* depicted in *Faust*, which, consciously or unconsciously, is an *opus alchymicum*.

43   The problem of opposites called up by the shadow plays a great – indeed, the decisive – role in alchemy, since it leads in the ultimate phase of the work to the union of opposites in the archetypal form of the *hieros gamos* or 'chymical wedding'. Here the supreme opposites, male and female (as in the Chinese *yang* and *yin*), are melted into a unity purified of all

opposition and therefore incorruptible. The prerequisite for this, of course, is that the artifex should not identify himself with the figures in the work but should leave them in their objective, impersonal state. So long as the alchemist was working in his laboratory he was in a favourable position, psychologically speaking, for he had no opportunity to identify himself with the archetypes as they appeared, since they were all projected immediately into the chemical substances. The disadvantage of this situation was that the alchemist was forced to represent the incorruptible substance as a chemical product – an impossible undertaking which led to the downfall of alchemy, its place in the laboratory being taken by chemistry. But the psychic part of the work did not disappear. It captured new interpreters, as we can see from the example of *Faust*, and also from the signal connection between our modern psychology of the unconscious and alchemical symbolism.

From: 'Religious Ideas in Alchemy' (1937) (*CW* 12)

451　The Christian receives the fruits of the Mass for himself personally and for the circumstances of his own life in the widest sense. The alchemist, on the other hand, receives the *fructus arboris immortalis* [fruit of the immortal tree] not merely for himself but first and foremost for the King or the King's Son, for the perfecting of the coveted substance. He may play a part in the *perfectio*, which brings him health, riches, illumination, and salvation; but since he is the redeemer of God and not the one to be redeemed, he is more concerned to perfect the substance than himself. Moral qualities he takes for granted and considers them only in so far as they help or hinder the *opus*. We could say that he lays the whole emphasis on the effect *ex opere operantis* (of the work of the operator), naturally to a much higher degree than the Church, since he takes the place of the Christ who sacrifices himself in the Mass. One should not for a moment suppose that he presumes to the role of redeemer from religious megalomania. He does so even less than the officiating priest who figuratively sacrifices Christ. The alchemist always stresses his humility and begins his treatises with invocations to God. He does not dream of identifying himself with Christ; on the contrary, it is the coveted substance, the *lapis*, that he likens to Christ. It is not really a question of identification at all, but of the hermeneutic *sicut* – 'as' or 'like' – which characterizes the analogy. For medieval man, however, analogy was not so much a logical figure as a secret identity, a remnant of primitive thinking which is still very much alive. An instructive example of this is the rite of hallowing the fire on the Saturday before Easter.[14] The fire is 'like unto' Christ, an *imago Christi*. The stone from which the spark is struck is the 'cornerstone' – another *imago*; and the spark that leaps from the stone is yet again an *imago Christi*. The analogy with the extraction of the *pneuma* from the stone in the saying of Ostanes forces itself upon us. We are already familiar with the idea of *pneuma* as fire, and with Christ as fire, and fire as the earth's inner counter-element; but the 'firestone' from which the spark is struck is also analogous to the rocky sepulchre, or the stone before it. Here Christ lay as one asleep or in the fetters of death during the three days of his descent into hell, when he went down to the *ignis gehennalis*, from which he rises again as the New Fire.

452   Without knowing it, the alchemist carries the idea of the *imitatio* a stage further and reaches the conclusion we mentioned earlier, that complete assimilation to the Redeemer would enable him, the assimilated, to continue the work of redemption in the depths of his own psyche. This conclusion is unconscious, and consequently the alchemist never feels impelled to assume that Christ is doing the work in him. It is by virtue of the wisdom and art which he himself has acquired, or which God has bestowed upon him, that he can liberate the world-creating Nous or Logos, lost in the world's materiality, for the benefit of mankind. The artifex himself bears no correspondence to Christ; rather he sees this correspondence to the Redeemer in his wonderful stone. From this point of view, alchemy seems like a continuation of Christian mysticism carried on in the subterranean darkness of the unconscious – indeed some mystics pressed the materialization of the Christ figure even to the appearance of the stigmata. But this unconscious continuation never reached the surface, where the conscious mind could have dealt with it. All that appeared in consciousness were the symbolic symptoms of the unconscious process. Had the alchemist succeeded in forming any concrete idea of his unconscious contents, he would have been obliged to recognize that he had taken the place of Christ – or, to be more exact, that he, regarded not as ego but as self,[15] had taken over the work of redeeming not man but God. He would then have had to recognize not only himself as the equivalent of Christ, but Christ as a symbol of the self. This tremendous conclusion failed to dawn on the medieval mind. What seems like a monstrous presumption to the Christian European would have been self-evident to the spirit of the Upanishads. Modern man must therefore consider himself fortunate not to have come up against Eastern ideas until his own spiritual impoverishment was so far gone that he did not even notice what he was coming up against. He can now deal with the East on the quite inadequate and therefore innocuous level of the intellect, or else leave the whole matter to Sanskrit specialists.

417   In the figure of the divine hero, God himself wrestles with his own imperfect, suffering, living creation; he even takes its suffering condition upon himself and, by this sacrificial act, accomplishes the *opus magnum*, the ἄθλον [prize] of salvation and victory over death. As regards the actual performance of this entirely metaphysical work, man is powerless to do anything really decisive. He looks to his Redeemer, full of faith and confidence, and does what he can in the way of 'imitation'; but this never

reaches the point where man himself becomes the Redeemer – or at least his own redeemer. Yet a complete imitation and re-establishment of Christ in the believer would necessarily lead to such a conclusion. But this is out of the question. Were such an approximation to occur, then Christ would have re-established himself in the believer and replaced the latter's personality. We should have to be satisfied with this statement were it not for the existence of the Church. The institution of the Church means nothing less than the everlasting continuation of the life of Christ and its sacrificial function. In the *officium divinum* or, in Benedictine parlance, the *opus divinum*, Christ's sacrifice, the redeeming act, constantly repeats itself anew while still remaining the unique sacrifice that was accomplished, and is accomplished ever again, by Christ himself inside time and outside all time. This *opus supernaturale* is represented in the sacrifice of the Mass. In the ritual act the priest as it were shows forth the mystical event, but the real agent is Christ, who sacrifices himself everywhere always. Though his sacrificial death occurred in time it is an essentially timeless occurrence. In the Thomist view the Mass is not a real *immolatio* (sacrifice) of the body of Christ but a 're-presentation' of his sacrificial death.[16] Such an interpretation would be sufficient and consistent were it not for the transubstantiation of the offered substances, the bread and wine. This offering is meant as a *sacrificium*, literally a 'making sacred'. The etymology of the German word for sacrifice, *Opfer*, is obscure, it being a moot point whether it comes from *offerre* (to offer) or from *operari* (to effect, to be active). In its ancient usage *operari Deo* meant to serve the god or to sacrifice to him. But if the *Opfer* is an *opus*, then it is far more than an *oblatio*, the offering of such a modest gift as bread and wine. It must be an effectual act, giving the ritual words spoken by the priest a causal significance. The words of the consecration (*qui pridie quam pateretur* etc.) are therefore to be taken not merely as representative, but as the *causa efficiens* of the transubstantiation. That is why the Jesuit Lessius (d. 1623) called the words of the consecration the 'sword' with which the sacrificial lamb is slaughtered.[17] The so-called theory of mactation (slaughtering) occupies an important place in the literature of the Mass, though it has not been generally accepted in its more objectionable outgrowths. Perhaps the clearest of all is the Greek ritual as described by the Archbishop Nikolaus Kabasilas of Thessalonika (d. 1363).[18] In the first (preparatory) part of the Mass the bread and wine are placed not on the main altar but on the πρόθεσις, a sort of sideboard. There the priest cuts a piece off the loaf and repeats the text 'He is led as a lamb to the slaughter.' Then he lays it on the table and repeats, 'The lamb of God is sacrificed.' The sign of the cross is then imprinted on the bread and a small lance stabbed into its side, to the text 'But one of the soldiers with a spear pierced his side and forthwith came there out blood and water.' At these words water and wine are mixed in the chalice. Then comes the *oblatio* in solemn procession, with the priest carrying the offering. (Here the δ'ῶρον, the gift, represents the giver: Christ the sacrificiant is also the sacrificed.) Thus the priest re-enacts the traditional event, and in so far as Christ, in the sacramental state, possesses a *vita corporea actualis*[19] (an actual bodily life) one could say that a physical slaying[20] (*mortificatio*) of his body has taken place. This happens as a result of the consecrating words spoken by the priest, and the destruction of the offering, the *oblatio occisi ad cultum Dei* (the offering up of the slain to the service of God), brings about the transubstantiation. The latter is a transmutation of the elements, which pass from a natural, soiled, imperfect material state into a subtle body. The bread, which must be wheaten, signifies the body, and the wine, representing blood, the soul. After the transubstantiation a piece of the Host is mingled with the wine, thus producing the *coniunctio* of the soul with the body and establishing the living body of Christ, namely the unity of the Church.

From: 'The Personification of the Opposites', *Mysterium coniunctionis* (1955–6) (*CW* 14)

122

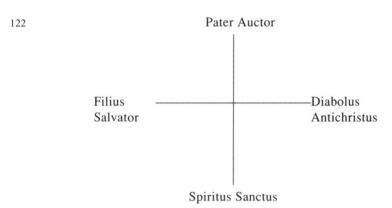

347   In spite of their undoubtedly 'heretical methods' the alchemists showed by their positive attitude to the Church that they were cleverer than certain apostles of enlightenment. Also – very much in contrast to the rationalistic tendencies of today – they displayed, despite its 'tortuousness', a remarkable understanding of the imagery upon which the Christian cosmos is built. This world of images, in its historical form, is irretrievably lost to modern man; its loss has spiritually impoverished the masses and compelled them to find pitiful substitutes, as poisonous as they are worthless. No one can be held responsible for this development. It is due rather to the restless tempo of spiritual growth and change, whose motive forces go far beyond the horizon of the individual. He can only hope to keep pace with it and try to understand it so far that he is not blindly swallowed up by it. For that is the alarming thing about mass movements, even if they

are good, that they demand and must demand blind faith. The Church can never explain the truth of her images because she acknowledges no point of view but her own. She moves solely within the framework of her images, and her arguments must always beg the question. The flock of harmless sheep was ever the symbolic prototype of the credulous crowd, though the Church is quick to recognize the wolves in sheep's clothing who lead the faith of the multitude astray in order to destroy them. The tragedy is that the blind trust which leads to perdition is practised just as much inside the Church and is praised as the highest virtue. Yet our Lord says: 'Be ye therefore wise as serpents',[21] and the Bible itself stresses the cleverness and cunning of the serpent. But where are these necessary if not altogether praiseworthy qualities developed and given their due? The serpent has become a byword for everything morally abhorrent, and yet anyone who is not as smart as a snake is liable to land himself in trouble through blind faith.

288   A feature worthy of special notice is that in the *opus* there is an ascent followed by a descent, whereas the probable Gnostic–Christian prototype depicts first the descent and then the ascent. There are numerous evidences of this in the literature and I do not need to cite them here. I will quote only the words of one of the great Greek Fathers, St Basil, who says in his explanation of Psalm 17:10[22] ('And he bowed the heavens and came down, and a black cloud was under his feet'): 'David says here: God came down from heaven to help me and to chastise his enemies. But he clearly prophesies the incarnation [ἐνανθρώπησις] of Christ when he says: He bowed the heavens and came down. For he did not break through the heavens and did not make the mystery manifest, but came down to earth secretly, like rain upon the fleece,[23] because the incarnation was secret and unknown, and his coming into the world-order [ἐν τῇ οἰκονομίᾳ] was hidden.'[24] Commenting on the next verse ('And he was borne upon the cherubim, and he flew'), Basil says: 'For in ascending he rose above the Cherubim, whom David named also the wings of the wind, on account of their winged and stormy nature. By the wings of the wind is also meant the cloud which took him up.'[25] Irenaeus sums up the mystery in the lapidary saying: 'For it is He who descended and ascended for the salvation of men.'[26]

289   In contrast to this, in alchemy the ascent comes first and then the descent. I would mention the ascent and descent of the soul in the *Rosarium* illustrations[27] and above all the exordium in the *Tabula smaragdina*, whose authority held sway throughout the Middle Ages:

IV.   Its father is the sun, its mother the moon; the wind hath carried it in his belly; its nurse is the earth.

VI.   Its power is complete when it is turned towards the earth.

VIII. It ascendeth from the earth to heaven, and descendeth again to the earth, and receiveth the power of the higher and lower things. So wilt thou have the glory of the whole world.[28]

290   These articles (whose subject is sometimes masculine and sometimes neuter) describe the 'sun–moon child' who is laid in the cradle of the four elements, attains full power through them and the earth, rises to heaven and receives the power of the upper world, and then returns to earth, accomplishing, it seems, a triumph of wholeness (*gloria totius mundi*). The words 'So wilt thou have' are evidently addressed to the Philosopher, for he is the artifex of the *filius philosophorum*. If he succeeds in transforming the arcane substance he will simultaneously accomplish his own wholeness, which will manifest itself as the glory of the whole world.

291   There can be no doubt that the arcane substance, whether in neuter or personified form, rises from the earth, unites the opposites, and then returns to earth, thereby achieving its own transformation into the elixir. 'He riseth up and goeth down in the tree of the sun', till he becomes the elixir, says the *Consilium coniugii*.[29] The text continues:

> Someone hath said,[30] And when I rise naked to heaven, then shall I come clothed upon the earth, and shall perfect all minerals.[31] And if we are baptized in the fountain of gold and silver, and the spirit of our body [i.e. the arcane substance] ascends into heaven with the father and the son, and descends again, then shall our souls revive, and my animal body will remain white, that is, [the body] of the moon.[32]

292   Here the union of opposites consists in an ascent to heaven and a descent to earth in the bath of the tincture. The earthly effect is first a perfection of minerals, then a resuscitation of souls and a transfiguration of the animal body, which before was dark. A parallel passage in the *Consilium* runs:

> His soul rises up from it[33] and is exalted to the heavens, that is, to the spirit, and becomes the rising sun (that is, red), in the waxing moon, and of solar nature.[34] And then the lantern with two lights,[35] which is the water of life, will return to its origin, that is, to earth. And it becomes of low estate, is humbled and decays, and is joined to its beloved,[36] the terrestrial sulphur.[37]

293   This text describes the ascent of the soul of the arcane substance, the incombustible sulphur. The soul as Luna attains its *plenilunium*, its sunlike brilliance, then wanes into the *novilunium* and sinks down into the embrace of the terrestrial sulphur, which here signifies death and corruption. We are reminded of the gruesome conjunction at the new moon in Maier's *Scrutinium chymicum*, where the woman and the dragon embrace in the grave.[38] The description Dorn gives in his *Physica Trismegisti* is also to the point: 'In the end it will come to pass that this earthly, spagyric birth clothes itself with heavenly nature by its ascent, and then by its descent visibly puts on the nature of the centre of the earth, but nonetheless the nature of the heavenly centre which it acquired by the ascent is secretly preserved.'[39] This 'birth' (*foetura*) conquers the 'subtile and spiritual sickness in the human mind and also all bodily defects, within as well as

without'. The medicament is produced 'in the same way as the world was created'. Elsewhere Dorn remarks that the *foetus spagyricus* is forced by the fire to rise up to heaven (*caelum*), by which he means from the bottom of the vessel to the top, and from there it descends again after attaining the necessary degree of ripeness, and returns to earth: 'This spirit becomes corporeal again, after having become spirit from a body.'[40]

From: 'The Paradoxa', *Mysterium coniunctionis* (1955–6) (*CW* 14)

86   Only with Christianity did the 'metaphysical' opposites begin to percolate into man's consciousness, and then in the form of an almost dualistic opposition that reached its zenith in Manichaeism. This heresy forced the Church to take an important step: the formulation of the doctrine of the *privatio boni*, by means of which she established the identity of 'good' and 'being'. Evil as a μὴ ὄν (something that does not exist) was laid at man's door – *omne bonum a Deo, omne malum ab homine* (God is the fount of all goodness, mankind is the root of all evil).[41] This idea, together with that of Original Sin, formed the foundation of a moral consciousness which was a novel development in human history: one half of the polarity, till then essentially metaphysical, was reduced to a psychic factor, which meant that the devil had lost the game if he could not pick on some moral weakness in man. Good, however, remained a metaphysical substance that originated with God and not with man. Original Sin had corrupted a creature originally good. As interpreted by dogma, therefore, good is still wholly projected but evil only partly so, since the passions of men are its main source. Alchemical speculation continued this process of integrating metaphysical projections in so far as it began to dawn on the adept that both opposites were of a psychic nature. They expressed themselves first of all in the duplicity of Mercurius, which, however, was cancelled out in the unity of the stone. The lapis was – *Deo concedente* – made by the adept and was recognized as an equivalent of *homo totus*. This development was extremely important, because it was an attempt to integrate opposites that were previously projected.

NOTES

1 Cf. Neumann, *The Origins and History of Consciousness*, pp. 220ff.
2 *Aion*, pp. 162ff.
3 [The term 'nothing but' (*nichts als*), which occurs frequently in Jung to denote the habit of explaining something unknown by reducing it to something apparently known and thereby devaluing it, is borrowed from William James, *Pragmatism*, p. 16: 'What is higher is explained by what is lower and treated for ever as a case of "nothing but" – nothing but something else of a quite inferior sort.']
4 The dogma that man is formed in the likeness of God weighs heavily in the scales in any assessment of man – not to mention the Incarnation.

5 The fact that the devil too can take possession of the soul does not diminish its significance in the least.

6 It is therefore psychologically quite unthinkable for God to be simply the 'wholly other', for a 'wholly other' could never be one of the soul's deepest and closest intimacies – which is precisely what God is. The only statements that have psychological validity concerning the God-image are either paradoxes or antinomies.

7 Tertullian, *Apologeticus*, xvii: 'Anima naturaliter christiana'.

8 Since it is a question here of human effort, I leave aside acts of grace which are beyond man's control.

9 [See *Jung on the East*, ed. J. J. Clarke (London: Routledge, 1994), pp. 192–3.]

10 Zöckler ('Probabilismus', p. 67) defines it as follows: 'Probabilism is the name generally given to that way of thinking which is content to answer scientific questions with a greater or lesser degree of probability. The moral probabilism with which alone we are concerned here consists in the principle that acts of ethical self-determination are to be guided not by conscience but according to what is probably right, i.e. according to whatever has been recommended by any representative or doctrinal authority.' The Jesuit probabilist Escobar (d. 1669) was, for instance, of the opinion that if the penitent should plead a probable opinion as the motive of his action, the father-confessor would be obliged to absolve him even if he were not of the same opinion. Escobar quotes a number of Jesuit authorities on the question of how often one is bound to love God in a lifetime. According to one opinion, loving God once shortly before death is sufficient: another says once a year or once every three or four years. He himself comes to the conclusion that it is sufficient to love God once at the first awakening of reason, then once every five years, and finally once in the hour of death. In his opinion the large number of different moral doctrines forms one of the main proofs of God's kindly providence, 'because they make the yoke of Christ so light' (Zöckler, p. 68). Cf. also Harnack, *History of Dogma*, VII, pp. 101ff.

11 Cf. Genesis 1: 2.

12 The reader will find a collection of these myth motifs in Lang, *Hat ein Gott die Welt erschaffen?* Unfortunately, philological criticism will have much to take exception to in this book, interesting though it is for its Gnostic trend.

13 In alchemical writings the word 'Mercurius' is used with a very wide range of meaning, to denote not only the chemical element mercury or quicksilver, Mercury (Hermes) the god, and Mercury the planet, but also – and primarily – the secret 'transforming substance' which is at the same time the 'spirit' in-dwelling in all living creatures . . . It would be misleading to use the English 'Mercury' and 'mercury', because there are innumerable passages where neither word does justice to the wealth of implications. It has therefore been decided to retain the Latin 'Mercurius' as in the German text, and to use the personal pronoun (since 'Mercurius' is personified), the word 'quicksilver' being employed only where the chemical element (Hg) is plainly meant. [*Author's note for the English edn.*]

14 The rite of blessing the New Fire seems to have originated in France: at any rate it was already known there in the eighth century, although it was not yet practised in Rome, as is proved by a letter from Pope Zacharias to St Boniface. It appears to have reached Rome only in the ninth century (see 'Feuerweihe', in Braun, *Liturgisches Handlexikon*).

15 Although I take every available opportunity to point out that the concept of the self, as I have defined it, is not identical with the conscious, empirical personality, I am always meeting with the misunderstanding which equates the self with the ego. Owing to the fundamentally indefinable nature of human personality, the self must remain a borderline concept, expressing a reality to which no limits can be set.

16 Hauck, *Realencyklopädie*, XII, p. 689, 35: 'Celebratio huius sacramenti est imago quaedam repraesentativa passionis Christi, quae est vera eius immolatio' ('The celebration of the sacrament is a kind of image that represents Christ's passion, which is his true immolation').

17 This point of view finds acceptance in the Beuron edition of the Missal (p. x).

18 Kramp, *Die Opferanschauungen der römischen Messliturgie*, p. 114.

19 *Vita corporea actualis sensitiva aut a sensibus pendens* (a real bodily life, apprehended by the senses or dependent on the senses) (Cardinal Álvarez Cienfuegos, S.J., d. 1739, in Hauck, *Realencyklopädie*, XII, p. 693, 59).

20 Cf. sacrifice of the lamb in the 'Vita S. Brendan', from *La légende latine de S. Brandaines* (based on 11th–13th cent. MSS), p. 12: 'Dixitque sanctus Brendanus fratribus: Faciamus hic *opus divinum*, et sacrificemus Deo agnum immaculatum, quia hodie cena Domini est. Et ibi manserunt usque in Sabbatum sanctum Pasche. Invenerunt eciam ibi multos greges ovium unius coloris, id est albi, ita ut non possent terram videre pre multitudine ovium. Convocatis autem fratribus, vir sanctus dixit eis: Accipite que sunt necessaria at diem festum de grege. Illi autem acceperunt unam ovem et cum illam ligassent per cornua, sequebatur quasi domestica, sequens illorum vestigia. At ille: Accepite, inquit, unum agnum immaculatum. Qui cum viri Dei mandata complessent, paraverunt omnia ad opus diei crastine' ('And St Brendan said to the brothers: 'Let us peform here the divine work and sacrifice to God an immaculate lamb, for today is the supper of the Lord.' And they remained there until Holy Saturday. They also found there many flocks of sheep of one colour, i.e. white, so that they could not see the ground because of the great number of sheep. The holy man called the brothers together and said to them: 'Take from the flock what you need for the feast day.' And they took one sheep, and when they had bound it by the horns, it followed as if it were a domestic animal, following in their footsteps. And he said: 'Take an immaculate lamb.' And when they had done the bidding of the man of God, they prepared everything for the work of the following day').

Ibid., p. 34: 'Confestim tunc cantaverunt tres psalmos: Miserere mei, Deus, et Domine refugium, et Deus, deus meus. Ad terciam vero alios tres: Omnes gentes. Deus in nomine. Dilexi quoniam, cum alleluya. Deinde immolaverunt agnum immaculatum, et omnes venerunt ad communionem dicentes: Hoc sacrum corpus Domini, et Salvatoris nostri, sanguinem sumite vobis in vitam aeternam' ('At once they sang three psalms: 'Have mercy on me, O God', and 'Lord, thous hast been our refuge', and 'O God, my God'; and at terce three others: 'O clap your hands, all ye nations', 'Save me, O God, by thy name', and 'I have loved, because', with alleluia. Then they sacrificed an immaculate lamb, and they all came to communion, saying: 'This is the sacred body of the Lord our Saviour, take the blood unto you for life eternal').

21 Matthew 10: 16.

22 DV; AV, 18: 9.

23 πόκος = 'wool, fleece' (L. *vellus*). The passage refers to Psalm 71: 6 (Vulgate): 'Descendet sicut pluvia in vellus' (DV: 'He shall come down like rains upon the fleece'), and Judges 6: 37: 'Ponam hoc vellus lanae in aera' (DV: 'I will put this fleece of wool on the floor').

24 Pitra, *Analecta sacra*, V, pp. 85f.

25 Refers to Acts 1: 9: 'and a cloud received him out of their sight'.

26 *Adv. haer.*, III, VI, 2 (*The Writings of Irenaeus*, I, p. 270).

27 Reproduced in my 'Psychology of the Transference', figs 7 and 9.

28 Cf. *Tabula smaragdina* (ed. Ruska), p. 2.

29 *Ars chemica*, p. 118.

30 This 'someone', as is clear from the later text (in *Bibliotheca chemica*), is the 'beloved' in the Song of Songs, i.e. Luna. She speaks here to Sol.

31 Possibly an allusion to the *Tabula smaragdina.*
32 'Consil. coniug.', p. 128; or remain 'in the golden tree', p. 211. There may be a reference here to John 3: 13: 'And no one has ascended into heaven except him who has descended from heaven' (DV).
33 I.e. from the *sulphur nostrum* previously referred to.
34 'In Luna crescente, in naturam solarem.' This could also be translated: 'waxing in Luna into the nature of the sun'.
35 The light of sun *and* moon.
36 The 1566 edn has 'figitur amanti eum'. I read 'eam'.
37 'Consil. coniug.', p. 165 (commentary in Senior, *De chemia*, p. 15). Cf. the 'transposition of the lights' in the Cabala.
38 Emblema L, p. 148: 'The dragon slays the woman and she him, and together they are bespattered with blood.'
39 *Theatr. chem.*, I, p. 409.
40 Ibid., p. 431. Dorn adds: 'It was hidden of old by the Philosophers in the riddle: Make the fixed, said they, volatile, and the volatile fixed, and you will have the whole magistery.'
41 Cf. *Aion*, paras 80ff.

6   The body and subtle body in alchemy

From: *Nietzsche's Zarathustra* (1988), 2: 967–8

The body is the original animal condition; we are all animals in the body, and so we should have animal psychology in order to be able to live in it. Yes, if we had no body then we could live with contracts and marvellous laws which everybody could observe and a marvellous morality which everybody could easily fulfil. But since we have a body it is indispensable that we exist also as an animal, and each time we invent a new increase of consciousness we have to put a new link in the chain that binds us to the animal, till finally it will become so long that complications will surely ensue. For when the chain between man and animal has grown so long that we lose sight of the animal, anything can happen in between, the chain will snarl up somewhere. That has happened already and therefore we doctors have to find in a conscious individual the place where the chain begins; we have to go back to find out where it has been caught or what has happened to the animal at the other end of the line. Then we have to shorten it perhaps, or disentangle it, in order to improve the relationship between the consciousness that went too far ahead and the animal left behind. This figure of the chain is not my own invention. I found it the other day in a book by an old alchemistic doctor, as the so-called symbol of Avicenna;[1] the alchemists were mostly doctors and they developed their peculiar kind of psychology by means of very apt symbols. This one consists of an eagle flying high in the air, and from his body falls a chain which is attached to a toad creeping along on the earth. The eagle of course represents the air, the spirit, and in alchemy it had a very particular meaning. The eagle would remind any alchemist of the phoenix, the self-renewing god, an Egyptian inheritance.

Now, what the living body represents is a great problem. Of course the historical symbolism, as far as we know it, refers to the animal. The life of the body is animal life. There is no difference in principle between the physiology of the monkey and our own physiology; we have the physiology of an animal with warm blood. Another analogy is with the plant and so with the tree. Therefore the cross of Christ is also called the tree; Christ was crucified upon the tree. And an old legend says that the wood for the cross was taken from the tree of paradise which was cut down and made into the two pillars, Aachim and Boas, in front of Solomon's temple. Then these were thrown away, and discovered again, and made into the cross. So Christ was sacrificed on the original Tree of Life, and in the *transitus* he carried it. The plant or the tree always refers to a non-animal growth or development and this would be spiritual development. The life of the body is animal life: it is instinctive, contains warm blood and is able to move about. Then within the body is spiritual or mental development, and that is always expressed as the growth of a flower or a miraculous plant or an extraordinary tree, like the tree that grows from above, the roots in heaven and the branches down towards the earth. That is Western as well as Eastern symbolism. The famous tree of yoga grows from above, and Ruysbroek, the Flemish mystic, uses the same symbol for the spiritual development within the Christian mysticism.[2] So in the one case the body or the corpse would mean the animal – we have to carry the sacrificed animal – and another aspect is that we have to carry our spiritual development which is also a part of nature, which has to do with nature just as much.

Then there is a further point to consider. Occasionally in my experience with patients it is less a matter of a corpse than of the dead thing generally, a sort of preoccupation with the dead. This hangs together with the fact that the body is a sort of conglomeration of ancestral units called Mendelian units. Your face, for instance, obviously consists of certain units inherited from your family; your nose comes from an ancestor in the eighteenth century, and your eyes are perhaps from a relative in the seventeenth century. The characteristic protruding lower lip of the Spanish Habsburgs dates from the time of Maximilian; that is a Mendelian unit which occasionally appears in a very pronounced way in certain individuals. There is also an insane streak in the Spanish Habsburgs, which appeared in the fifteenth century and then disappeared, and then, according to the Mendelian law, it appeared again after two hundred years. Then there is an English family named Whitelock, which is characterized by the fact that most of the members, particularly the male members, have a tuft of white hair in the centre of the skull; therefore they are called Whitelock. That is again a unit of a particular tenacity. So our whole body consists of inherited units from our father's or mother's side, from our particular clan or tribe for centuries past.

Now, each unit has also a psychical aspect, because the psyche represents the life or the living essence of the body. So the psyche of man contains all these units too in a way, a psychological representation; a certain trait of character is peculiar to the grandfather, another one to a great-great-grandfather, and so on. Just as much as the body derives from the ancestors, the psyche derives from them. It is like a sort of puzzle, somewhat disjointed, not properly welded together to begin with, and then the mental development of the character, the development of the personality, consists in putting the puzzle together. The puzzle is represented in dreams sometimes by the motif of a swarm of small particles, little animals or flies or small fishes or particles of minerals, and those disjointed and disparate elements have to be brought together again by means of a peculiar process. This is the main theme of alchemy. It begins with the idea of totality, which is depicted as a circle. This is called 'chaos', or the *massa confusa*, and it consists of all sorts of elements, a chaotic collection, but all in one mass. The task of the alchemist begins there. These particles are to be arranged by means of the squaring of the circle. The symbolic idea is to arrange the particles in a sort of crystal-like axis, which is called the quaternity, or the *quaternion*, or the *quadrangulum*, the four, and to each point a particular quality is given.

That is what we would call the differentiation of the psychological functions. You see, it is a fact that certain people start with an intuitive gift, for instance, which will become their main function, the function by means of which they adapt. A man who is born with a good brain will naturally use his intelligence to adapt; he will not use his feelings, which are not then developed. And a man who is very musical will surely use his musical gift in making his career and not his philosophical faculty, which is practically non-existent. So one will use his feeling, another one his sense of reality, and so on, and each time there will be a one-sided product. The study of these one-sided human products led me to the idea of the four functions, and nowadays we think that we should have not only one differentiated function but should take into consideration that there are others, and that a real adaptation to the world needs four functions – or at least more than one. And this is something like the ideas of those old alchemists who wanted to produce out of chaos a symmetrical arrangement of the quaternity. The four quarters of the circle indicate the fire, the air, the water and the earth regions, and when they are arranged they will make in the centre the *quinta essentia*, the fifth essence; the four essences are in the corners and in the centre is the fifth. That is the famous concept of the *quinta essentia*, a new unit which is also called the *rotundum*, the roundness, or the round complete thing. It is again that circle of the beginning, but this circle now has the *anima mundi*, the soul of the world, which was hidden in chaos. At first all the elements were completely mixed in that round chaos, and the centre was hidden; then the alchemist disentangles these elements and arranges them in a regular figure, like a crystal. That is the idea of the philosopher's stone in which the original round thing appears again, and this time it is the spiritual body, the ethereal thing, the *anima mundi*, the redeemed microcosmos.

The motif of the swarm of little fishes or other little objects is also found in alchemy, representing the disjointed elements. And it is often in children's dreams. I have dealt with such a case in one of my dream seminars: a child who died unexpectedly about a year after she had produced a series of the most extraordinary dreams, practically all containing the swarm motif. There was a cosmological dream where it was clearly visible how the swarm comes into existence, or how it is synthesized, and how it is dissolved into the swarm. The Mendelian units join together physiologically as well as psychically and then disintegrate again. That anticipated her death: her psyche was loosely connected, and when something adverse happened it dissolved into these units. Now, each of those particles is a Mendelian unit inasmuch as it is living; for instance, your nose is living. You live inasmuch as these Mendelian units are living. They have souls, are endowed with psychic life, the psychic life of that ancestor; or you can call it part of an ancestral soul. So inasmuch as you are like your nose, or can concentrate upon your nose, you become at once identical with the grandfather who had your nose. If your brain happens to be exactly like that of the great-grandfather, you are identical with him, and nothing can help you there – you have to function as if you were entirely possessed by him. It is difficult, or quite impossible, to indicate the size of Mendelian units; some are bigger, some are smaller, and so you have either large areas or small areas of ancestral souls included within you. At all events, you are a collection of ancestral spirits, and the psychological problem is how to find yourself in that crowd. Somewhere you are also a spirit – somewhere you have the secret of your particular pattern.

Now, that is in this circle of chaos but you don't know where, and then you have to go through that whole procedure of the squaring of the circle in order to find out the *quinta essentia* which is the self. The alchemists said it was of a celestial blue colour because it was heaven, and since it was round, globular, they called it 'heaven in ourselves'. That is their idea of the self. As we are contained in the heaven, so we are contained in the self, and the self is the *quinta essentia*. Now, when someone is threatened with dissolution, it is just as if these particles could not be united, as if the ancestral souls would not come together. I am telling you all this in order to explain that other aspect of the dead: it is not only the dead body, but the spirits of the dead. So if a primitive wants to become a medicine man, a superior man, he must be able to talk to the dead, must be able to reconcile them. For the dead are the makers of illnesses, causing all the trouble to the tribe; and then the medicine man is called upon because he is supposed to be able to talk to the ancestral spirits and make a compromise with them, to lay them or to integrate them properly. That is necessary for everybody in order to develop mentally and spiritually. He has to collect these spirits and make them into a whole, integrate them; and that difficult task, the integration process, is called the carrying of the corpse of the ancestors, or the burden of the ancestors.

From: 'Paracelsus as a Spiritual Phenomenon' (1942) (*CW* 13)

190   At the end of the process, says Paracelsus, a 'physical lightning' will appear, the 'lightning of Saturn' will separate from the lightning of Sol, and what appears in this lightning pertains 'to longevity, to that un-doubtedly great Iliaster'.[3] This process does not take anything away from the body's weight but only from its 'turbulence', and that 'by virtue of the

translucent colours'.[4] 'Tranquillity of mind' as a goal of the opus is stressed also by other alchemists. Paracelsus has nothing good to say about the body. It is 'bad and putrid'.

From: *Nietzsche's Zarathustra* (1988), 2: 1067–8

One is also continually baffled by the use of the word 'spirit' or *spiritus* in the alchemical concept. For instance, they say: 'If thou dost not succeed in making the body a spirit, thou hast not accomplished the work.' You see, in that case it would mean originally, inasmuch as the procedure was chemical, 'If thou has not succeeded in making the body, a metal, into an oxide, thou hast not succeeded in accomplishing the work.' That is, the oxide is a volatile substance. If mercury is boiled, it always ascends and becomes a condensation again in those parts of the retort that are cooler; and then they say that the mercury in the state of boiling is the body, and the vapour of mercury, which ascends and transcends, is the spirit. When substances are heated, they usually oxidize or change their quality, and that change of quality was understood as what they called 'sublimation'; it was like becoming a different being. You see, certain bodies change so much through oxidation that a naive person could not possibly recognize the relationship; therefore those old chemists thought that they produced new bodies, and the new body, caused by heating up the former body, was the spirit, a *spiritus*. But they used this word 'spirit' absolutely indiscriminately even in their mystical texts, where they also talked about making the body a *pneuma*. Now *pneuma* is a wind, a volatile compound, a changeable compound, or it is really the spirit – I mean the spirit in its metaphysical or philosophical or religious sense – and you simply are unable to make sure which they meant. Presumably they meant that the spirit – what we now call 'spirit' or what the Bible calls 'spirit' – is a subtle body. You don't get away from that; it is just a subtle body. So you can make a spirit out of matter, can de-materialize – what they call 'subtilize' matter to such an extent that it becomes a spirit, not a disembodied spirit but a spirit that is a subtle body.

Now, since this subtle body was made by heat, they assumed that through the fire they imparted fire-substance to the body so that it became partially like fire, and 'fire' was another symbol for the soul. In Heraclitus you find a passage where it says that the noblest soul is the essence of fire – it is of the most intense radiation and splendour and quite dry – and therefore he says it is death to a spirit, or a soul, to become water. He also says that souls of alcoholics turn to water; they become waterlogged or humid and they die.[5] So the idea was that the real spirit, the essence of life, of the soul, was fire. And by giving fire to substances they assumed that they became half spiritual, or subtle bodies. The fire means, of course, intensity, so if you submit to intensity, say to an intense emotion, you would change into a subtle body. Therefore, to subtilize or sublimate a man, you must expose him to the fire;

first he must be cleansed from impurity by the ablution with water, and then exposed to the fire.

That idea is older than Christianity, and you remember that saying in the New Testament: 'I indeed baptize you with water unto repentance: but he that cometh after me is mightier than I, whose shoes I am not worthy to bear: he shall baptize you with the Holy Ghost, and with fire.' You find that saying already in alchemistic texts of the first century – the famous text of Komarios for instance[6] – and these are all connected with pre-Christian traditions; and though we have no evidence, the texts being no longer extant, we know the names of people who were great authorities on these matters in the first and second centuries BC. And, as I said, we have authentic texts from the first century, where we find those ideas. When a man is subjected to a great emotion, it means that he is subjected to the fire, and the contact with the fire can give him the nature of a subtle body; the fire can subtilize him, or it may destroy him. This idea is expressed also in the non-canonical saying of Jesus: 'He who is near to me is near to the fire; and he who is far from me is far from the kingdom.' For he is the fire, the greatest intensity, and whoever touches upon this intensity is subtilized, made pneumatic, made into a volatile body.

Now, the more Nietzsche becomes intense, the more he is identical with the flame Zarathustra; and the more he exposes himself to that fire, the more he becomes volatile, the more his body is burned up. The alchemists say that all the superfluities must be burned up and therefore the action of the fire must be strong; not so strong at first, in order not to burn up too much, but later on in the process the fire must be increased, become more intense, and then all superfluities are burned away. Then one becomes subtilized; then one is a subtle body, a spirit.

From: 'The Psychology of the Transference' (1946) (*CW* 16)

486   After all this there can be no more doubt that the black darkness is washed away by the *aqua sapientiae* of 'our science', namely the God-given gift of the royal art and the knowledge it bestows. The *mundificatio* (purification) means, as we have seen, the removal of the superfluities that always cling to merely natural products, and especially to the symbolic unconscious contents which the alchemist found projected into matter. He therefore acted on Cardan's rule that the object of the work of interpretation is to reduce the dream material to its most general principles.[7] This is what the laboratory worker called the *extractio animae*, and what in the psychological field we would call the working-through of the idea contained in the dream. We know that this requires a necessary premise or hypothesis, a certain intellectual structure by means of which 'apper-

ceptions' can be made. In the case of the alchemist, such a premise was ready to hand in the *aqua* (*doctrinae*), or the God-inspired *sapientia* which he could also acquire through a diligent study of the 'books', the alchemical classics. Hence the reference to the books, which at this stage of the work must be avoided or destroyed 'lest your hearts be rent asunder'. This singular exhortation, altogether inexplicable from the chemical point of view, has a profound significance here. The absolvent water or *aqua sapientiae* had been established in the teachings and sayings of the masters as the *donum Spiritus Sancti* which enables the philosopher to understand the *miracula operis*. Therefore he might easily be tempted to assume that philosophical knowledge is the highest good. The psychological equivalent of this situation is when people imagine that they have reached the goal of the work once the unconscious contents have been made conscious and theoretically evaluated. In both cases this would be arbitrarily to define 'spirit' as a mere matter of thinking and intuition. Both disciplines, it is true, are aiming at a 'spiritual' goal: the alchemist undertakes to produce a new, volatile (hence aerial or 'spiritual') entity endowed with *corpus, anima, et spiritus*, where *corpus* is naturally understood as a 'subtle' body or 'breath body'; the analyst tries to bring about a certain attitude or frame of mind, a certain 'spirit' therefore. But because the body, even when conceived as the *corpus glorificationis*, is grosser than *anima* and *spiritus*, a 'remnant of earth' necessarily clings to it, albeit a very subtle one.[8] Hence an attitude that seeks to do justice to the unconscious as well as to one's fellow-human beings cannot possibly rest on knowledge alone, in so far as this consists merely of thinking and intuition. It would lack the function that perceives values, i.e. feeling, as well as the *fonction du réel*, i.e. sensation, the sensible perception of reality.[9]

503   The process of differentiating the ego from the unconscious,[10] then, has its equivalent in the *mundificatio*, and, just as this is the necessary condition for the return of the soul to the body, so the body is necessary if the unconscious is not to have destructive effects on the ego-consciousness, for it is the body that gives bounds to the personality. The unconscious can be integrated only if the ego holds its ground. Consequently, the alchemist's endeavour to unite the *corpus mundum*, the purified body, with the soul is also the endeavour of the psychologist once he has succeeded in freeing the ego-consciousness from contamination with the unconscious. In alchemy the purification is the result of numerous distillations; in psychology too it comes from an equally thorough separation of the ordinary ego-personality from all inflationary admixtures of unconscious material. This task entails the most painstaking self-examination and self-education, which can, however, be passed on to others by one who has acquired the discipline himself. The process of psychological differentiation is no light work; it needs the tenacity and patience of the alchemist, who must purify the body from all superfluities in the fiercest heat of the furnace, and pursue

Mercurius 'from one bride chamber to the next'. As alchemical symbolism shows, a radical understanding of this kind is impossible without a human partner. A general and merely academic 'insight into one's mistakes' is ineffectual, for then the mistakes are not really seen at all, only the idea of them. But they show up acutely when a human relationship brings them to the fore and when they are noticed by the other person as well as by oneself. Then and then only can they really be felt and their true nature recognized. Similarly, confessions made to one's secret self generally have little or no effect, whereas confessions made to another are much more promising.

From: 'The Personification of the Opposites', *Mysterium coniunctionis* (1955–6) (*CW* 14)

318   The effect of Christian baptism is the washing-away of sin and the acceptance of the neophyte into the Church as the earthly kingdom of Christ, sanctification and rebirth through grace, and the bestowal of an 'indelible character' on the baptized. The effect of the *aqua permanens* is equally miraculous. The 'Gloria mundi' says: 'The mystery of every thing is life, which is water; for water dissolves the body into spirit and summons a spirit from the dead.'[11] Dissolution into spirit, the body's volatilization or sublimation, corresponds chemically to evaporation, or at any rate to the expulsion of evaporable ingredients like quicksilver, sulphur, etc. Psychologically it corresponds to the conscious realization and integration of an unconscious content. Unconscious contents lurk somewhere in the body like so many daemons of sickness, impossible to get hold of, especially when they give rise to physical symptoms the organic causes of which cannot be demonstrated. The 'spirit' summoned from the dead is usually the spirit Mercurius, who, as the *anima mundi*, is inherent in all things in a latent state. It is clear from the passage immediately following that it is salt of which it is said: 'And that is the thing which we seek: all our secrets are contained in it.' Salt, however, 'takes its origin from Mercurius', so salt is a synonym for the arcane substance. It also plays an important part in the Roman rite: after being blessed it is added to the consecrated water, and in the ceremony of baptism a few grains of the consecrated salt are placed in the neophyte's mouth with the words: 'Receive the salt of wisdom: may it be a propitiation for thee unto eternal life.'

From: *Nietzsche's Zarathustra* (1988), 2: 441–5

Very little is known about this strange concept of the subtle body. Mead has written a book about it.[12] You see, when we speak of the unconscious we mean the psychological unconscious, which is a possible concept; we are then

dealing with certain factors in the unconscious which we really can understand and discriminate. But the part of the unconscious which is designated
as the subtle body becomes more and more identical with the functioning of
the body, and therefore it grows darker and darker and ends in the utter
darkness of matter; that aspect of the unconscious is exceedingly incomprehensible. I only mentioned it because in dealing with Nietzsche's
concept of the self, one has to include a body, so one must include not only
the shadow – the psychological unconscious – but also the physiological
unconscious, the so-called somatic unconscious which is the subtle body. You
see, somewhere our unconscious becomes material, because the body is the
living unit, and our conscious and our unconscious are embedded in it: they
contact the body. Somewhere there is a place where the two ends meet and
become interlocked. And that is the place where one cannot say whether it is
matter, or what one calls 'psyche'. Now everything that can be represented
to the conscious is psychological, but if a thing cannot be made conscious,
or can only be expressed by vague analogies or hints, it is so dark that one
doesn't know whether it has to do with the top or the bottom of the system,
whether it leads into the body or into the air.

According to the old Gnostic system, the *pneuma* is above, that part of the
unconscious which is divine; then below would come the body which was
called *hyle*, or *sarx*, as Paul calls the flesh in the New Testament, and between
the two there is the human or the psychological sphere. The Latin words for
pneuma are *spiritus* and in another connection *animus*, not to be mistaken for
the specific *animus* concept in our psychology. Then with the psyche would
be the *anima*, with the connotation of the breath of life, the living flame, the
living warmth of the body. This *anima* has a spiritual side, called in China
the *shen*, and their concept of *kuei* would be the somatic or corporeal part.
This region contains the psychology of the subtle body because it reaches
into the *sarx*. Now, when you look at man you see the body, the *sarx*, and
only by inference do you come to the psychological side; you get reflected
rays of light from a body of flesh, and you hear a voice, vibrations of the air,
and they give you the necessary hints to conclude as to the psyche. If you are

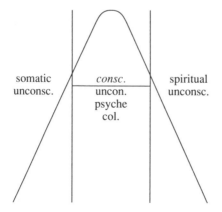

somatic
unconsc.

consc.
uncon.
psyche
col.

spiritual
unconsc.

inside yourself, in your own body, then you are in the psyche, which is the centre. It would be about like this. The mountain would be the conscious and the unconscious, and the spiritual would be on one side and the somatic on the other. The greatest intensity of life is in the centre and the darkness is on either side, on the spiritual side as well as on the side of matter.

You may have read that famous Gnostic work *Pistis Sophia*.[13] *Pistis* means fidelity, confidence, trust, loyalty, wrongly translated by 'belief' or 'creed', and Sophia is the woman wisdom of God. She is God's wife in a way, and therefore has also been understood as the so-called *theotokos*, the mother of God – that is the term used in the Greek Orthodox church for Mother Mary – and certain Gnostics held that Sophia was the mother of the spiritual Jesus. The man Jesus has of course been born of an earthly woman, but the spiritual Jesus that descended into him when he was baptized by John was born out of Sophia. They were convinced that the man Jesus who was hanging on the cross was only the material body, that during his struggle in the garden, hours before his crucifixion, the God had departed from him. So the God was never crucified. The body was hanging on the cross and not the God–man, the proof being that Christ himself said, 'My God, my God, why hast thou forsaken me?' That is the belief of the *Doketic* form of Christianity, a very important branch which for a while threatened the development of the orthodox Christian dogma.[14] I mention this because all these ideas of the subtle body play a great role in the New Testament. The body, or *sarx*, to St Paul is the gross, biological, physiological body, the corruptible body; but he speaks also of the incorruptible body which we put on with Christ, because Christ is in a way the soul or the *pneuma*, the incorruptible body that is beyond space and time.[15]

You see, the subtle body – assuming that there is such a thing – necessarily must be beyond space and time. Every real body fills space because it consists of matter, while the subtle body is said not to consist of matter, or it is matter which is so exceedingly subtle that it cannot be perceived. So it must be a body which does not fill space, a matter which is beyond space, and therefore it would be in no time. You know, we can only have a notion of time by the measure of distance; for instance, to move from this end of the room to the other needs a certain length of time, but if there is no extension, no change, there is no time; even if that moment stands still for ten thousand eternities, there is no time because nothing happens. This idea of the subtle body is very important, and it is marvellous to encounter it in a text which naively comes from the wholeness of man . . . I usually do not deal with that concept simply because it is too difficult; I content myself with things of which I can really know something. It is beyond our grasp *per definition*; the subtle body is a transcendental concept which cannot be expressed in terms of our language or our philosophical views, because they are all inside the categories of time and space.[16]

So we can only talk primitive language as soon as we come to the question of the subtle body, and that is everything else but scientific. It means speaking in images. Of course, we can talk such a language, but whether it is comprehensible is an entirely different question. And you know I believe in science, I believe in that which man can do. I also remember what Mephistopheles says to the student who went away with the devil's good advice. The devil smiles behind his back and says:

Scorn reason and science if you can,
The highest powers yet bestowed on man![17]

Science is the highest power of man, for we can do just what we can do, and when we try to deal with things which are beyond our comprehension, we are overstepping our competence. You see, there are plenty of secrets – only a few fools, morbid intellects, think we have solved all the riddles; anybody with even the smallest amount of imagination knows that the world is a great enigma, and psychology is one of the foremost enigmas. And you can touch one with your hands in this question of the subtle body. Now, [one of our participants] asks: 'Are there not two uses of the expression "subtle body"? At times, it seems to be used as a synonym for the diamond body. Isn't the other, more primitive meaning of "subtle body" a kind of ghost-like body, like a framework, halfway between spirit and matter, which everyone possesses and in which the various centres are located? Is the diamond body something which *may* develop *in* this subtle body?'

Such questions will inevitably arise as soon as you begin to talk of the subtle body. Is the subtle body identical with what Chinese yoga calls the diamond body, or is it rather the *kuei* of Chinese philosophy, the somatic unconscious? Well, the diamond body is the equivalent of the concept of the self. Therefore it is expressed by the stone of the highest value, and it is also called the golden germ, the golden child, *Hiranyagarbha* in Sanskrit. According to Chinese yoga, it comes from the lead of the water region, which is not of a precious nature. It is the heavy cold metal of a low nature which is supposed to be deep down in the body, the *muladhara*, or in *svadhisthana*, the water centre; out of this common or vulgar body the alchemistic procedure produces gold or the diamond body, the everlasting body. In the language of medieval alchemy it would have been the philosopher's stone or the eagle (*aurum nostrum*, '*our* gold'); for those old alchemists were by no means making ordinary gold. There was no making of bodies. They started from bodies and tried to develop something out of the water region into a substance of highest value, something with the qualities of light. Yet it is located in the centre – the psyche – between body and spirit– and consists of both. So in that respect one can say the concept of the diamond body is really identical with the idea of the subtle body. Naturally, the subtle body is a primitive formulation and the diamond body is the expression for a finished product of the same nature.

The Chinese yoga procedure and alchemy are much alike, but alchemy is a most mistaken name; it had better be called the 'yoga process'. It is a process of transmutation which creates out of the subtle body within, something which is equal to the subtle body, yet it is of very great value. The matter out of which it is created can also be of little value, so the alchemists said that it could be found everywhere, quite ordinary, even despicable, a stone that is *eiectus in viam*, thrown out into the street. It is the stone, rejected by the builders, which became the cornerstone. They even find it in the *Sterquilinium*, the dung heap, as you can read in their literature. Therefore when Meyrink read those old alchemistic treatises about sorcerers making gold and God knows what, he was so impressed that he bought an ancient water-closet, a little outhouse, and dug up the *fond*; it was two or three hundred years old and he went to the very bottom of it in order to find the substance for the stone, because the old texts say you can find it in such disreputable places.[18] It is funny that many old things, even manuscripts, have been found in that way. I am not a bit sure whether the famous Oxyrhynchus papyri were not found in such a place and that they had not been put to a most disreputable use before.

From: 'The Conjunction', *Mysterium coniunctionis* (1955–6) (*CW* 14)

663   Mercurius usually stands for the arcane substance, whose synonyms are the *panacea* and the 'spagyric medicine'. Dorn identifies the latter with the 'balsam'[19] of Paracelsus, which is a close analogy of the μύρον of the Basilidians. In the *De vita longa* of Paracelsus, balsam as an *elixir vitae* is associated with the term *gamonymus*, which might be rendered 'having the name of matrimony'.[20] Dorn thinks that the balsam, which 'stands higher than nature', is to be found in the human body and is a kind of etheric substance.[21] He says it is the best medicament not only for the body but also for the mind (*mens*). Though it is a corporeal substance, as a combination of the spirit and soul of the spagyric medicine it is essentially spiritual:[22]

> We conclude that meditative philosophy consists in the overcoming of the body by mental union [*unio mentalis*]. This first union does not as yet make the wise man, but only the mental disciple of wisdom. The second union of the mind with the body shows forth the wise man, hoping for and expecting that blessed third union with the first unity [i.e. the *unus mundus*, the latent unity of the world]. May Almighty God grant that all men be made such, and may He be one in All.[23]

664   It is significant for the whole of alchemy that in Dorn's view a mental union was not the culminating-point but merely the first stage of the procedure. The second stage is reached when the mental union, that is, the unity of spirit and soul, is conjoined with the body. But a consummation

of the *mysterium coniunctionis* can be expected only when the unity of spirit, soul and body is made one with the original *unus mundus*.

670   Although the esoteric symbolism of the *coniunctio* occupies a prominent position, it does not cover all aspects of the *mysterium*. In addition we have to consider the symbolism of death and the grave, and the motif of conflict. Obviously, very different if not contradictory symbolisms were needed to give an adequate description of the paradoxical nature of the conjunction. In such a situation one can conclude with certainty that none of the symbols employed suffices to express the whole. One therefore feels compelled to seek a formula in which the various aspects can be brought together without contradiction. Dorn attempted to do this with the means that were then at his disposal. He could do so the more easily as the current idea of *correspondentia* came to his aid. For a man of those times there was no intellectual difficulty in postulating a 'truth' which was the same in God, in man and in matter. With the help of this idea he could see at once that the reconciliation of hostile elements and the union of alchemical opposites formed a 'correspondence' to the *unio mentalis* which took place simultaneously in the mind of man, and not only in man but in God ('that He may be one in All'). Dorn correctly recognized that the entity in which the union took place is the psychological authority which I have called the self. The *unio mentalis*, the interior oneness which today we call individuation, he conceived as a psychic equilibration of opposites 'in the overcoming of the body', a state of equanimity transcending the body's affectivity and instinctuality.[24] The spirit (*animus*), which is to unite with the soul, he called a 'spiracle [*spiraculum*] of eternal life', a sort of 'window into eternity' (Leibniz), whereas the soul is an organ of the spirit and the body an instrument of the soul. The soul stands between good and evil and has the 'option' of both. It animates the body by a 'natural union', just as, by a 'supernatural union', it is endowed with life by the spirit.[25]

671   But, in order to bring about their subsequent reunion, the mind (*mens*) must be separated from the body – which is equivalent to 'voluntary death'[26] – for only separated things can unite. By this separation (*distractio*) Dorn obviously meant a discrimination and dissolution of the 'composite', the composite state being one in which the affectivity of the body has a disturbing influence on the rationality of the mind. The aim of this separation was to free the mind from the influence of the 'bodily appetites and the heart's affections', and to establish a spiritual position which is supraordinate to the turbulent sphere of the body. This leads at first to a dissociation of the personality and a violation of the merely natural man.

672   This preliminary step, in itself a clear blend of Stoic philosophy and Christian psychology, is indispensable for the differentiation of consciousness.[27] Modern psychotherapy makes use of the same procedure when it objectifies the affects and instincts and confronts consciousness with them.

But the separation of the spiritual and the vital spheres, and the subordination of the latter to the rational standpoint, is not satisfactory inasmuch as reason alone cannot do complete or even adequate justice to the irrational facts of the unconscious. In the long run it does not pay to cripple life by insisting on the primacy of the spirit, for which reason the pious man cannot prevent himself from sinning again and again and the rationalist must constantly trip up over his own irrationalities. Only the man who hides the other side in artifical unconsciousness can escape this intolerable conflict. Accordingly, the chronic duel between body and spirit seems a better though by no means ideal solution. The advantage, however, is that both sides remain conscious. Anything conscious can be corrected, but anything that slips away into the unconscious is beyond the reach of correction and, its rank growth undisturbed, is subject to increasing degeneration. Happily, nature sees to it that the unconscious contents will irrupt into consciousness sooner or later and create the necessary confusion. A permanent and uncomplicated state of spiritualization is therefore such a rarity that its possessors are canonized by the Church.

673 Since the soul animates the body, just as the soul is animated by the spirit, she tends to favour the body and everything bodily, sensuous and emotional. She lies caught in 'the chains' of Physis, and she desires 'beyond physical necessity'. She must be called back by the 'counsel of the spirit' from her lostness in matter and the world. This is a relief to the body too, for it not only enjoys the advantage of being animated by the soul but suffers under the disadvantage of having to serve as the instrument of the soul's appetites and desires. Her wish-fantasies impel it to deeds to which it would not rouse itself without this incentive, for the inertia of matter is inborn in it and probably forms its only interest except for the satisfaction of physiological instincts. Hence the separation means withdrawing the soul and her projections from the bodily sphere and from all environmental conditions relating to the body. In modern terms it would be a turning-away from sensuous reality, a withdrawal of the fantasy-projections that give 'the ten thousand things' their attractive and deceptive glamour. In other words, it means introversion, introspection, meditation and the careful investigation of desires and their motives. Since, as Dorn says, the soul 'stands between good and evil', the disciple will have every opportunity to discover the dark side of his personality, his inferior wishes and motives, childish fantasies and resentments, etc.; in short, all those traits he habitually hides from himself. He will be confronted with his shadow, but more rarely with the good qualities, of which he is accustomed to make a show anyway. He will learn to know his soul, that is, his *anima* who conjures up a delusory world for him. He attains this knowledge, Dorn supposes, with the help of the spirit, by which are meant all the higher mental faculties such as reason, insight and moral discrimination. But, in so far as the spirit is also a 'window into eternity' and, as the *anima rationalis*, immortal, it conveys to the soul a certain 'divine

influx' and the knowledge of higher things, wherein consists precisely its supposed animation of the soul. This higher world has an impersonal character and consists on the one hand of all those traditional, intellectual and moral values which educate and cultivate the individual, and, on the other, of the products of the unconscious, which present themselves to consciousness as archetypal ideas. Usually the former predominate. But when, weakened by age or by criticism, they lose their power of conviction, the archetypal ideas rush in to fill the gap. Freud, correctly recognizing this situation, called the traditional values the 'super-ego', but the archetypal ideas remained unknown to him, as the belief in reason and the positivism of the nineteenth century never relaxed their hold. A materialistic view of the world ill accords with the reality and autonomy of the psyche.

674 The *arcanum* of alchemy is one of these archetypal ideas that fills a gap in the Christian view of the world, namely, the unbridged gulf between the opposites, in particular between good and evil. Only logic knows a *tertium non datur*; nature consists entirely of such 'thirds', since she is represented by effects which resolve an opposition – just as a waterfall mediates between 'above' and 'below'. The alchemists sought for that effect which would heal not only the disharmonies of the physical world but the inner psychic conflict as well, the 'affliction of the soul'; and they called this effect the *lapis Philosophorum*.

679 The second stage of conjunction, the re-uniting of the *unio mentalis* with the body, is particularly important, as only from here can the complete conjunction be attained – union with the *unus mundus*. The reuniting of the spiritual position with the body obviously means that the insights gained should be made real. An insight might just as well remain in abeyance if it is simply not used. The second stage of conjunction therefore consists in making a reality of the man who has acquired some knowledge of his paradoxical wholeness.

680 The great difficulty here, however, is that no one knows how the paradoxical wholeness of man can ever be realized. That is the crux of individuation, though it becomes a problem only when the loophole of 'scientific' or other kinds of cynicism is not used. Because the realization of the wholeness that has been made conscious is an apparently insoluble task and faces the psychologist with questions which he can answer only with hesitation and uncertainty, it is of the greatest interest to see how the more unencumbered symbolical thinking of a medieval 'philosopher' tackled this problem. The texts that have come down to us do not encourage the supposition that Dorn was conscious of the full range of his undertaking. Although in general he had a clear grasp of the role the adept played in the alchemical process, the problem did not present itself to him in all its acuteness, because only a part of it was enacted in the moral and psychological sphere, while for the rest it was hypostatized in the form of

certain magical properties of the living body, or as a magical substance hidden within it. This projection spread over the problem a kind of mist which obscured its sharp edges. The alchemists still believed that metaphysical assertions could be proved (even today we have still not entirely freed ourselves from this somewhat childish assumption), and they could therefore entrench themselves behind seemingly secure positions in the Beyond, which they were confident would not be shaken by any doubts. In this way they were able to procure for themselves considerable alleviations. One has only to think what it means if in the misery and incertitude of a moral or philosophical dilemma one has a *quinta essentia*, a *lapis* or a *panacea* so to say, in one's pocket! We can understand this *deus ex machina* the more easily when we remember with what passion people today believe that psychological complications can be made magically to disappear by means of hormones, narcotics, insulin shocks and convulsion thereapy. The alchemists were as little able to perceive the symbolical nature of their ideas of the *arcanum* as we to recognize that the belief in hormones and shocks is a symbol. We would indignantly dismiss such an interpretation as a nonsensical suggestion.

NOTES

1 Avicenna (980–1037), Islamic physician and philosopher, interpreter of Aristotle.
2 Jan van Ruysbroek (1293–1381), Flemish mystic. See, for instance, *The Spiritual Espousals*, tr. Eric Colledge (New York, 1953), pt I, B, a.
3 There is only *one* flash of lightning, which changes the darkness of Saturn into the brightness of Jupiter. Ruland (*Lexicon*, p. 153) states: 'Metallic fulmination is, with the higher metals, a process of purging. . . . Fulmination is a metallic gradation, with excoction, educing the pure part, the perfection thereof being indicated by an irradiating splendour.'
4 The colours refer to the *cauda* pavonis, which appears just before the completion of the opus.
5 Heraclitus often contrasted noble fire with ignoble wetness; e.g. 'It is delight, or rather death, to become wet'; and 'Fire . . . will judge and seize upon all things' (Freeman, fragments 74, 66).
6 Matthew 3:11. The fullest description of how, for Komarios, baptism may be in both of the opposites, fire and water, comes in *CW* 14, paras 316–17. Komarios, or Comarius, was a first-century alchemist.
7 Cardan, *Somniorum synesiorum*: 'Unumquodque somnium ad sua generalia deducendum est.'
8 '. . . subtilietur lapis, donec in ultimam subtilitatis puritatem deveniat et ultimo volatilis fiat' ('The stone should be subtilized until it reaches the ultimate purity of refinement and becomes, in the end, volatile'): *Rosarium*, p. 351. Or again (ibid., p. 285): 'Sublimatio est duplex: Prima est remotio superfluitatis, ut remaneant partes purissimae a faecibus elementaribus segregatae sicque virtutem quintae essentiae possideant. Et haec sublimatio est corporum in spiritum reductio cum scilicet corporalis densitas transit in spiritus subtilitatem' ('Sublimation is twofold: The first is the removal of the superfluous so that the purest parts shall remain, free from elementary dregs, and shall possess the quality of the quintessence. The other sublimation is the reduction of the bodies to spirit, i.e. when the corporeal density is transformed into a spiritual subtlety').

9 Cf. *Psychological Types*, definitions 21 (in Baynes edn, def. 20), 35, 47, 53.

10 This process is described in the second of my *Two Essays*.

11 *Mus. herm.*, p. 262 (Waite, I, p. 211). This opinion is put into the mouth of 'Socrates', and corresponds more or less to Sermo XVI of the *Turba*.

12 G. R. S. Mead, *The Doctrine of the Subtle Body in Western Tradition* (London, 1919).

13 This third-century work centres on the legend of 'the twin Jesus'. Mary is represented as telling Jesus that when he was a child, a spirit descended, identical in appearance to the child he sought as brother, and in an embrace the two became one. See *Apocrypha* XXIII, and *Pistis Sophia*, tr. G. R. S. Mead (London, 1896), pp. 188–919.

14 *Doketic*: see Z, 16 May 1934, n. 20.

15 I Corinthians 15: 53–4.

16 Jung often contrasted the empirical or experimental approach with the transcendental, meaning by the latter 'approximately the same as Kant meant when he called the thing-in-itself, a merely negative, border-line concept' (*CW* 13, para. 82).

17 Spoken by Mephistopheles dressed in Faust's long robe (*Faust*, tr. Alice Raphael (New York, 1932), Act II, Sc. ii).

18 Gustav Meyrink, author of *Das Grüne Gesicht* (The Green Face) (Leipzig, 1916), once bought a house in Prague famous for its still having an alchemical dung heap wherein the priceless philosopher's stone might lie buried. Meyrink read old alchemy and dug in the dung heap for the stone.

19 Balsam occurs in Zosimos as a synonym for the *aqua permanens* (Berthelot, *Alch. grecs*, III, xxv, 1).

20 Cf. 'Paracelsus as a Spiritual Phenomenon', para. 171.

21 'For there is in man's body a certain substance comformable to the ethereal, which preserves the other elemental parts in it and causes them to continue' ('Phil. meditativa', *Theatr. chem.*, I, p. 456).

22 'And we do not deny that our spagyric spirit clothes it' (ibid.). A synonym for balsam is the wine that is 'duplex', i.e. both 'philosophic' and 'common' (ibid., p. 464).

23 Ibid., p. 456.

24 'Therefore the mind is well said to be composed when the spirit and the soul are joined by such a bond that the bodily appetites and the heart's affections are restrained' ('Phil. medit.', *Theatr. chem.*, I, p. 451).

25 Ibid., pp. 451f.

26 Here Dorn cites the *verbum Dei*: 'He that loveth his soul shall lose it, and he that hateth his soul preserveth it for ever' (p. 453). Cf. Matthew 16: 25, Luke 27: 33, and John 23: 25.

27 Cf. the parallel in Wei Po-yang: 'Closed on all sides, its interior is made up of intercommunicating labyrinths. The protection is so complete as to turn back all that is devilish and undesirable. . . . Cessation of thought is desirable and worries are preposterous. The divine *ch'i* (air, spirit, ethereal essence) fills the quarters. . . . Whoever retains it will prosper and he who loses it, will perish.' (p. 238.)

7 Opposites and the *coniunctio*

From: 'The Psychology of the Transference' (1946) (*CW* 16)

501   If there is such a thing as an unconscious that is not personal – i.e. does not consist of individually acquired contents, whether forgotten, subliminally perceived, or repressed – then there must also be processes going on in this non-ego, spontaneous archetypal events which the conscious mind can only perceive when they are projected. They are immemorially strange and unknown, and yet we seem to have known them from everlasting; they are also the source of a remarkable fascination that dazzles and illuminates at once. They draw us like a magnet and at the same time frighten us; they manifest themselves in fantasies, dreams, hallucinations and in certain kinds of religious ecstasy. The *coniunctio* is one of these archetypes. The absorptive power of the archetype explains not only the widespread incidence of this motif but also the passionate intensity with which it seizes upon the individual, often in defiance of all reason and understanding.

From: 'The Components of the Coniunctio', *Mysterium coniunctionis* (1955–6) (*CW* 14)

1   The factors which come together in the *coniunctio* are conceived as opposites, either confronting one another in enmity or attracting one another in love.[1] To begin with they form a dualism; for instance the opposites are *humidum* (moist) / *siccum* (dry), *frigidum* (cold) / *calidum* (warm), *superiora* (upper, higher) / *inferiora* (lower), *spiritus–anima* (spirit–soul) / *corpus* (body), *coelum* (heaven) / *terra* (earth), *ignis* (fire) / *aqua* (water), bright / dark, *agens* (active) / *patiens* (passive), *volatile* (volatile, gaseous) / *fixum* (solid), *pretiosum* (precious, costly; also *carum*, dear) / *vile* (cheap, common), *bonum* (good) / *malum* (evil), *manifestum* (open) / *occultum* (occult; also *celatum*, hidden), *oriens* (East) / *occidens* (West), *vivum* (living) / *mortuum* (dead, inert), *masculus* (masculine) / *foemina* (feminine), Sol / Luna. Often the polarity is arranged as a *quaternio* (quaternity), with the two opposites crossing one another, as for

instance the four elements or the four qualities (moist, dry, cold, warm), or the four directions and seasons,[2] thus producing the cross as an emblem of the four elements and symbol of the sublunary physical world.[3] This fourfold Physis, the cross, also appears in the signs for earth ♁, Venus ♀, Mercury ☿, Saturn ♄, and Jupiter ♃.[4]

2   The opposites and their symbols are so common in the texts that it is superfluous to cite evidence from the sources. On the other hand, in view of the ambiguity of the alchemists' language, which is *tam ethice quam physice* (as much ethical as physical), it is worthwhile to go rather more closely into the manner in which the texts treat of the opposites. Very often the masculine–feminine opposition is personified as King and Queen (in the *Rosarium philosophorum* also as Emperor and Empress), or as *servus* (slave) or *vir rubeus* (red man) and *mulier candida* (white woman);[5] in the *Visio Arislei* they appear as Gabricus (or Thabritius) and Beya, the King's son and daughter.[6] Theriomorphic symbols are equally common and are often found in the illustrations.[7] I would mention the eagle and toad ('the eagle flying through the air and the toad crawling on the ground'), which are the 'emblem' of Avicenna in Michael Maier,[8] the eagle representing Luna 'or Juno, Venus, Beya, who is fugitive and winged like the eagle, which flies up to the clouds and receives the rays of the sun in his eyes'. The toad 'is the opposite of air, it is a contrary element, namely earth, whereon alone it moves by slow steps, and does not trust itself to another element. Its head is very heavy and gazes at the earth. For this reason it denotes the philosophic earth, which cannot fly [i.e. cannot be sublimated], as it is firm and solid. Upon it as a foundation the golden house[9] is to be built. Were it not for the earth in our work the air would fly away, neither would the fire have its nourishment, nor the water its vessel.'[10]

3   Another favourite theriomorphic image is that of the two birds or two dragons, one of them winged, the other wingless. This allegory comes from an ancient text, *De Chemia Senioris antiquissimi philosophi libellus*.[11] The wingless bird or dragon prevents the other from flying. They stand for Sol and Luna, brother and sister, who are united by means of the art.[12] In Lambspringk's 'Symbols'[13] they appear as the astrological Fishes which, swimming in opposite directions, symbolize the spirit/soul polarity. The water they swim in is *mare nostrum* (our sea) and is interpreted as the body.[14] The fishes are 'without bones and cortex'.[15] From them is produced a *mare immensum*, which is the *aqua permanens* (permanent water). Another symbol is the stag and unicorn meeting in the 'forest'.[16] The stag signifies the soul, the unicorn spirit, and the forest the body. The next two pictures in Lambspringk's 'Symbols' show the lion and lioness,[17] or the wolf and dog, the latter two fighting; they too symbolize soul and spirit. In Lambspringk's Figure VII [not shown here] the opposites are symbolized by two birds in a wood, one fledged, the other unfledged. Whereas in the earlier pictures the conflict seems to be between spirit and soul, the two birds signify the conflict between spirit and body, and in

Figure VIII [not shown here] the two birds fighting do in fact represent that conflict. The opposition between spirit and soul is due to the latter having a very fine substance. It is more akin to the 'hylical' body and is *densior et crassior* (denser and grosser) than the spirit.

4   The elevation of the human figure to a king or a divinity, and on the other hand its representation in subhuman, theriomorphic form, are indications of the *transconscious character* of the pairs of opposites. They do not belong to the ego-personality but are supraordinate to it. The ego-personality occupies an intermediate position, like the *anima inter bona et mala sita* (soul placed between good and evil). The pairs of opposites constitute the phenomenology of the paradoxical *self*, man's totality. That is why their symbolism makes use of cosmic expressions like *coelum/ terra*.[18] The intensity of the conflict is expressed in symbols like fire and water,[19] height and depth,[20] life and death.[21]

From: 'The Personification of the Opposites', *Mysterium coniunctionis* (1955–6) (*CW* 14)

104   The alchemist's endeavours to unite the opposites culminate in the 'chymical marriage', the supreme act of union in which the work reaches its consummation. After the hostility of the four elements has been overcome, there still remains the last and most formidable opposition, which the alchemist expressed very aptly as the relationship between male and female. We are inclined to think of this primarily as the power of love, of passion, which drives the two opposite poles together, forgetting that such a vehement attraction is needed only when an equally strong resistance keeps them apart. Although enmity was put only between the serpent and the woman (Genesis 3: 15), this curse nevertheless fell upon the relationship of the sexes in general. Eve was told: 'Thy desire shall be to thy husband, and he shall rule over thee.' And Adam was told: 'Cursed is the ground for thy sake . . . because thou has hearkened unto the voice of thy wife' (3: 16f–17). Primal guilt lies between them, an *interrupted state of enmity*, and this appears unreasonable only to our rational mind but not to our psychic nature. Our reason is often influenced far too much by purely physical considerations, so that the union of the sexes seems to it the only sensible thing, and the urge for union the most sensible instinct of all. But if we conceive of nature in the higher sense as the totality of all phenomena, then the physical is only one of her aspects, the other is pneumatic or spiritual. The first has always been regarded as feminine, the second as masculine. The goal of the one is union, the goal of the other is discrimination. Because it overvalues the physical, our contemporary reason lacks spiritual orientation, that is, *pneuma*. The alchemists seem to have had an inkling of this, for how otherwise could they have come upon that strange myth of the country of the King of the Sea, where only like

pairs with like and the land is unfruitful?[22] It was obviously a realm of innocent friendship, a kind of paradise or golden age, to which the 'Philosophers', the representatives of the physical, felt obliged to put an end with their good advice. But what happened was not by any means a natural union of the sexes; on the contrary it was a 'royal' incest, a sinful deed that immediately led to imprisonment and death and only afterwards restored the fertility of the country. As a parable the myth is certainly ambiguous; like alchemy in general, it can be understood spiritually as well as physically, *tam moralis quam chymica*.[23] The physical goal of alchemy was gold, the *panacea*, the elixir of life; the spiritual one was the rebirth of the (spiritual) light from the darkness of Physis: healing self-knowledge and the deliverance of the pneumatic body from the corruption of the flesh.

110   In alchemy, the sun signifies first of all gold, whose sign it shares. But just as the 'philosophical' gold is not the 'common' gold,[24] so the sun is neither just the metallic gold[25] nor the heavenly orb.[26] Sometimes the sun is an active substance hidden in the gold and is extracted as the *tinctura rubea* (red tincture). Sometimes, as the heavenly body, it is the possessor of magically effective and transformative rays. As gold and a heavenly body[27] it contains an active sulphur of a red colour, hot and dry.[28] Because of this red sulphur the alchemical sun, like the corresponding gold, is red.[29] As every alchemist knew, gold owes its red colour to the admixture of Cu (copper), which he interpreted as Kypris (the Cyprian, Venus), mentioned in Greek alchemy as the transformative substance.[30] Redness, heat and dryness are the classical qualities of the Egyptian Set (Greek Typhon), the evil principle which, like the alchemical sulphur, is closely connected with the devil. And just as Typhon has his kingdom in the forbidden sea, so the sun, as *sol centralis* has its sea, its 'crude perceptible water', and as *sol coelestis* its 'subtle imperceptible water'. This sea water (*aqua pontica*) is extracted from sun and moon. Unlike the Typhonian sea, the life-giving power of this water is praised, though this does not mean that it is invariably good.[31] It is the equivalent of the two-faced Mercurius, whose poisonous nature is often mentioned. The Typhonian aspect of the active sun-substance, of the red sulphur, of the water 'that does not make the hands wet',[32] and of the 'sea water' should not be left out of account. The author of the *Novum lumen chemicum* cannot suppress a reference to the latter's paradoxical nature: 'Do not be disturbed because you sometimes find contradictions in my treatises, after the custom of the philosophers; these are necessary, if you understand that no rose is found without thorns.'[33]

111   The active sun-substance also has favourable effects. As the so-called 'balsam' it drips from the sun and produces lemons, oranges, wine and, in the mineral kingdom, gold.[34] In man the balsam forms the 'radical moisture, from the sphere of the supracelestial waters'; it is the 'shining' or 'lucent body' which 'from man's birth enkindles the inner warmth, and

from which come all the motions of the will and the principle of all appetition'. It is a 'vital spirit', and it has 'its seat in the brain and its governance in the heart'.[35]

112   In the *Liber Platonis quartorum*, a Sabaean treatise, the *spiritus animalis* or solar sulphur is still a πνεῦμα πάρεδρον, a ministering spirit or familiar who can be conjured up by magical invocations to help with the work.[36]

113   From what has been said about the active sun-substance it should be clear that Sol in alchemy is much less a definite chemical substance than a *virtus*, a mysterious power[37] believed to have a generative[38] and transformative effect. Just as the physical sun lightens and warms the universe, so, in the human body, there is in the heart a sunlike *arcanum* from which life and warmth stream forth.[39] 'Therefore Sol', says Dorn, 'is rightly named the first after God, and the father and begetter of all,[40] because in him the seminal and formal virtue of all things whatsoever lies hid.'[41] This power is called 'sulphur'.[42] It is a hot, daemonic principle of life, having the closest affinities with the sun in the earth, the 'central fire' or *ignis gehennalis* (fire of hell). Hence there is also a *Sol niger* (a black sun), which coincides with the *nigredo* and *putrefactio*, the state of death.[43] Like Mercurius, Sol in alchemy is ambivalent.

116   After all this, we can say that the alchemical Sol, as a 'certain luminosity' (*quaedam luminositas*), is in many respects equal to the *lumen naturae*. This was the real source of illumination in alchemy, and from alchemy Paracelsus borrowed this same source in order to illuminate the art of medicine. Thus the concept of Sol has not a little to do with the growth of modern consciousness, which in the last two centuries has relied more and more on the observation and experience of natural objects. Sol therefore seems to denote an important psychological fact. Consequently, it is well worthwhile delineating its peculiarities in greater detail on the basis of the very extensive literature.

117   Generally Sol is regarded as the masculine and active half of Mercurius, a supraordinate concept whose psychology I have discussed in a separate study.[44] Since, in his alchemical form, Mercurius does not exist in reality, he must be an unconscious projection, and because he is an absolutely fundamental concept in alchemy he must signify the unconscious itself. He is by his very nature the unconscious, where nothing can be differentiated; but, as a *spiritus vegetativus* (living spirit), he is an active principle and so must always appear in reality in differentiated form. He is therefore fittingly called 'duplex', both active and passive. The 'ascending', active part of him is called Sol, and it is only through this that the passive part can be perceived. The passive part therefore bears the name of Luna, because she borrows her light from the sun.[45] Mercurius demonstrably corresponds to the cosmic Nous of the classical philosophers. The human mind is a derivative of this and so, likewise, is the diurnal life of the psyche, which we call consciousness.[46] Consciousness requires as its necessary counterpart a dark, latent, non-manifest side,

the unconscious, whose presence can be known only by the light of consciousness.[47]

218   Luna is thus the sum and essence of the metals' natures, which are all taken up in her shimmering whiteness. She is multi-natured, whereas Sol has an exceptional nature as the 'seventh from the six spiritual metals'. He is 'in himself nothing other than pure fire'.[48] This role of Luna devolves upon the *anima*, as she personifies the plurality of archetypes, and also upon the Church and the Blessed Virgin, who, both of lunar nature, gather the many under their protection and plead for them before the *Sol iustitiae*. Luna is the 'universal receptacle of all things', the 'first gateway of heaven',[49] and William Mennens[50] says that she gathers the powers of all the stars in herself as in a womb, so as then to bestow them on sublunary creatures.[51] This quality seems to explain her alleged effect in the *opus ad Lunam*, where she gives the tincture the character and powers of all the stars. The 'Fragment from the Persian Philosphers' says: 'With this tincture all the dead are revived, so that they live for ever, and this tincture is the first created ferment,[52] namely that "to the moon",[53] and it is the light of all lights and the flower and fruit of all lights,[54] which lighteth all things.'[55]

219   This almost hymn-like paean to the *materia lapidis* or the tincture refers in the first instance to Luna, for it is during her work of whitening that the illumination takes place. She is the 'mother in this art'. In her water 'Sol is hidden like a fire'[56] – a parallel to the conception of Selene as the μήτηρ τοῦ κόσμου [mother of the world] in Plutarch. On the first day of the month of Phamenoth, Osiris enters into Selene, and this is evidently equivalent to the synodos in the spring. 'Thus they make the power of Osiris to be fixed in the moon.'[57] Selene, Plutarch says, is male– female and is impregnated by Helios. I mention these statements because they show that the moon has a double light, outside a feminine one but inside a masculine one which is hidden in it as a fire. Luna is really the mother of the sun, which means, psychologically, that the unconscious is pregnant with consciousness and gives birth to it. It is the night, which is older than the day:

> Part of the darkness which gave birth to light,
> That proud light which is struggling to usurp
> The ancient rank and realm of Mother Night.[58]

220   From the darkness of the unconscious comes the light of illumination, the *albedo*. The opposites are contained in it *in potentia*, hence the hermaphroditism of the unconscious, its capacity for spontaneous and autochthonous reproduction. This idea is reflected in the 'Father–Mother' of the Gnostics,[59] as well as in the naive vision of Brother Klaus[60] and the modern vision of Maitland,[61] the biographer of Anna Kingsford.

329   As to the importance of salt in the *opus*, Johannes Grasseus says of the

arcane substance: 'And this is the Lead of the Philosophers, which they also call the lead of the air. In it is found the shining white dove, named the salt of the metals, wherein is the whole magistery of the work. This [dove] is the pure, chaste, wise and rich Queen of Sheba.'[62] Here salt, arcane substance (the paradoxical 'lead of the air'), the white dove (*spiritus sapientiae*), wisdom and femininity appear in one figure. The saying from the 'Gloria mundi' is quite clear: 'No man can understand this Art who does not know the salt and its preparation.'[63] For the 'Aquarium sapientum' the *sal sapientiae* comes from the *aqua benedicta* or *aqua pontica*, which, itself an extract, is named 'heart, soul and spirit'. At first the *aqua* is contained in the *prima materia* and is 'of a blood-red colour; but after its preparation it becomes of a bright, clear, transparent white, and is called by the sages the Salt of Wisdom'.[64] Khunrath boldly summarizes these statements about the salt when he says: 'Our water cannot be made without the salt of wisdom, for it is the salt of wisdom itself, say the philosophers; a fire and a salt fire, the true Living Universal Menstruum.' 'Without salt the work has no success.'[65] Elsewhere he remarks: 'Not without good reason has salt been adorned by the wise with the name of Wisdom.' Salt is the *lapis*, a 'mystery to be hidden'.[66] Vigenerus says that the Redeemer chose his disciples 'that they might be the salt of men and proclaim to them the pure and incorruptible doctrine of the gospel'. He reports the 'Cabalists' as saying that the *computatio*[67] of the Hebrew word for salt (*melach*) gives the number 78. This number could be divided by any divisor and still give a word that referred to the divine Name. We will not pursue the inferences he draws from this but will only note that for all those reasons salt was used 'for the service of God in all offerings and sacrifices'.[68] Glauber calls Christ the *sal sapientiae* and says that his favourite disciple John was 'salted with the salt of wisdom'.[69]

134   Because of the singular role it plays in alchemy, sulphur deserves to be examined rather more closely. The first point of interest, which we have already touched on, is its relation to Sol: it was called the *prima materia* of Sol, Sol being naturally understood as the gold. As a matter of fact, sulphur was sometimes identified with gold.[70] Sol therefore derives from sulphur. The close connection between them explains the view that sulphur was the 'companion of Luna'.[71] When the gold (Sol) and his bride (Luna) are united, 'the coagulating sulphur, which in the corporal gold was turned outwards [*extraversum*], is turned inwards [i.e. introverted].[72] This remark indicates the psychic double nature of sulphur (*sulphur duplex*); there is a red and a white sulphur, the white being the active substance of the moon, the red that of the sun.[73] The specific 'virtue' of sulphur is said to be greater in the red variety.[74] But its duplicity also has another meaning: on the one hand it is the *prima materia*, and in this form it is burning and corrosive (*adurens*), and 'hostile' to the matter of the stone; on the other hand, when

'cleansed of all impurities, it is the matter of our stone'.[75] Altogether, sulphur is one of the innumerable synonyms for the *prima materia*[76] in its dual aspect, i.e. as both the initial material and the end-product. At the beginning it is 'crude' or 'common' sulphur, at the end it is a sublimation product of the process.[77]

138   In view of the significance of sulphur it is worth our while to take a look at its effects as described by the alchemists. Above all, it burns and consumes: 'The little power of this sulphur is sufficient to consume a strong body.'[78] The 'strong body' is the sun, as is clear from the saying 'Sulphur blackens the sun and consumes it.' Then, it causes or signifies the *putrefactio*, 'which in our day was never seen', says the *Rosarium*.[79] A third capacity is that of coagulating,[80] and a fourth and fifth those of tincturing (*tingere, colorare*) and maturing (*maturare*).[81] Its 'putrefying' effect is also understood as its ability to 'corrupt'. Sulphur is the 'cause of imperfection in all metals', the 'corrupter of perfection', 'causing the blackness in every operation'; 'too much sulphurousness is the cause of corruption', it is 'bad and not well mixed', of an 'evil, stinking odour and of feeble strength'. Its substance is dense and tough and its corruptive action is due on the one hand to its combustibility and on the other to its 'earthy feculence'. 'It hinders perfection in all its works.'[82]

139   These unfavourable accounts evidently impressed one of the adepts so much that, in a marginal note, he added 'diabolus' to the *causae corruptionis*.[83] This remark is illuminating: it forms the counterpoint to the luminous role of sulphur, for sulphur is a 'Lucifer' or 'Phosphorus' (light-bringer), from the most beautiful star in the chymic firmament down to the *candelulae*, 'little bits of sulphurous tow such as old women sell for lighting fires'.[84] In addition to so many other qualities, sulphur shares this extreme paradox with Mercurius, besides having like him a connection with Venus, though here the allusion is veiled and more discreet: 'Our Venus is not the common sulphur, which burns and is consumed with the combustion of the fire and of the corruption; but the whiteness of Venus of the Sages is consumed with the combustion of the white and the red [*albedinis et rubedinis*], and this combustion is the entire whitening [*dealbatio*] of the whole work. Therefore two sulphurs are mentioned and two quicksilvers,[85] and these the Philosophers have named one and one,[86] and they rejoice in one another,[87] and the one contains the other.'[88]

151   I would like to conclude my remarks on sulphur. This arcane substance has provided occasion for some general reflections, which are not altogether fortuitous in that sulphur represents the active substance of the sun or, in psychological language, the *motive factor in consciousness*: on the one hand the will, which can best be regarded as a dynamism subordinated to consciousness, and on the other hand compulsion, an involuntary motivation or impulse ranging from mere interest to possession proper. The unconscious dynamism would correspond to sulphur, for

compulsion is the great mystery of human life. It is the thwarting of our conscious will and of our reason by an inflammable element within us, appearing now as a consuming fire and now as life-giving warmth.

152   The *causa efficiens et finalis* of this lack of freedom lies in the unconscious and forms that part of the personality which still has to be added to the conscious man in order to make him whole. At first sight it is but an insignificant fragment – a *lapis exilis, in via eiectus* [an insignificant stone, cast in the road], and often inconvenient and repellent because it stands for something that demonstrates quite plainly our secret inferiority. This aspect is responsible for our resistance to psychology in general and to the unconscious in particular. But together with this fragment, which could round out our consciousness into a whole, there is in the unconscious an already existing wholeness, the *homo totus* of the Western and the *Chên-yên* (true man) of Chinese alchemy, the round primordial who represents the greater man within, the Anthropos, who is akin to God. This inner man is of necessity partly unconscious, because consciousness is only part of a man and cannot comprehend the whole. But the whole man is always present, for the fragmentation of the phenomenon 'Man' is nothing but an effect of consciousness, which consists only of supraliminal ideas. No psychic content can become conscious unless is possesses a certain energy-charge. If this falls, the content sinks below the threshold and becomes unconscious. The possible contents of consciousness are then sorted out, as the energy-charge separates those capable of becoming conscious from those that are not. This separation gives rise on the one hand to consciousness, whose symbol is the sun, and on the other hand to the shadow, corresponding to the *umbra solis.*

153   Compulsion, therefore, has two sources: the shadow and the Anthropos. This is sufficient to explain the paradoxical nature of sulphur: as the 'corrupter' it has affinities with the devil, while on the other hand it appears as a parallel of Christ.

From: 'The Psychology of the Transference' (1946) (*CW* 16)

353   The fact that the idea of the mystic marriage plays such an important part in alchemy is not so surprising when we remember that the term most frequently employed for it, *coniunctio*, referred in the first place to what we now call chemical combination, and that the substances or 'bodies' to be combined were drawn together by what we would call affinity. In days gone by, people used a variety of terms which all expressed a human, and more particularly an erotic, relationship, such as *nuptiae, matrimonium, coniugium, amicitia, attractio, adulatio*. Accordingly the bodies to be combined were thought of as *agens et patiens*, as *vir* or *masculus*, and as

femina, mulier, femineus; or they were described more picturesquely as dog and bitch,[89] horse (stallion) and donkey,[90] cock and hen,[91] and as the winged and wingless dragon.[92] The more anthropomorphic and theriomorphic the terms become, the more obvious is the part played by creative fantasy and thus by the unconscious, and the more we see how the natural philosphers of old were tempted, as their thoughts explored the dark, unknown qualities of matter, to slip away from a strictly chemical investigation and to fall under the spell of the 'myth of matter'. Since there can never be absolute freedom from prejudice, even the most objective and impartial investigator is liable to become the victim of some unconscious assumption upon entering a region where the darkness has never been illuminated and where he can recognize nothing. This need not necessarily be a misfortune, since the idea which then presents itself as a substitute for the unknown will take the form of an archaic though not inapposite analogy. Thus Kekulé's vision of the dancing couples,[93] which first put him on the track of the structure of certain carbon compounds, namely the benzene ring, was surely a vision of the *coniunctio*, the mating that had preoccupied the minds of the alchemists for seventeen centuries. It was precisely this image that had always lured the mind of the investigator away from the problem of chemistry and back to the ancient myth of the royal or divine marriage; but in Kekulé's vision it reached its chemical goal in the end, thus rendering the greatest imaginable service both to our understanding of organic compounds and to the subsequent unprecedented advances in synthetic chemistry. Looking back, we can say that the alchemists had keen noses when they made this *arcanum arcanorum* [mystery of mysteries],[94] this *donum Dei et secretum altissimi* [gift of God and secret of the Most High],[95] this inmost mystery of the art of gold-making, the climax of their work. The subsequent confirmation of the other idea central to gold-making – the transmutability of chemical elements – also takes a worthy place in this belated triumph of alchemical thought. Considering the eminently practical and theoretical importance of these two key ideas, we might well conclude that they were intuitive anticipations whose fascination can be explained in the light of later developments.

354   We find, however, that alchemy did not merely change into chemistry by gradually discovering how to break away from its mythological premises, but that it also became, or had always been, a kind of mystic philosphy. The idea of the *coniunctio* served on the one hand to shed light on the mystery of chemical combination, while on the other it became the symbol of the *unio mystica*, since, as a mythologem, it expresses the archetype of the union of opposites. Now the archetypes do not represent anything external, non-psychic, although they do of course owe the concreteness of their imagery to impressions received from without. Rather, independently of, and sometimes in direct contrast to, the outward forms they may take, they represent the life and essence of a non-individual psyche. Although this psyche is innate in every individual it can

be neither modified nor possessed by him personally. It is the same in the individual as it is in the crowd and ultimately in everybody. It is the precondition of each individual psyche, just as the sea is the carrier of the individual wave.

355   The alchemical image of the *coniunctio*, whose practical importance was proved at a later stage of development, is equally valuable from the psychological point of view: that is to say, it plays the same role in the exploration of the darkness of the psyche as it played in the investigation of the riddle of matter. Indeed, it could never have worked so effectively in the material world had it not already possessed the power to fascinate and thus to fix the attention of the investigator along those lines. The *coniunctio* is an *a priori* image that occupies a prominent place in the history of man's mental development. If we trace this idea back we find it has two sources in alchemy, one Christian, the other pagan. The Christian source is unmistakably the doctrine of Christ and the Church, *sponsus* and *sponsa*, where Christ takes the role of Sol and the Church that of Luna.[97] The pagan source is on the one hand the *hieros gamos*,[98] on the other the marital union of the mystic with God.[99] These psychic experiences and the traces they have left behind in tradition explain much that would otherwise be totally unintelligible in the strange world of alchemy and its secret language.

356   As we have said, the image of the *coniunctio* has always occupied an important place in the history of the human mind. Recent developments in medical psychology have, through observation of the mental processes in neuroses and psychoses, forced us to become more and more thorough in our investigation of the psychic background, commonly called the unconscious. It is psychotherapy above all that makes such investigations necessary, because it can no longer be denied that morbid disturbances of the psyche are not to be explained exclusively by the changes going on in the body or in the conscious mind; we must adduce a third factor by way of explanation, namely hypothetical unconscious processes.[100]

357   Practical analysis has shown that unconscious contents are invariably projected at first upon concrete persons and situations. Many projections can ultimately be integrated back into the individual once he has recognized their subjective origin; others resist integration, and although they may be detached from their original objects, they thereupon transfer themselves to the doctor. Among these contents the relation to the parent of opposite sex plays a particularly important part, i.e. the relation of son to mother, daughter to father, and also that of brother to sister.[101] As a rule this complex cannot be integrated completely, since the doctor is nearly always put in the place of the father, the brother, and even (though naturally more rarely) the mother. Experience has shown that this projection persists with all its original intensity (which Freud regarded as aetiological), thus creating a bond that corresponds in every respect to the initial infantile relationship, with a tendency to recapitulate all the experiences of childhood on the doctor. In other words, the neurotic

maladjustment of the patient is now *transferred* to him.[102] Freud, who was the first to recognize and describe this phenomenon, coined the term 'transference neurosis'.[103]

358   This bond is often of such intensity that we could almost speak of a 'combination'. When two chemical substances combine, both are altered. This is precisely what happens in the transference. Freud rightly recognized that this bond is of the greatest therapeutic importance in that it gives rise to a *mixtum compositum* of the doctor's own mental health and the patient's maladjustment. In Freudian technique the doctor tries to ward off the transference as much as possible – which is understandable enough from the human point of view, though in certain cases it may considerably impair the therapeutic effect. It is inevitable that the doctor should be influenced to a certain extent and even that his nervous health should suffer.[104] He quite literally 'takes over' the sufferings of his patient and shares them with him. For this reason he runs a risk – and must run it in the nature of things.[105] The enormous importance that Freud attached to the transference phenomenon became clear to me at our first personal meeting in 1907. After a conversation lasting many hours there came a pause. Suddenly he asked me out of the blue, 'And what do you think about the transference?' I replied with the deepest conviction that it was the alpha and omega of the analytical method, whereupon he said, 'Then you have grasped the main thing.'

359   The great importance of the transference has often led to the mistaken idea that it is absolutely indispensable for a cure, that it must be demanded from the patient, so to speak. But a thing like that can no more be demanded than faith, which is only valuable when it is spontaneous. Enforced faith is nothing but spiritual cramp. Anyone who thinks that he must 'demand' a transference is forgetting that this is only one of the therapeutic factors, and that the very word 'transference' is closely akin to 'projection' – a phenomenon that cannot possibly be demanded.[106] I personally am always glad when there is only a mild transference or when it is practically unnoticeable. Far less claim is then made upon one as a person, and one can be satisfied with other therapeutically effective factors. Among these the patient's own insight plays an important part, also his goodwill, the doctor's authority, suggestion,[107] good advice,[108] understanding, sympathy, encouragement, etc. Naturally the more serious cases do not come into this category.

360   Careful analysis of the transference phenomenon yields an extremely complicated picture with such startlingly pronounced features that we are often tempted to pick out one of them as the most important and then exclaim by way of explanation: 'Of course, it's nothing but . . . !' I am referring chiefly to the erotic or sexual aspect of transference fantasies. The existence of this aspect is undeniable, but it is not always the only one and not always the essential one. Another is the will to power (described by Adler), which proves to be coexistent with sexuality, and it is often

very difficult to make out which of the two predominates. These two aspects alone offer sufficient grounds for a paralysing conflict.

361   There are, however, other forms of instinctive *concupiscentia* that come more from 'hunger', from wanting to possess; others again are based on the instinctive negation of desire, so that life seems to be founded on fear or self-destruction. A certain *abaissement du niveau mental* [lowering of mental level], i.e. a weakness in the hierarchical order of the ego, is enough to set these instinctive urges and desires in motion and bring about a dissociation of personality – in other words, a multiplication of its centres of gravity. (In schizophrenia there is an actual fragmentation of personality.) These dynamic components must be regarded as real or symptomatic, vitally decisive or merely syndromal, according to the degree of their predominance. Although the strongest instincts undoubtedly demand concrete realization and generally enforce it, they cannot be considered exclusively biological since the course they actually follow is subject to powerful modifications coming from the personality itself. If a man's temperament inclines him to a spiritual attitude, even the concrete activity of the instincts will take on a certain symbolical character. This activity is no longer the mere satisfaction of instinctual impulses, for it is now associated with or complicated by 'meanings'. In the case of purely syndromal instinctive processes, which do not demand concrete realization to the same extent, the symbolical character of their fulfilment is all the more marked. The most vivid examples of these complications are probably to be found in erotic phenomenology. Four stages of eroticism were known in the late classical period: Hawwah (Eve), Helen (of Troy), the Virgin Mary, and Sophia. The series is repeated in Goethe's *Faust*: in the figures of Gretchen as the personification of a purely instinctual relationship (Eve); Helen as an *anima* figure;[109] Mary as the personification of the 'heavenly', i.e. Christian or religious, relationship; and the 'eternal feminine' as an expression of the alchemical Sapientia. As the nomenclature shows, we are dealing with the heterosexual Eros or anima-figure in four stages, and consequently with four stages of the Eros cult. The first stage – Hawwah, Eve, earth – is purely biological; woman is equated with the mother and only represents something to be fertilized. The second stage is still dominated by the sexual Eros, but on an aesthetic and romantic level where woman has already acquired some value as an individual. The third stage raises Eros to the heights of religious devotion and thus spiritualizes him: Hawwah has been replaced by spiritual motherhood. Finally, the fourth stage illustrates something which unexpectedly goes beyond the almost unsurpassable third stage: Sapientia. How can wisdom transcend the most holy and the most pure? Presumably only by virtue of the truth that the less sometimes means the more. This stage represents a spiritualization of Helen and consequently of Eros as such. That is why Sapientia was regarded as a parallel to the Shulamite in the Song of Songs.

From: 'The Conjunction', *Mysterium coniunctionis* (1955–6) (*CW* 14)

654   Herbert Silberer rightly called the *coniunctio* the 'central idea' of the alchemical procedure.[110] This author correctly recognized that alchemy was, in the main, symbolical, whereas the historian of alchemy Eduard von Lippmann, a chemist, did not mention the term *coniunctio* even in his index.[111] Anyone who has but a slight acquaintance with the literature knows that the adepts were ultimately concerned with a union of the substances – by whatever names these may have been called. By means of this union they hoped to attain the goal of the work: the production of the gold or a symbolical equivalent of it. Although the *coniunctio* is unquestionably the primordial image of what we today would call chemical combination, it is hardly possible to prove beyond a doubt that the adept thought as concretely as the modern chemist. Even when he spoke of a union of the 'natures', or of an 'amalgam' of iron and copper, or of a compound of sulphur and mercury, he meant it at the same time as a symbol: iron was Mars and copper was Venus, and their fusion was at the same time a love-affair. The union of the 'natures' which 'embrace one another' was not physical and concrete, for they were 'celestial natures' which multiplied 'by the command of God'.[112] When 'red lead' was roasted with gold it produced a 'spirit', that is, the compound became 'spiritual',[113] and from the 'red spirit' proceeded the 'principle of the world'.[114] The combination of sulphur and mercury was followed by the 'bath' and 'death'.[115] By the combination of copper and *aqua permanens*, which was usually quicksilver, we think only of an amalgam. But for the alchemists it meant a secret, 'philosphical' sea, since for them the *aqua permanens* was primarily a symbol or a philosphical postulate which they hoped to discover – or believed they had discovered – in the various 'fluids'. The substances they sought to combine in reality always had – on account of their unknown nature – a numinous quality which tended towards phantasmal personification. They were substances which, like living organisms, 'fertilized one another and thereby produced the living being sought by the Philosophers'.[116] The substances seemed to them hermaphroditic, and the conjunction they strove for was a philosphical operation, namely the union of form and matter.[117] This inherent duality explains the duplications that so often occur, e.g. two sulphurs, two quicksilvers.[118]

658   The *coniunctio* does not always take the form of a direct union, since it needs – or occurs in – a medium: 'Only through a medium can the transition take place',[119] and 'Mercurius is the medium of conjunction.'[120] Mercurius is the soul (*anima*), which is the 'mediator between body and spirit'.[121] The same is true of the synonyms for Mercurius, the green lion[122] and the *aqua permanens* or spiritual water,[123] which are likewise media of conjunction. The *Consilium coniugii* mentions as a connective agent the sweet smell or 'smoky vapour',[124] recalling Basilides' idea of the sweet

smell of the Holy Ghost.[125] Obviously this refers to the 'spiritual' nature of Mercurius, just as the spiritual water, also called *aqua aëris* (aerial water or air–water), is a life-principle and the 'marriage-maker' between man and woman.[126] A common synonym for the water is the 'sea', as the place where the chymical marriage is celebrated.

659   Mercurius, however, is not just the medium of conjunction but also that which is to be united, since he is the essence or 'seminal matter' of both man and woman. *Mercurius masculinus* and *Mercurius foemineus* are united in and through *Mercurius menstrualis*, which is the 'aqua'.[127] Dorn gives the 'philosphical' explanation of this in his *Physica Trismegisti*: In the beginning God created *one* world (*unus mundus*).[128] This he divided into two – heaven and earth. 'Beneath this spiritual and corporeal binarius lieth hid a third thing, which is the bond of holy matrimony. This same is the medium enduring until now in all things, partaking of both their extremes, without which it cannot be at all, nor they without this medium be what they are, one thing out of three.'[129] The division into two was necessary in order to bring the 'one' world out of the state of potentiality into reality. Reality consists of a multiplicity of things. But one is not a number; the first number is two, and with it multiplicity and reality begin.

172   Psychologically, the union of consciousness (Sol) with its feminine counterpart the unconscious (Luna) has undesirable results to begin with: it produces poisonous animals such as the dragon, serpent, scorpion, basilisk and toad;[130] then the lion, bear, wolf, dog,[131] and finally the eagle[132] and the raven. The first to appear are the cold-blooded animals, then warm-blooded predators, and lastly birds of prey or ill-omened scavengers. The first progeny of the *matrimonium luminarium* are all, therefore, rather unpleasant. But that is only because there is an evil darkness in both parents which comes to light in the children, as indeed often happens in real life. I remember, for instance, the case of a twenty-year-old bank clerk who embezzled several hundred francs. His old father, the chief cashier at the same bank, was much pitied, because for forty years he had discharged his highly responsible duties with exemplary loyalty. Two days after the arrest of his son he decamped to South America with a million. So there must have been 'something in the family'. We have seen in the case of Sol that he either possesses a shadow or is even a *Sol niger*. As to the position of Luna, we have already been told what this is when we discussed the new moon. In the 'Epistola Solis ad Lunam crescentem'[133] Sol cautiously says: 'If you do me no hurt, O moon.'[134] Luna has promised him complete dissolution while she herself 'coagulates', i.e. becomes firm, and is clothed with his blackness (*induta fuero nigredine tua*).[135] She assumes in the friendliest manner that her blackness comes from *him*. The matrimonial wrangle has already begun. Luna is the 'shadow of the sun, and with corruptible bodies she is consumed, and through her corruption . . . is the Lion eclipsed'.[136]

173   According to the ancient view, the moon stands on the borderline between the eternal, ethereal things and the ephemeral phenomena of the earthly, sublunar realm.[137] Macrobius says: 'The realm of the perishable begins with the moon and goes downwards. Souls coming into this region begin to be subject to the numbering of days and to time. . . . There is no doubt that the moon is the author and contriver of mortal bodies.'[138] Because of her moist nature, the moon is also the cause of decay.[139] The loveliness of the new moon, hymned by the poets and Church Fathers, veils her dark side, which, however, could not remain hidden from the fact-finding of the empiricist.[140] The moon, as the star nearest to the earth, partakes of the earth and its sufferings, and her analogy with the Church and the Virgin Mary as mediators has the same meaning.[141] She partakes not only of the earth's sufferings but of its daemonic darkness as well.[142]

From: 'The Components of the Coniunctio', *Mysterium coniunctionis* (1955–6) (*CW* 14)

15   The *Turba* says (Sermo LIX):

Nevertheless the Philosophers have put to death the woman who slays her husbands, for the body of that woman is full of weapons and poison. Let a grave be dug for that dragon, and let that woman be buried with him, he being chained fast to that woman; and the more he winds and coils himself about her, the more will he be cut to pieces by the female weapons which are fashioned in the body of the woman. And when he sees that he is mingled with the limbs of the woman, he will be certain of death, and will be changed wholly into blood. But when the Philosophers see him changed into blood, they leave him a few days in the sun, until his softness is consumed, and the blood dries, and they find that poison. What then appears, is the hidden wind.[143]

The *coniunctio* can therefore take more gruesome forms than the relatively harmless one depicted in the *Rosarium*.[144]

From: 'The Psychology of the Transference' (1946) (*CW* 16)

465   The reader should not imagine that the psychologist is in any position to explain what 'higher copulation' is, or the *coniunctio*, or 'psychic pregnancy', let alone the 'soul's child'. Nor should one feel annoyed if the newcomer to this delicate subject, or one's own cynical self, gets disgusted with these – as he thinks them – phoney ideas and brushes them aside with a pitying smile and an offensive display of tact. The unprejudiced scientific

inquirer who seeks the truth and nothing but the truth must guard against rash judgements and interpretations, for here he is confronted with *psychological facts* which the intellect cannot falsify and conjure out of existence. There are among one's patients intelligent and discerning persons who are just as capable as the doctor of giving the most disparaging interpretations, but who cannot avail themselves of such a weapon in the face of these insistent facts. Words like 'nonsense' only succeed in banishing little things – not the things that thrust themselves tyrannically upon you in the stillness and loneliness of the night. The images welling up from the unconscious do precisely that. What we choose to call this fact does not affect the issue in any way. If it is an illness, then this *morbus sacer* must be treated according to its nature. The doctor can solace himself with the reflection that he, like the rest of his colleagues, does not only have patients who are curable, but chronic ones as well, where curing becomes nursing. At all events the empirical material gives us no sufficient grounds for always talking about 'illness'; on the contrary, one comes to realize that it is a moral problem and often one wishes for a priest who, instead of confessing and proselytizing, would just listen, obey and put this singular matter before God so that He could decide.

466   *Patientia et mora* [patience and lack of haste] are absolutely necessary in this kind of work. One must be able to wait on events. Of work there is plenty – the careful analysis of dreams and other unconscious contents. Where the doctor fails, the patient will fail too, which is why the doctor should possess a real knowledge of these things and not just opinions, the offscourings of our modern philosphy for everyman. In order to augment this much-needed knowledge, I have carried my researches back to those earlier times when naive introspection and projection were still at work, mirroring a psychic hinterland that is virtually blocked for us today. In this way I have learned much for my own practice, especially as regards understanding the formidable fascination of the contents in question. These may not always strike the patient as particularly fascinating, so he suffers instead from a proportionately strong compulsive tie in whose intensity he can rediscover the force of those subliminal images. He will, however, try to interpret the tie rationalistically, in the spirit of the age, and consequently does not perceive and will not admit the irrational foundations of his transference, namely the archetypal images.

NOTES

1 Ripley says: 'The coniunctio is the uniting of separated qualities or an equalizing of principle' ('Duodecim portarum axiomata philosophica', *Theatr. chem.*, II, p. 128).
2 Cf. The representation of the *tetrameria* in Stolcius de Stolcenberg, *Viridarium chymicum*, fig. XLII.
3 Cf. 'Consilium coniugii', *Ars chemica*, p. 79: 'In this stone are the four elements, and it is to be compared to the world and the composition of the world'; also

Michael Maier, *De circulo physico quadrato*, p. 17: 'Nature, I say, when she turned about the golden circle, by that movement made its four qualities equal, that is to say, she squared that homogeneous simplicity turning back on itself, or brought it into an equilateral rectangle, in such a way that contraries are bound together by contraries, and enemies by enemies, as if with everlasting bonds, and are held in mutual embrace.' Petrus Bonus says: 'The elements are conjoined in the circle in true friendship' (*Bibliotheca chemica*, II, p. 35).

4 Cf. John Dee, 'Monas hieroglyphica', *Theatr. chem.*, II, p. 220.

5 Cf. 'Consilium coniugii', *Ars chemica*, pp. 69f., and 'Clangor buccinae', *Artis auriferae*, I, p. 484. In the Cabala the situation is reversed: red denotes the female, white (the left side) the male. Cf. Mueller, *Der Sohar und seine Lehre*, pp. 20f.

6 'Aenigmata ex visione Arislei', *Art. aurif.*, I, pp. 146ff. Union of sun and moon: Petrus Bonus (ed. Lacinius), *Pretiosa margarita novella* (1546), p. 112. The archetype of the heavenly marriage plays a great role here. On a primitive level this motif can be found in shamanism. Cf. Eliade, *Shamanism*, p. 75.

7 The most complete collection of the illustrations that appeared in printed works is Stolcius de Stolcenberg's *Viridarium chymicum figuris cupro incisis adornatum* (Frankfurt, 1624).

8 *Symbola aureae mensae*, p. 192.

9 The 'treasure-house' (*gazophylacium, domus thesauraria*) of philosophy, which is a synonym for the *aurum philosophorum*, or lapis. Cf. von Franz, *Aurora consurgens*, pp. 101ff. The idea goes back to Alphidius (see 'Consilium coniugii', *Ars chemica*, p. 108) and ultimately to Zosimos, who describes the *lapis* as a shining white temple of marble (Berthelot, *Alch. grecs*, III, i, 5).

10 *Symb. aur. mensae*, p. 200.

11 The printing is undated, but it probably comes from Samuel Emmel's press at Strasbourg and may be contemporaneous with *Ars chemica*, which was printed there in 1566 and matches our libellus as regards type, paper and format. The author, Senior Zadish filius Hamuel, may perhaps have been one of the Harranites of the tenth century, or at least have been influenced by them. If the *Clavis maioris sapientiae* mentioned by Stapleton ('Muhammad bin Umail: His Date, Writings, and Place in Alchemical History') is identical with the Latin treatise of the same name, traditionally ascribed to Artefius, this could be taken as proved, since that treatise contains a typical Harranite astral theory. Ruska ('Studien zu M. ibn Umail') groups Senior with the *Turba* literature that grew up on Egyptian soil.

12 Senior says: 'I joined the two luminaries in marriage and it became as water having two lights' (*De chemia*, pp. 15f.).

13 *Musaeum hermeticum*, p. 343. (Cf. Waite, *The Hermetic Museum Restored and Enlarged*, I, pp. 276f.)

14 *Corpus* (as *corpus nostrum*) usually means the chemical 'body' or 'substance', but morally it means the human body. 'Sea' is a common symbol of the unconscious. In alchemy, therefore, the 'body' would also symbolize the unconscious.

15 'Aenigmata philosophorum II', *Art. aurif.*, I, p. 149. Cf. *Aion*, paras 195, 213 n. 51.

16 See *Psychology and Alchemy*, fig. 240.

17 They also appear in the 'XI Clavis' of Basilius Valentinus, *Chymische Schrifften*, p. 68, and in *Viridarium*, figs XI, LV, LXII. Variants are lion and snake (*Viridarium*, fig. XII), lion and bird (fig. LXXIV), lion and bear (figs XCIII and CVI).

18 Cf. Petrus Bonus, 'Pretiosa margarita novella', *Theatr. chem.*, V, pp. 647f.: 'Hermes: At the end of the world heaven and earth must be joined together, which is the philosophical word.' Also *Mus. herm.*, p. 803 (Waite, II, p. 263).

19 Ms Incipit: 'Figurarum Aegyptiorum Secretarum' (18th cent.; author's collection).
20 'Thus the height is hidden and the depth is made manifest' (*Mus. herm.*, p. 652).
21 Cf. the oft-repeated saying: 'From the dead he makes the living' (Mylius, *Philosophia reformata*, p. 191).
22 'Visio Arislei', *Art. aurif.*, I, pp. 146ff.
23 Maier, *Symb. aur. mensae*, p. 156.
24 Senior, *De chemia*, p. 92.
25 'Gold and silver in their metallic form are not the matter of our stone', ('Tractatus aureus', *Mus. herm.*, p. 32) (Waite, I, p. 33).
26 Because gold is not subject to oxidization, Sol is an arcanum described in the 'Consilium coniugii' as follows: 'A substance equal, permanent, fixed for the length of eternity' (*Ars chemica*, p. 58). 'For Sol is the root of incorruption', 'Verily there is no other foundation of the Art than the sun and its shadow' (ibid., p. 138).
27 Rupescissa, *La Vertu et la propriété de la quinte essence*, p. 19: 'Jceluy soleil est vray or . . ... L'or de Dieu est appelé par les Philosophes, Soleil; car il est fils du Soleil du Ciel, et est engendré par les influences du Soleil ès entrailles et veines de la terre.'
28 Sulphur is even identical with fire. Cf. 'Consil. coniugii' (*Ars chemica*, p. 217): 'Know therefore that sulphur is fire, that is, Sol.' In Mylius (*Phil. ref.*, p. 185) Sol is identical with sulphur, i.e. the alchemical Sol signifies the active substance of the sun or of the gold.
29 'Our Sol is ruddy and burning' (Zacharias, 'Opusculum', *Theatr. chem.*, I, p. 840). Bernardus Trevisanus goes so far as to say: 'Sol is nothing other than sulphur and quicksilver' (ibid., Flamel's annotations, p. 860).
30 Olympiodorus (Berthelot, *Alch. grecs*, II, iv, 43): 'Smear [with it] the leaves of the shining goddess, the red Cyprian.'
31 Cf. the sulphur parable, where the water is 'most dangerous'.
32 Hoghelande, *Theatr. chem.*, I, p. 181.
33 *Mus. herm.*, pp. 581f. (Waite, II, p. 107).
34 Steeb, *Coelum sephiroticum*, p. 50. Paracelsus, in 'De natura rerum' (Sudhoff, XI, p. 330), says: 'Now the life of man is none other than an astral balsam, a balsamic impression, a heavenly and invisible fire, an enclosed air' (*De vita longa*, ed. Bodenstein, fol. c 7ᵛ): '[Treating of a certain invisible virtue] he calls it balsam, surpassing all bodily nature, which preserves the two bodies by conjunction, and upholds the celestial body together with the four elements.'
35 Steeb, p. 117. The moon draws 'universal form and natural life' from the sun. (Dorn, 'Physica genesis', *Theatr. chem.*, I, p. 397).
36 *Theatr. chem.*, V. p. 130.
37 'It were vain to believe, as many do, that the sun is merely a heavenly fire' (Dorn, 'Physica Trismegisti', *Theatr. chem.*, I, p. 423).
38 The alchemists still believed with Proclus that the sun generates the gold. Cf. Proclus, *Commentaries on the Timaeus of Plato*, 18 B (tr. Taylor), I, p. 36.
39 Dorn ('Phys. Trismeg.', p. 423) says: 'As the fount of life of the human body, it is the centre of man's heart, or rather that secret thing which lies hid within it, wherein the natural heat is active.'
40 Zosimos (Berthelot, *Alch. grecs*, III, xxi, 3) cites the saying of Hermes: 'The sun is the maker of all things.'
41 'Phys. Trismeg.', p. 423. The Codex Berol. Lat. 532 (fol. 154ᵛ) says of the germ-cell of the egg: 'The sun-point, that is, the germ of the egg, which is in the yolk.'
42 'The first and most powerful male and universal seed is, by its nature, sulphur, the first and most powerful cause of all generation. Wherefore Paracelsus says that the sun and man through man generate man' (Dorn, ibid.).

43 The alchemical sun also rises out of the darkness of the earth, as in *Aurora consurgens*, pp. 125f.: 'This earth made the moon . . . then the sun arose . . . after the darkness which thou has appointed therein before the sunrise.'

44 'The Spirit Mercurius'.

45 Cf. the ancient idea that the sun corresponds to the right eye and the moon to the left (Olympiodorus in Berthelot, *Alch. grecs*, II, iv, 51).

46 Just as for the natural philosophers of the Middle Ages the sun was the god of the physical world, so the 'little god of the world' is consciousness.

47 Consciousness, like the sun, is an 'eye of the world' (cf. Pico della Mirandola, 'Disputationes adversus astrologos', lib. III, cap. X, p. 88^r.) In his *Heptaplus* (Expositio 7, cap. IV, p. 11^r) he says: 'Since Plato calls the Sun . . . the visible son of God, why do we not understand that we are the image of the invisible son? And if he is the true light enlightening every mind, he hath as his most express image this Sun, which is the light of the image enlightening every body.'

48 'Congeries Paracelsicae', *Theatr. chem.*, I, p. 642.

49 Penotus in 'De medicament. chem.', *Theatr. chem.*, I, p. 681.

50 'Aurei velleris Libri tres', *Theatr. chem.*, V, p. 321.

51 A parallel to the Maria Mediatrix of the Church, who dispenses grace.

52 Presumably ether as the *quinta essentia*.

53 The 'opus ad Lunam' is the whitening (*albedo*), which is compared with sunrise.

54 That is, of all luminaries, i.e. stars.

55 *Art. aurif.*, I, p. 398.

56 'Gloria mundi', *Mus. herm.*, p. 280 (Waite, I, p. 225).

57 'Isis and Osiris', 43, *Moralia* (tr. Babbitt, V, pp. 104f.).

58 Goethe, *Faust* (tr. MacNeice), p. 48 (mod.).

59 For instance, in Marcus the Gnostic. Cf. Hippolytus, *Elenchos*, VI, 42, 2 (Legge, II, p. 44).

60 Cf. 'Brother Klaus', pars. 485f.

61 *Anna Kingsford: Her Life, Letters, Diary, and Work*, I, p. 130. I have quoted this vision at some length in my 'Commentary on *The Secret of the Golden Flower*', para. 40.

62 'Arca arcani', *Theatr. chem.*, VI, p. 314.

63 *Mus. herm.*, p. 216 (Waite, I, p. 176).

64 *Mus. herm.*, p. 88 (Waite, I, p. 80).

65 *Hyleal. Chaos*, pp. 229, 254.

66 *Amphitheatrum*, p. 197. The *lapis*, however, corresponds to the self.

67 By 'computatio' is meant the 'isopsephia', that is, the sum which results from the numerical values of the letters in a word, this word being then equated with another word having the same numerical value.

68 'De igne et sale', *Theatr. chem.*, VI, pp. 129f.

69 *De natura salium*, pp. 25 and 51. Christ as *sal sapientiae* [salt of wisdom] is another symbol of the self.

70 Laurentius Ventura, 'De ratione confic. lap.', *Theatr. chem.*, II, pp. 334f.

71 'Figurarum Aegyptiorum', (MS, 18th cent., author's possession).

72 'Introitus apertus', *Mus. herm.*, p. 652 (Waite, II, p. 165).

73 'Tractatus aureus', *Mus. herm.*, p. 33 (Waite, I, p. 34); Mylius, *Phil. ref.*, p. 54.

74 Ventura, *Theatr. chem.*, II, p. 342.

75 'Tract. aureus', *Mus. herm.*, p. 24 (Waite, I, p. 26).

76 Ibid., pp. 11 and 21 (Waite, I, pp. 14 and 23); Aegidius de Vadis, 'Dialogus', *Theatr. chem.*, II, p. 100; Ripley, 'Axiomata philosophica', *Theatr. chem.*, II, p. 125.

77 Ripley, *Theatr. chem.*, II, p. 125. As *sulphur incremabile*, it is an end-product in *Theatr. chem.*, II, p. 302, and also in 'De sulphure', *Mus. herm.*, p. 622 (Waite II, p. 142).

78 *Turba*, p. 125, line 10.
79 *Art. aurif.*, II, p. 229.
80 Zacharius, 'Opusculum', *Theatr. chem.*, I, p. 842.
81 'De sulphure', *Mus. herm.*, p. 632 (Waite, II, p. 149).
82 Mylius, *Phil. ref.*, pp. 61ff.
83 In my copy of *Phil. ref.*, p. 62. In Glauber (*De natura salium*, pp. 41 and 43) sulphur is the 'exceeding black devil of hell' who quarrels with the salt.
84 'De sulphure', *Mus. herm.*, p. 640 (Waite, II, p. 155). *Candelulae* are 'Elychnia of Sulphur, in which threads or morsels of wood are inserted' (Ruland, *Lexicon*, Latin edn, p. 457).
85 The higher and the lower, the subtle and the coarse, the spiritual and the material.
86 They are one and the same, however. As above so below, and vice versa. Cf. *Tabula smaragdina*.
87 'Nature rejoices in nature', according to the axiom of Democritus.
88 An allusion to the *uroboros*. The text of this passage is in 'Rosinus ad Sarratantam', *Art. aurif.*, I, p. 302.
89 'Accipe canem corascenum masculum et caniculum Armeniae' ('Take a Corascene dog and an Armenian bitch') ('De alchimiae difficultatibus', *Theatr. chem.*, I, p. 163). A quotation from Kalid (in the *Rosarium*, *Artis auriferae*, II, p. 248) runs: 'Accipe canem coetaneum et catulam Armeniae' ('Take a Coetanean dog and an Armenian bitch'). In a magic papyrus, Selene (moon) is called κύων (bitch) (Paris MS Z 2280, in Preisendanz, *Papryi Graecae magicae*, I, p. 142). In Zosimos, dog and wolf (Berthelot, *Alch. grecs*, III, xii, 9). [No translation of the words *corascenum* and *coetaneum* has been attempted, as we are advised that they are probably corrupt, or may indicate geographical names. – EDITORS.]
90 Zosimos, in Berthelot, *Alch. grecs*, III, xii, 9.
91 The classical passage is to be found in Senior, *De chemia*, p. 8: 'Tu mei indiges, sicut gallus gallinae indiget' ('You need me as the cock needs the hen').
92 Numerous pictures exist in the literature.
93 Kekulé, *Lehrbuch der organischen Chemie*, I, pp. 624f., and Fierz-David, *Die Entwicklungsgeschichte der Chemie*, pp. 235ff.
94 Zacharias, 'Opusculum', *Theatr. chem.*, I, p. 826.
95 'Consilium coniugii', *Ars chemica*, p. 259. Cf. *Aurora consurgens*, I, ch. II: 'Est namque donum et sacramentum Dei atque res divina' ('For she [Wisdom] is a gift and sacrament of God and a divine matter').
96 This does not contradict the fact that the *coniunctio* motif owes its fascination primarily to its archetypal character.
97 Cf. the detailed account in Rahner, 'Mysterium lunae'.
98 A collection of the classical sources is to be found in Klinz, Ιερὸς γάμος.
99 Bousset, *Hauptprobleme der Gnosis*, pp. 69ff., 263f., 315ff.; Leisegang, *Der heilige Geist*, I, p. 235.
100 I call unconscious processes 'hypothetical' because the unconscious is by definition not amenable to direct observation and can only be inferred.
101 I am not considering the so-called homosexual forms, such as father–son, mother–daughter, etc. In alchemy, as far as I know, this variation is alluded to only once, in the 'Visio Arislei' (*Art. aurif.*, I, p. 147): 'Domine quamvis rex sis, male tamen imperas et regis: masculos namque masculis coniunxisti, sciens quod masculi non gignunt' ('Lord, though thou art king, yet thou rulest and governest badly; for thou has joined males with males, knowing that males do not produce offspring').
102 Freud says (*Introductory Lectures*, Part III, p. 455): 'The decisive part of the work is achieved by creating in the patient's relation to the doctor – in the 'transference' – new editions of the old conflicts; in these the patient would like to behave in the same way as he did in the past. . . . In place of the patient's true

illness there appears the artificially constructed transference illness, in place of the various unreal objects of his libido there appears a single, and once more imaginary, object in the person of the doctor.' It is open to doubt whether the transference is always constructed artificially, since it is a phenomenon that can take place quite apart from any treatment, and is moreover a very frequent natural occurrence. Indeed, in any human relationship that is at all intimate, certain transference phenomena will almost always operate as helpful or disturbing factors.

103 'Provided only that the patient shows compliance enough to respect the necessary conditions of the analysis, we regularly succeed in giving all the symptoms of the illness a new transference meaning and in replacing his ordinary neurosis by a "transference-neurosis"' ('Remembering, Repeating, and Working Through', p. 154.) Freud puts down a little too much to his own account here. A transference is not by any means always the work of the doctor. Often it is in full swing before he has even opened his mouth. Freud's conception of the transference as a 'new edition of the old disorder', a 'newly created and transformed neurosis', or a 'new, artificial neurosis' (*Introductory Lectures*, III, p. 444), is right in so far as the transference of a neurotic patient is equally neurotic, but this neurosis is neither new nor artificial nor created: it is the same old neurosis, and the only new thing about it is that the doctor is now drawn into the vortex, more as its victim than as its creator.

104 Freud had already discovered the phenomenon of the 'counter-transference'. Those acquainted with his technique will be aware of its marked tendency to keep the person of the doctor as far as possible beyond the reach of this effect. Hence the doctor's preference for sitting behind the patient, also his pretence that the transference is a product of his technique, whereas in reality it is a perfectly natural phenomenon that can happen to him just as it can happen to the teacher, the clergyman, the general practitioner and – last but not least – the husband. Freud also uses the expression 'transference-neurosis' as a collective term for hysteria, hysterical fears and compulsion neuroses (ibid., p. 445).

105 The effects of this on the doctor or nurse can be very far-reaching. I know of cases where, in dealing with borderline schizophrenics, short psychotic intervals were actually 'taken over', and during these periods it happened that the patients were feeling more than ordinarily well. I have even met a case of induced paranoia in a doctor who was analysing a woman patient in the early stages of latent persecution mania. This is not so astonishing since certain psychic disturbances can be extremely infectious if the doctor himself has a latent predisposition in that direction.

106 Freud himself says ('Observations on Transference-Love', p. 380) of this: 'I can hardly imagine a more senseless proceeding. In doing so, an analyst robs the phenomenon of the element of spontaneity which is so convincing and lays up obstacles for himself in the future which are hard to overcome.' Here Freud stresses the 'spontaneity' of the transference, in contrast to his views quoted above. Nevertheless those who 'demand' the transference can fall back on the following cryptic utterance of their master ('Fragment of an Analysis of a Case of Hysteria', p. 116): 'If the theory of analytic technique is gone into, it becomes evident that transference is [something necessarily demanded]' ['. . . that transference is an inevitable necessity', as in the authorized translation, is to stretch the meaning of Freud's 'etwas notwendig Gefordertes' – TRANS.]

107 Suggestion happens of its own accord, without the doctor's being able to prevent it or taking the slightest trouble to produce it.

108 'Good advice' is often a doubtful remedy, but generally not dangerous because it has so little effect. It is one of the things the public expects in the *persona medici*.

109 Simon Magus' Helen (Selene) is another excellent example.
110 *Problems of Mysticism and its Symbolism*, p. 121.
111 *Entstehung und Ausbreitung der Alchemie.*
112 *Turba*, ed. Ruska, p. 119.
113 Ibid., p. 127.
114 Ibid.
115 P. 126.
116 Berthelot, *Alch. grecs*, III, xI, 2.
117 Aegidius de Vadis, 'Dialogus' (*Theatr. chem.*, II, p. 99): 'But minerals and vegetables are of hermaphrodite nature in that they have twofold sex. Nonetheless, there comes about between them a conjunction of form and matter, as with animals.'
118 'Rosinus ad Sarratantam' (*Art. aurif.*, I, p. 302): 'Wherefore there are said to be two sulphurs and two quicksilvers, and they are such that they are called one and one, and they rejoice together, and the one contains the other.'
119 Dorn, 'Physica Trismegisti', *Theatr. chem.*, I, p. 418. Cf. his remark 'tertium esse necessarium' ('Congeries Paracelsicae', *Theatr. chem.*, I, p. 577).
120 Ventura, *Theatr. chem.*, II, p. 320.
121 Ibid., p. 332.
122 Ripley, 'Axiomata philosophica', *Theatr. chem.*, II, p. 125. Similarly in *Mus. herm.*, p. 39 (Waite, I, p. 42).
123 *Art. aurif.*, I, p. 281.
124 *Ars chemica*, p. 74. The counterpart of the 'Luna odorifera' mentioned here is the *odor sepulcrorum* (stench of the graves).
125 Μύρον εὐωδέστατον (Hippolytus, *Elenchos*, VII, 22, 14).
126 'The aerial water existing between earth and heaven is the life of everything. For that water dissolves the body into spirit, makes the dead to live, and brings about the marriage between man and woman.'
127 'Exercit. in Turbam', *Art. aurif.*, I, pp. 160f.
128 'In a way not unlike that in which God in the beginning created one world by meditation alone, so likewise he created one world, from which all things came into being by adaptation' (*Theatr. chem.*, I, p. 417).

   'Also, as there is only one God and not many, so he willed at first in his mind to create from nothing one world, and then to bring it about that all things which he created should be contained in it, that God in all things might be one' (ibid., p. 415).
129 Ibid., p. 418.
130 A milder form of these is the salamander.
131 Often mentioned as the 'Corascene dog' (sun) and the 'Armenian bitch' (moon).
132 Said to devour its own wings or feathers. The eagle is therefore a variant of the *uroboros*.
133 Senior, *De chemia*, p. 9.
134 Sol is mindful of the dangerous role of Luna: 'No one torments me but my sister' ('Exercitationes in Turbam', *Art. aurif.*, I, p. 173.
135 Song of Songs 1: 5, 'I am black, but comely', and 1: 6, 'I am black because the sun has burnt me' is sometimes quoted.
136 'Consil. coniugii', *Ars chemica*, p. 136.
137 *Commentary on the Dream of Scipio*, I, xxi, p. 181: 'The moon, being the boundary of ether and air, is also the demarcation between the divine and the mortal.'
138 Ibid., I, xi, p. 131.
139 The heat and dew of the moon 'turn flesh rotten' (Macrobius, *Saturnalia*, lib. VII, cap. XVI).
140 The empirical method of physicians is a heresy, according to Isidore of Seville

(*Liber etymologiarum*, IV, cap. IV, fol. xxiʳ). There are three medical heresies, and of this one he says: 'The second empirical method, the method of trial and error, was discovered by Aesculapius.'

141 Cf. Rahner, 'Das christliche Mysterium von Sonne und Mond', p. 400.

142 The mediating position of the moon and the Church is mentioned by the alchemist William Mennens ('Aureum vellus', *Theatr. chem.*, V, p. 460): '[This] comes about when the light of the Moon begins to increase up to its fifteenth day and then to decrease until its thirtieth, returning then into the horns, until no light at all appears in it. According to this view, the Moon in allegory . . . signifies the Church, which is bright on its spiritual side, but dark on its carnal.' Note the due emphasis he lays on the two aspects of the Moon. This is the spirit of scientific truth as contrasted with the retouchings of the kerygmatic point of view, which plays such an unfortunate role in the two great Christian confessions.

143 Ruska, *Turba*, p. 247. The wind is the *pneuma* hidden in the *prima materia*. The final illustration in Maier's *Scrutinium chymicum* shows this burial.

144 Cf. also the μάχη θηλεία (female combat) in *Carmen Archelai*, one of the *Carmina Heliodori* (p. 56, IV, lines 230f.) (ed. Goldschmidt), where the *materia* flees under the rain of projectiles and ends up as a 'corpse' in the grave.

8 Alchemy and psychotherapy

From: 'The Personification of the Opposites',
Mysterium coniunctionis (1955–6) (*CW* 14)

130   In view of the supreme importance of the ego in bringing reality to light,
we can understand why this infinitesimal speck in the universe was
personified as the sun, with all the attributes that this image implies. As
the medieval mind was incomparably more alive than ours to the divine
quality of the sun, we may assume that the totality character of the sun-
image was implicit in all its allegorical or symbolic applications. Among
the significations of the sun as totality the most important was its frequent
use as a God-image, not only in pagan times but in the sphere of
Christianity as well.

131   Although the alchemists came very close to realizing that the ego was
the mysteriously elusive arcane substance and the longed-for *lapis*, they
were not aware that with their sun-symbol they were establishing an
intimate connection between God and the ego. As already remarked,
projection is not a voluntary act; it is a natural phenomenon beyond the
interference of the conscious mind and peculiar to the nature of the human
psyche. If, therefore, it is this nature that produces the sun-symbol, nature
herself is expressing an identity of God and ego. In that case only
unconscious nature can be accused of blasphemy, but not the man who is
its victim. It is the rooted conviction of the West that God and the ego are
worlds apart. In India, on the other hand, their identity was taken as self-
evident. It was the nature of the Indian mind to become aware of the world-
creating significance of the consciousness[1] manifested in man.[2] The West,
on the contrary, has always emphasized the littleness, weakness and
sinfulness of the ego, despite the fact that it elevated one man to the status
of divinity. The alchemists at least suspected man's hidden godlikeness,
and the intuition of Angelus Silesius finally expressed it without disguise.

132   The East resolves these confusing and contradictory aspects by merging
the ego, the personal *atman*, with the universal *atman* and thus explaining
the ego as the veil of *maya*. The Western alchemist was not consciously
aware of these problems. But when his unspoken assumptions and his
symbols reached the plane of conscious gnosis, as was the case with
Angelus Silesius, it was precisely the littleness and lowliness of the ego[3]
that impelled him to recognize its identity with its extreme opposite.[4] It

was not the arbitrary opinions of deranged minds that gave rise to such insights, but rather the nature of the psyche itself, which, in East and West alike, expresses these truths either directly or clothed in transparent metaphors. This is understandable when we realize that a world-creating quality attaches to human consciousness as such. In saying this we violate no religious convictions, for the religious believer is at liberty to regard man's consciousness (through which, as it were, a second world-creation was enacted) as a divine instrument.

133   I must point out to the reader that these remarks on the significance of the ego might easily prompt him to charge me with grossly contradicting myself. He will perhaps remember that he has come across a very similar argument in my other writings. Only there it was not a question of ego but of the *self* or, rather, of the personal *atman* in contradistinction and in relation to the suprapersonal *atman*. I have defined the self as the totality of the conscious and the unconscious psyche, and the ego as the central reference-point of consciousness. It is an essential part of the self, and can be used *pars pro toto* when the significance of consciousness is borne in mind. But when we want to lay emphasis on the psychic totality it is better to use the term 'self'. There is no question of a contradictory definition, but merely of a difference of standpoint.

From: 'Rex and Regina', *Mysterium coniunctionis* (1955–6) (*CW* 14)

520   A personal ego seizes the reins of power to its own destruction, for mere egohood, despite possessing an *anima rationalis*, is not even sufficient for the guidance of personal life, let alone for the guidance of men. For this purpose it always needs a 'mythical' dominant, yet such a thing cannot simply be invented and then believed in. Contemplating our own times we must say that though the need for an effective dominant was realized to a large extent, what was offered was nothing more than an arbitrary invention of the moment. The fact that it was also believed in goes to prove the gullibility and cluelessness of the public and at the same time the profoundly felt need for a spiritual authority transcending ego-hood. An authority of this kind is never the product of rational reflection or an invention of the moment, which always remains caught in the narrow circle of ego-bound consciousness; it springs from traditions whose roots go far deeper both historically and psychologically. Thus a real and essentially religious renewal can be based, for us, only on Christianity. The extremely radical reformation of Hinduism by the Buddha assimilated the traditional spirituality of India in its entirety and did not thrust a rootless novelty upon the world. It neither denied nor ignored the Hindu pantheon swarming with millions of gods, but boldly introduced Man, who before that had not been represented at all. Nor did Christ, regarded simply as a Jewish reformer,

destroy the law, but made it, rather, into a matter of conviction. He likewise, as the regenerator of his age, set against the Graeco-Roman pantheon and the speculations of the philosophers the figure of Man, not intending it as a contradiction but as the fulfilment of a mythologem that existed long before him – the conception of the Anthropos with its complex Egyptian, Persian and Hellenistic background.

521   Any renewal not deeply rooted in the best spiritual tradition is ephemeral; but the dominant that grows from historical roots acts like a living being within the ego-bound man. He does not possess it, it possesses him; therefore the alchemists said that the artifex is not the master but rather the minister of the stone – clearly showing that the stone is indeed a king towards whom the artifex behaves as a subject.

522   Although the renewed king corresponds to a renewed consciousness, this consciousness is as different from its former state as the *filius regius* differs from the enfeebled old king. Just as the old king must forgo his power and make way for the little upstart ego, so the ego, when the renewed king returns, must step into the background. It still remains the *sine qua non* of consciousness,[5] but it no longer imagines that it can settle everything and do everything by the force of its will. It no longer asserts that where there's a will there's a way. When lucky ideas come to it, it does not take the credit for them, but begins to realize how dangerously close it had been to an inflation. The scope of its willing and doing becomes commensurate with reality again after an Ash Wednesday has descended upon its presumptuousness.[6]

523   We can compare the logical sequence of psychological changes with the alchemical symbolism as follows:

Ego-bound state with feeble dominant	Sick king, enfeebled by age, about to die
Ascent of the unconscious and/or descent of the ego into the unconscious	Disappearance of the king in his mother's body, or his dissolution in water
Conflict and synthesis of conscious and unconscious	Pregnancy, sick-bed, symptoms, display of colours
Formation of a new dominant; circular symbols (e.g. mandala) of the self	King's son, hermaphrodite, rotundum[7]

518   What the nature is of that unity which in some incomprehensible way embraces the antagonistic elements eludes our human judgement, for the simple reason that nobody can say what a being is like that unites the full range of consciousness with that of the unconscious. Man knows no more than his consciousness, and he knows himself only so far as this extends. Beyond that lies an unconscious sphere with no assignable limits, and it too belongs to the phenomenon Man. We might therefore say that perhaps

the One is like a man, that is, determined and determinable and yet undetermined and indeterminable. Always one ends up with paradoxes when knowledge reaches its limits. The ego knows it is part of this being, but only a part. The symbolic phenomenology of the unconscious makes it clear that although consciousness is accorded the status of spiritual kingship with all its attendant dangers, we cannot say what kind of king it will be. This depends on two factors: on the decision of the ego, and the assent of the unconscious. Any dominant that does not have the approval of the one or the other proves to be unstable in the long run. We know how often in the course of history consciousness has subjected its highest and most central ideas to drastic revision and correction, but we know little or nothing about the archetypal processes of change which, we may suppose, have taken place in the unconscious over the millennia, even though such speculations have no firm foundation. Nevertheless the possibility remains that the unconscious may reveal itself in an unexpected way at any time.

540   But a conscious attitude that renounces its ego-bound intentions – not in imagination only, but in truth – and submits to the suprapersonal decrees of fate, can claim to be serving a king. This more exalted attitude raises the status of the *anima* from that of a temptress to a psychopomp.[8] The transformation of the kingly substance from a lion into a king has its counterpart in the transformation of the feminine element from a serpent into a queen. The coronation, apotheosis and marriage signalize the equal status of conscious and unconscious that becomes possible at the highest level – a *coincidentia oppositorum* [meeting of opposites] with redeeming effects.

541   It would certainly be desirable if a psychological explanation and clarification could be given of what seems to be indicated by the mythologem of the marriage. But the psychologist does not feel responsible for the existence of what cannot be known; as the handmaid of truth he must be satisfied with establishing the existence of these phenomena, mysterious as they are. The union of conscious and unconscious symbolized by the royal marriage is a mythological idea which on a higher level assumes the character of a psychological concept. I must expressly emphasize that the psychological concept is definitely not derived from the mythologem, but solely from practical investigation of both the historical and the case material. What this empirical material looks like has been shown in the dream-series given in *Psychology and Alchemy*. It serves as a paradigm in place of hundreds of examples, and it may therefore be regarded as more than an individual curiosity.

542   The psychological union of opposites is an intuitive idea which covers the phenomenology of this process. It is not an 'explanatory' hypothesis for something that, by definition, transcends our powers of conception. For, when we say that conscious and unconscious unite, we are saying in effect that this process is inconceivable. The unconscious is unconscious and therefore can be neither grasped nor conceived. The union of opposites

is a transconscious process and, in principle, not amenable to scientific explanation. The marriage must remain the 'mystery of the queen', the secret of the art, of which the *Rosarium* reports King Solomon as saying:

> This is my daughter, for whose sake men say that the Queen of the South came out of the east, like the rising dawn, in order to hear, understand, and behold the wisdom of Solomon. Power, honour, strength, and dominion are given into her hand; she wears the royal crown of seven glittering stars, like a bride adorned for her husband, and on her robe is written in golden lettering, in Greek, Arabic and Latin: 'I am the only daughter of the wise, utterly unknown to the foolish.'[9]

543   The Queen of Sheba, Wisdom, the royal art and the 'daughter of the philosophers' are all so interfused that the underlying psychologem clearly emerges: the art is queen of the alchemist's heart, she is at once his mother, his daughter and his beloved, and in his art and its allegories the drama of his own soul, his individuation process, is played out.

514   Medical psychology has recognized today that it is a therepeutic necessity, indeed, the first requisite of any thorough psychological method, for consciousness to confront its shadow.[10] In the end this must lead to some kind of union, even though the union consists at first in an open conflict, and often remains so for a long time. It is a struggle that cannot be abolished by rational means.[11] When it is wilfully repressed it continues in the unconscious and merely expresses itself indirectly and all the more dangerously, so no advantage is gained. The struggle goes on until the opponents run out of breath. What the outcome will be can never be seen in advance. The only certain thing is that both parties will be changed; but what the product of the union will be it is impossible to imagine. The empirical material shows that it usually takes the form of a subjective experience which, according to the unanimous testimony of history, is always of a religious order. If, therefore, the conflict is consciously endured and the analyst follows its course without prejudice, he will unfailingly observe compensations from the unconscious which aim at producing a unity. He will come across numerous symbols similar to those found in alchemy – often, indeed, the very same. He will also discover that not a few of these spontaneous formations have a numinous quality in harmony with the mysticism of the historical testimonies. It may happen, besides, that a patient, who till then had shut his eyes to religious questions, will develop an unexpected interest in these matters. He may, for instance, find himself getting converted from modern paganism to Christianity or from one creed to another, or even getting involved in fundamental theological questions which are incomprehensible to a layman. It is unnecessary for me to point out here that not every analysis leads to a conscious realization of the conflict, just as not every surgical operation is as drastic as a resection of the stomach. There is a minor surgery, too, and in the same way there is a minor psychotherapy whose operations are harmless and

require no such elucidation as I am concerned with here. The patients I have in mind are a small minority with certain spiritual demands to be satisfied, and only these patients undergo a development which presents the doctor with the kind of problem we are about to discuss.

515   Experience shows that the union of antagonistic elements is an irrational occurrence which can fairly be described as 'mystical', provided that one means by this an occurrence that cannot be reduced to anything else or regarded as in some way unauthentic. The decisive criterion here is not rationalistic opinions or regard for accepted theories, but simply and solely the value for the patient of the solution he has found and experienced. In this respect the doctor, whose primary concern is the preservation of life, is in an advantageous position, since he is by training an empiricist and has always had to employ medicines whose healing power he knew even though he did not understand how it worked. Equally, he finds all too often that the scientifically explained and attested healing power of his medicine does not work in practice.

516   If, now, the alchemists meant by their old king that he was God himself, this also applies to his son. They themselves must have shrunk from thinking out the logical consequences of their symbolism, otherwise they would have had to assert that God grows old and must be renewed through the art. Such a thought would have been possible at most in the Alexandrian epoch, when gods sprang up like mushrooms. But for medieval man it was barely conceivable.[12] He was far more likely to consider that the art would change something in himself, for which reason he regarded its product as a kind of φάρμακον [remedy]. Had he had any idea of 'psychology', he would almost certainly have called his healing medicament 'psychic' and would have regarded the king's renewal as a transformation of the conscious dominant – which naturally has nothing to do with a magical intervention in the sphere of the gods.

From: 'Epilogue' to *Psychology and Alchemy* (1944) (*CW* 12)

562   In a sense, the old alchemists were nearer to the central truth of the psyche than Faust when they strove to deliver the fiery spirit from the chemical elements, and treated the mystery as though it lay in the dark and silent womb of nature. It was still outside them. The upward thrust of evolving consciousness was bound sooner or later to put an end to the projection, and to restore to the psyche that which had been psychic from the beginning. Yet, ever since the Age of Enlightenment and in the era of scientific rationalism, what indeed was the psyche? It had become synonymous with consciousness. The psyche was 'what I know'. There was no psyche outside the ego. Inevitably, then, the ego identified with the contents accruing from the withdrawal of projections. Gone were the days

when the psyche was still for the most part 'outside the body' and imagined 'those greater things' which the body could not grasp. The contents that were formerly projected were now bound to appear as personal possessions, as chimerical phantasms of the ego-consciousness. The fire chilled to air, and the air became the great wind of Zarathustra and caused an inflation of consciousness which, it seems, can be damped down only by the most terrible catastrophe to civilization, another deluge let loose by the gods upon inhospitable humanity.

563   An inflated consciousness is always egocentric and conscious of nothing but its own existence. It is incapable of learning from the past, incapable of understanding contemporary events, and incapable of drawing right conclusions about the future. It is hypnotized by itself and therefore cannot be argued with. It inevitably dooms itself to calamities that must strike it dead. Paradoxically enough, inflation is a regression of consciousness into unconsciousness. This always happens when consciousness takes too many unconscious contents upon itself and loses the faculty of discrimination, the *sine qua non* of all consciousness. When fate, for four whole years, played out a war of monumental frightfulness on the stage of Europe – a war that *nobody* wanted – nobody dreamed of asking exactly who or what had caused the war and its continuation. Nobody realized that European man was possessed by something that robbed him of all free will. And this state of unconscious possession will continue undeterred until we Europeans become scared of our 'god-almightiness'. Such a change can begin only with individuals, for the masses are blind brutes, as we know to our cost. It seems to me of some importance, therefore, that a few individuals, or people individually, should begin to understand that there are contents which do not belong to the ego-personality, but must be ascribed to a psychic non-ego. This mental operation has to be undertaken if we want to avoid a threatening inflation. To help us, we have the useful and edifying models held up to us by poets and philosophers – models or *archetypi* that we may well call remedies for both men and the times. Of course, what we discover there is nothing that can be held up to the masses – only some hidden thing that we can hold up to ourselves in solitude and in silence. Very few people care to know anything about this; it is so much easier to preach the universal panacea to everybody else than to take it oneself, and, as we all know, things are never so bad when everybody is in the same boat. No doubts can exist in the herd; the bigger the crowd the better the truth – and the greater the catastrophe.

From: 'Rex and Regina', *Mysterium coniunctionis* (1955–6) (*CW* 14)

510   Just as the decay of the conscious dominant is followed by an irruption of chaos in the individual, so also in the case of the masses (Peasant Wars,

Anabaptists, French Revolution, etc.), and the furious conflict of elements in the individual psyche is reflected in the unleashing of primeval blood thirstiness and lust for murder on a collective scale. This is the sickness so vividly described in the *Cantilena*. The loss of the eternal images is in truth no light matter for the man of discernment. But since there are infinitely many more men of no discernment, nobody, apparently, notices that the truth expressed by the dogma has vanished in a cloud of fog, and nobody seems to miss anything. The discerning person knows and feels that his psyche is disquieted by the loss of something that was the life-blood of his ancestors. The undiscerning (ἄνοοι) miss nothing, and only discover afterwards in the papers (much too late) the alarming symptoms that have now become 'real' in the outside world because they were not perceived before inside, in oneself, just as the presence of the eternal images was not noticed. If they had been, a threnody for the lost god would have arisen, as once before in antiquity at the death of Great Pan.[13] Instead, all well-meaning people assure us that one has only to believe he is still there – which merely adds stupidity to unconsciousness. Once the symptoms are really outside in some form of sociopolitical insanity, it is impossible to convince anybody that the conflict is in the psyche of every individual, since he is now quite sure where his enemy is. Then, the conflict which remains an intrapsychic phenomenon in the mind of the discerning person, takes place on the plane of projection in the form of political tension and murderous violence. To produce such consequences the individual must have been thoroughly indoctrinated with the insignificance and worthlessness of his psyche and of psychology in general. One must preach at him from all the pulpits of authority that salvation always comes from outside and that the meaning of his existence lies in the 'community'. He can then be led docilely to the place where of his own natural accord he would rather go anyway: to the land of childhood, where one makes claims exclusively on others, and where, if wrong is done, it is always somebody else who has done it. When he no longer knows by what his soul is sustained, the potential of the unconscious is increased and takes the lead. Desirousness overpowers him, and illusory goals set up in the place of the eternal images excite his greed. The beast of prey seizes hold of him and soon makes him forget that he is a human being. His animal affects hamper any reflection that might stand in the way of his infantile wish-fulfilments, filling him instead with a feeling of a new-won right to existence and intoxicating him with the lust for booty and blood.

511   Only the living presence of the eternal images can lend the human psyche a dignity which makes it morally possible for a man to stand by his own soul, and be convinced that it is worth his while to persevere with it. Only then will he realize that the conflict is *in him*, that the discord and tribulation are his riches, which should not be squandered by attacking others; and that, if fate should exact a debt from him in the form of guilt, it is a debt to himself. Then he will recognize the worth of his psyche, for

nobody can owe a debt to a mere nothing. But when he loses his own values he becomes a hungry robber; the wolf, lion and other ravening beasts which for the alchemists symbolized the appetites that break loose when the black waters of chaos – i.e. the unconsciousness of projection – have swallowed up the king.[14]

From: 'The Psychology of the Transference' (1946) (*CW* 16)

364   The doctor, by voluntarily and consciously taking over the psychic sufferings of the patient, exposes himself to the overpowering contents of the unconscious and hence also to their inductive action. The case begins to 'fascinate' him. Here again it is easy to explain this in terms of personal likes and dislikes, but one overlooks the fact that this would be an instance of *ignotum per ignotius*. In reality these personal feelings, if they exist at all in any decisive degree, are governed by those same unconscious contents which have become activated. An unconscious tie is established and now, in the patient's fantasies, it assumes all the forms and dimensions so profusely described in the literature. The patient, by bringing an activated unconscious content to bear upon the doctor, constellates the corresponding unconscious material in him, owing to the inductive effect which always emanates from projections in greater or lesser degree. Doctor and patient thus find themselves in a relationship founded on mutual unconsciousness.

367   Even the most experienced psychotherapist will discover again and again that he is caught up in a bond, a combination resting on mutual unconsciousness. And though he may believe himself to be in possession of all the necessary knowledge concerning the constellated archetypes, he will in the end come to realize that there are very many things indeed of which his academic knowledge never dreamed. Each new case that requires thorough treatment is pioneer work, and every trace of routine then proves to be a blind alley. Consequently the higher psychotherapy is a most exacting business and sometimes it sets tasks which challenge not only our understanding or our sympathy, but the whole man. The doctor is inclined to demand this total effort from his patient, yet he must realize that this same demand only works if he is aware that it applies also to himself.

375   The transference, however, alters the psychological stature of the doctor, though this is at first imperceptible to him. He too becomes affected, and has as much difficulty in distinguishing between the patient and what has taken possession of him as has the patient himself. This leads both of them to a direct confrontation with the daemonic forces lurking in the darkness. The resultant paradoxical blend of positive and negative, of trust and fear, of hope and doubt, of attraction and repulsion, is character-

istic of the initial relationship. It is the νεῖκος καὶ φιλία (hate and love) of the elements, which the alchemists likened to the primeval chaos. The activated unconscious appears as a flurry of unleashed opposites and calls forth the attempt to reconcile them, so that, in the words of the alchemists, the great *panacea*, the *medicina catholica*, may be born.

From: 'Foreword' to 'The Psychology of the Transference' (1946) (*CW* 16)

It may seem strange to the reader that, in order to throw light on the transference, I should turn to something so apparently remote as alchemical symbolism. But anyone who has read my book *Psychology and Alchemy* will know what close connections exist between alchemy and those phenomena which must, for practical reasons, be considered in the psychology of the unconscious. Consequently he will not be surprised to learn that this phenomenon, shown by experience to be so frequent and so important, also has its place in the symbolism and imagery of alchemy. Such images are not likely to be conscious representations of the transference relationship; rather, they unconsciously take that relationship for granted, and for this reason we may use them as an Ariadne thread to guide us in our argument.

From: 'The Psychology of the Transference' (1946) (*CW* 16)

1 THE MERCURIAL FOUNTAIN

> We are the metals' first nature and only source/
> The highest tincture of the Art is made through us.
> No fountain and no water has my like/
> I make both rich and poor both whole and sick.
> For healthful can I be and poisonous.[15]

402   This picture goes straight to the heart of alchemical symbolism, for it is an attempt to depict the mysterious basis of the *opus*. It is a quadratic quaternity characterized by the four stars in the four corners. These are the four elements. Above, in the centre, there is a fifth star which represents the fifth entity, the 'One' derived from the four, the *quinta essentia*. The basin below is the *vas Hermeticum*, where the transformation takes place. It contains the *mare nostrum*, the *aqua permanens* or ὕδωρ θεῖον, the 'divine water'. This is the *mare tenebrosum*, the chaos. The vessel is also called the uterus[16] in which the *foetus spagyricus* (the homunculus) is gestated.[17] This basin, in contrast to the surrounding square, is circular, because it is the matrix of the perfect form into which the square, as an

ROSARIVM

Figure 8.1 The Mercurial fountain.
Source: From the *Rosarium philosophorum* (1550); reproduced in Jung's *Collected Works*, Vol. 16.

imperfect form, must be changed. In the square the elements are still separate and hostile to one another and must therefore be united in the circle. The inscription on the rim of the basin bears out this intention. It runs (filling in the abbreviations): 'Unus est Mercurius mineralis, Mercurius vegetabilis, Mercurius animalis' (*vegetabilis* should be translated as 'living' and *animalis* as 'animate' in the sense of having a soul, or even as 'psychic').[18] On the outside of the basin there are six stars which together with Mercurius represent the seven planets or metals. They are all as it were contained in Mercurius, since he is the *pater metallorum*. When personified, he is the unity of the seven planets, an Anthropos whose body is the world, like Gayomart, from whose body the seven metals flow into the earth. Owing to his feminine nature, Mercurius is also the mother of the seven, and not only of the six, for he is his own father and mother.[19]

2 KING AND QUEEN

419   As regards the psychology of this picture [Figure 8.2], we must stress above all else that it depicts a human encounter where love plays the decisive part. The conventional dress of the pair suggests an equally conventional attitude in both of them. Convention still separates them and hides their natural reality, but the crucial contact of left hands points to something 'sinister', illegitimate, morganatic, emotional and instinctive, i.e. the fatal touch of incest and its 'perverse' fascination. At the same time the intervention of the Holy Ghost reveals the hidden meaning of the incest, whether of brother and sister or of mother and son, as a repulsive symbol for the *unio mystica*. Although the union of close blood-relatives is everywhere taboo, it is yet the prerogative of kings (witness the incestuous marriages of the Pharaohs, etc.). Incest symbolizes union with one's own being, it means individuation or becoming a self, and, because this is so vitally important, it exerts an unholy fascination – not, perhaps, as a crude reality, but certainly as a psychic process controlled by the unconscious, a fact well known to anybody who is familiar with psychopathology. It is for this reason, and not because of occasional cases of human incest, that the first gods were believed to propagate their kind incestuously. Incest is simply the union of like with like, which is the next stage in the development of the primitive idea of self-fertilization.[20]

421   It would be quite natural to suppose that the king and queen represent a transference relationship in which the king stands for the masculine partner and the queen for the feminine partner. But this is by no means the case, because the figures represent contents which have been projected from the unconscious of the adept (and his *soror mystica* [mystical sister]). Now the adept is conscious of himself as a man, consequently his masculinity cannot be projected, since this only happens to unconscious contents. As it is primarily a question of man and woman here, the projected fragment of personality can only be the feminine component of

PHILOSOPHORVM.

Nota bene: In arte noſtri magiſterij nihil eſt *Secretum*
celatū à Philoſophis excepto ſecreto artis, quod *artis*
non licet cuiquam reuelare, quod ſi fieret ille ma
lediceretur, & indignationem domini incur⸗
reret, & apoplexia moreretur. ⫫ Quare om⸗
nis error in arte exiſtit, ex eo, quod debitam
C ij

Figure 8.2 King and Queen.
Source: From the *Rosarium philosophorum* (1550); reproduced in Jung's *Collected Works*,
Vol. 16.

the man, i.e. his *anima*.[21] Similarly, in the woman's case, only the masculine component can be projected. There is thus a curious counter-crossing of the sexes: the man (in this case the adept) is represented by the queen, and the woman (the *soror mystica*) by the king. It seems to me that the flowers forming the 'symbol' suggest this counter-crossing. The reader should therefore bear in mind that the picture shows two archetypal figures meeting, and that Luna is secretly in league with the adept, and Sol with his woman helper. The fact that the figures are royal expresses, like real royalty, their archetypal character; they are collective figures common to large numbers of people. If the main ingredient of this mystery were the enthronement of a king or the deification of a mortal, then the figure of the king might possibly be a projection and would in that case correspond to the adept. But the subsequent development of the drama has quite another meaning, so we can discount this possibility.[22]

422   The fact that, for reasons which can be proved empirically, king and queen play cross-roles and represent the unconscious contrasexual side of the adept and his *soror* leads to a painful complication which by no means simplifies the problem of transference. Scientific integrity, however, forbids all simplification of situations that are not simple, as is obviously the case here. The pattern of relationship is simple enough, but, when it comes to detailed description in any given case, it is extremely difficult to make out from which angle the relationship is being described and what aspect we are describing. The pattern is as follows:

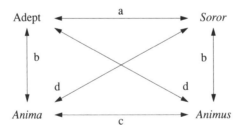

423   The direction of the arrows indicates the pull from masculine to feminine, and vice versa, and from the unconscious of one person to the conscious of the other, thus denoting a positive transference relationship. The following relationships have therefore to be distinguished, although in certain cases they can all merge into each other, and this naturally leads to the greatest possible confusion:

(a) an uncomplicated personal relationship.

(b) a relationship of the man to his *anima* and of the woman to her *animus*.

(c) a relationship of *anima* to *animus*, and vice versa.

(d) a relationship of the woman's *animus* to the man (which happens when the woman is identical with her *animus*), and of the man's *anima* to the woman (which happens when the man is identical with his *anima*).

424   In describing the transference problem with the help of this series of illustrations, I have not always kept these different possibilities apart; for in real life they are invariably mixed up and it would have put an intolerable strain on the explanation had I attempted a rigidly schematic exposition. Thus the king and queen each display every conceivable shade of meaning from the superhuman to the subhuman, sometimes appearing as a transcendental figure, sometimes hiding in the figure of the adept. The reader should bear this in mind if he comes across any real or supposed contradictions in the remarks which follow.

3 THE NAKED TRUTH

450   The text to this picture (Figure 8.3) is, with a few alterations, a quotation from the *Tractatus aureus*.[23] It runs: 'He who would be initiated into this art and secret wisdom must put away the vice of arrogance, must be devout, righteous, deepwitted, humane towards his fellows, of a cheerful countenance and a happy disposition, and respectful withal. Likewise he must be an observer of the eternal secrets that are revealed to him. My son, above all I admonish thee to fear God who seeth what manner of man thou art [*in quo dispositionis tuae visus est*] and in whom is help for the solitary, whosoever he may be [*adiuvatio cuiuslibet sequestrati*].'[24] And the *Rosarium* adds from Pseudo-Aristotle: 'Could God but find a man of faithful understanding, he would open his secret to him.'[25]

451   This appeal to obviously moral qualities makes one thing quite clear: the *opus* demands not only intellectual and technical ability as in the study and practice of modern chemistry; it is a moral as well as a psychological undertaking. The texts are full of such admonitions, and they indicate the kind of attitude that is required in the execution of a religious work. The alchemists undoubtedly understood the *opus* in this sense, though it is difficult to square our picture with such an exordium. The chaste disguises have fallen away.[26] Man and woman confront one another in unabashed naturalness. Sol says, 'O Luna, let[27] me be thy husband', and Luna, 'O Sol, I must submit to thee.'

452   Psychologically we can say that the situation has thrown off the conventional husk and developed into a stark encounter with reality, with no false veils or adornments of any kind. Man stands forth as he really is and shows what was hidden under the mask of conventional adaptation: the shadow. This is now raised to consciousness and integrated with the ego, which means a move in the direction of wholeness. Wholeness is not so much perfection as completeness. Assimilation of the shadow gives a man body, so to speak; the animal sphere of instinct, as well as the primitive or archaic psyche, emerges into the zone of consciousness and can no longer be repressed by fictions and illusions. In this way man becomes for himself the difficult problem he really is. He must always remain conscious of the fact that he is such a problem if he wants to

PHILOSOPHORVM.

feipfis fecundum equalitate infpiffentur. Solus
enim calor teperatus eft humiditatis infpiffatiuus
et mixtionis perfectiuus, et non fuper excedens.
Nã generatiões et procreationes rerũ naturaliũ
habent folũ fieri per teperatifsimũ calorẽ et equa
lẽ, vti eft folus fimus equinus humidus et calidus.

D

Figure 8.3 The naked truth.
Source: From the *Rosarium philosophorum* (1550); reproduced in Jung's *Collected Works*, Vol.
16.

develop at all. Repression leads to a one-sided development if not to stagnation, and eventually to neurotic dissociation. Today it is no longer a question of 'How can I get rid of my shadow?' – for we have seen enough of the curse of one-sidedness. Rather we must ask ourselves: 'How can man live with his shadow without its precipitating a succession of disasters?' Recognition of the shadow is reason enough for humility, for genuine fear of the abysmal depths in man. This caution is most expedient, since the man without a shadow thinks himself harmless precisely because he is ignorant of his shadow. The man who recognizes his shadow knows very well that he is not harmless, for it brings the archaic psyche, the whole world of the archetypes, into direct contact with the conscious mind and saturates it with archaic influences. This naturally adds to the dangers of 'affinity', with its deceptive projections and its urge to assimilate the object in terms of the projection, to draw it into the family circle in order to actualize the hidden incest situation, which seems all the more attractive and fascinating the less it is understood. The advantage of the situation, despite all its dangers, is that once the naked truth has been revealed the discussion can get down to essentials; ego and shadow are no longer divided but are brought together in an – admittedly precarious – unity. This is a great step forward, but at the same time it shows up the 'differentness' of one's partner all the more clearly, and the unconscious usually tries to close the gap by increasing the attraction, so as to bring about the desired union somehow or other. All this is borne out by the alchemical idea that the fire which maintains the process must be temperate to begin with and must then gradually be raised to the highest intensity.

4   IMMERSION IN THE BATH

453   A new motif appears in this picture [Figure 8.4]: the bath. In a sense this takes us back to the first picture of the Mercurial Fountain, which represents the 'upwelling'.

454   The immersion in the 'sea' signifies the *solutio* – 'dissolution' in the physical sense of the word and at the same time, according to Dorn, the solution of a problem.[28] It is a return to the dark initial state, to the amniotic fluid of the gravid uterus. The alchemists frequently point out that their stone grows like a child in its mother's womb; they call the *vas hermeticum* the uterus and its contents the foetus.

  . . . . In our pictures the bond is effected by the dove from above and by the water from below. These constitute the link – in other words, they are the soul. Thus the underlying idea of the psyche proves it be a half bodily, half spiritual substance, an *anima media natura*,[29] as the alchemists call it,[30] an hermaphroditic being[31] capable of uniting the opposites, but who is never complete in the individual unless related to another individual. The unrelated human being lacks wholeness, for he can achieve

ROSARIVM

corrũpitur, neꝗ ex imperfecto penitus fecundũ artem aliquid fieri poteſt. Ratio eſt quia ars prí mas diſpoſitiones inducere non poteſt, ſed lapis noſter eſt res media inter perfecta & imperfecta corpora, & quod natura ipſa incepit hoc per artem ad perfectionẽ deducitur. Si in ipſo Mercurio operari inceperis vbi natura reliquit imperſectum, inuenies in eo perfectionẽ et gaudebis.

Perfectum non alteratur, ſed corrumpitur. Sed imperfectum bene alteratur, ergo corrupſ tio vnius eſt generatio alterius.

Speculum

Figure 8.4 Immersion in the bath.
Source: From the *Rosarium philosophorum* (1550); reproduced in Jung's *Collected Works*, Vol. 16.

wholeness only through the soul, and the soul cannot exist without its other side, which is always found in a 'You'. Wholeness is a combination of I and You, and these show themselves to be parts of a transcendent unity whose nature can only be grasped symbolically, as in the symbols of the *rotundum*, the rose, the wheel, or the *coniunctio Solis et Lunae*.

455   Coming now to the psychology of the picture, it is clearly a descent into the unconscious. The immersion in the bath is another 'night sea journey',[32] as the *Visio Arislei* proves. There the philosophers are shut up with the brother–sister pair in a triple glass-house at the bottom of the sea by the *Rex Marinus*. Just as, in the primitive myths, it is so stiflingly hot in the belly of the whale that the hero loses his hair, so the philosophers suffer very much from the intense heat[33] during their confinement. The hero-myths deal with rebirth and apocatastasis, and the *Visio* likewise tells of the resuscitation of the dead Thabritius (Gabricus) or, in another version, of his rebirth.[34] The night sea-journey is a kind of *descensus ad inferos* – a descent into Hades and a journey to the land of ghosts somewhere beyond this world, beyond consciousness, hence an immersion in the unconscious. In our picture the immersion is effected by the rising-up of the fiery, chthonic Mercurius, presumably the sexual libido which engulfs the pair[35] and is the obvious counterpart to the heavenly dove. The latter has always been regarded as a love-bird, but it also has a purely spiritual significance in the Christian tradition accepted by the alchemists. Thus the pair are united *above* by the symbol of the Holy Ghost, and it looks as if the immersion in the bath were also uniting them *below*, i.e. in the water which is the counterpart of spirit ('It is death for souls to become water', says Heraclitus). Opposition and identity at once – a philosophical problem only when taken as a psychological one!

5 THE CONJUNCTION

O Luna, folded in my sweet embrace/
Be you as strong as I, as fair of face.
O Sol, brightest of all lights known to men/
And yet you need me, as the cock the hen.

457   The sea has closed over the king and queen [Figure 8.5], and they have gone back to the chaotic beginnings, the *massa confusa*. Physis has wrapped the 'man of light' in a passionate embrace. As the text says: 'Then Beya [the maternal sea] rose up over Gabricus and enclosed him in her womb, so that nothing more of him was to be seen. And she embraced Gabricus with so much love that she absorbed him completely into her own nature, and dissolved him into atoms.'

459   The psychology of this central symbol is not at all simple. On a superficial view it looks as if natural instinct had triumphed. But if we

CONIVNCTIO SIVE
Coitus.

O Luna durch meyn vmbgeben/vnd suffe mynne/
Wirstu schon/starck/vnd gewaltig als ich byn·

O Sol/ du bist vber alle liecht zu erkennen/
So bedarsstu doch mein als der han der hennen.

ARISLEVS IN VISIONE.

Coniunge ergo filium tuum Gabricum dile=
ctiorem tibi in omnibus filijs tuis cum sua sorore
Beya

Figure 8.5 The conjunction.
Source: From the *Rosarium philosophorum* (1550); reproduced in Jung's *Collected Works*, Vol. 16.

examine it more closely we note that the coitus is taking place in the water, the *mare tenebrositatis* [sea of darkness], i.e. the unconscious.

460   As to the frank eroticism of the pictures, I must remind the reader that they were drawn for medieval eyes and that consequently they have a symbolical rather than a pornographic meaning. Medieval hermeneutics and meditation could contemplate even the most delicate passages in the Song of Songs without taking offence and view them through a veil of spirituality. Our pictures of the *coniunctio* are to be understood in this sense: union on the biological level is a symbol of the *unio oppositorum* at its highest. This means that the union of opposites in the royal art is just as real as coitus in the common acceptation of the word, so that the *opus* becomes an analogy of the natural process by means of which instinctive energy is transformed, at least in part, into symbolical activity. The creation of such analogies frees instinct and the biological sphere as a whole from the pressure of unconscious contents. Absence of symbolism, however, overloads the sphere of instinct.[36] The analogy contained in Figure 8.5 is a little too obvious for our modern taste, so that it almost fails in its purpose.

461   As every specialist know, the psychological parallels encountered in medical practice often take the form of fantasy-images which, when drawn, differ hardly at all from our pictures. The reader may remember the typical case I mentioned earlier, where the act of conception was represented symbolically and, exactly nine months later, the unconscious, as though influenced by a *suggestion à échéance*, produced the symbolism of a birth, or of a new-born child, without the patient's being conscious of the preceding psychic conception or having consciously reckoned the period of her 'pregnancy'. As a rule the whole process passes off in a series of dreams and is discovered only retrospectively, when the dream material comes to be analysed. Many alchemists compute the duration of the *opus* to be that of a pregnancy, and they liken the entire procedure to such a period of gestation.[37]

6 DEATH

Here King and Queen are lying dead/
In great distress the soul is sped.

467   *Vas hermeticum*, fountain, and sea have here become sarcophagus and tomb. King and queen are dead and have melted into a single being with two heads. The feast of life is followed by the funereal threnody. Just as Gabricus dies after becoming united with his sister, and the son–lover always comes to an early end after consummating the *hieros gamos* with the mother-goddess of the Near East, so, after the *coniunctio oppositorum*, deathlike stillness reigns. When the opposites unite, all energy ceases: there is no more flow. The waterfall has plunged to its full depth in that

PHILOSOPHORVM.

CONCEPTIOSEV PVTRE
factio

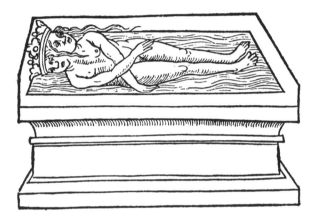

Hye ligen kṏnig vnd kṏningin dot/
Die ſele ſcheydt ſich mit groſſer not.

ARISTOTELES REX ET
Philoſophus.

Vnquam vidi aliquod animatum creſcere
Nſine putrefactione, niſi autem fiat putri⸗
dum inuanum erit opus alchimicum.

Figure 8.6 Death.
Source: From the *Rosarium philosophorum* (1550); reproduced in Jung's *Collected Works*,
Vol. 16.

torrent of nuptial joy and longing; now only a stagnant pool remains, without wave or current. So at least it appears, looked at from the outside. As the legend tells us, the picture represents the *putrefactio*, the corruption, the decay of a once living creature. Yet the picture [Figure 8.6] is also entitled 'Conceptio'. The text says: *Corruptio unius generatio est alterius* (the corruption of one is the generation of the other),[38] an indication that this death is an interim stage to be followed by a new life. No new life can arise, say the alchemists, without the death of the old. They liken the art to the work of the sower, who buries the grain in the earth: it dies only to waken to new life.[39]

7 THE ASCENT OF THE SOUL

Here is the divsion of the four elements/
As from the lifeless corpse the soul ascends.

476   This picture [Figure 8.7] corresponds psychologically to a dark state of disorientation. The decomposition of the elements indicates dissociation and the collapse of the existing ego-consciousness. It is closely analogous to the schizophrenic state, and it should be taken very seriously because this is the moment when latent psychoses may become acute, i.e. when the patient becomes aware of the collective unconscious and the psycic non-ego. This collapse and disorientation of consciousness may last a considerable time and it is one of the most difficult transitions the analyst has to deal with, demanding the greatest patience, courage and faith on the part of both doctor and patient. It is a sign that the patient is being driven along willy-nilly without any sense of direction, that, in the truest sense of the word, he is in an utterly *soulless* condition, exposed to the full force of autoerotic affects and fantasies.

477   This critical state, when the conscious mind is liable to be submerged at any moment in the unconscious, is akin to the 'loss of soul' that frequently attacks primitives. It is a sudden *abaissement du niveau mental*, a slackening of the conscious tension, to which primitive man is especially prone because his consciousness is still relatively weak and means a considerable effort for him. Hence his lack of will-power, his inability to concentrate and the fact that, mentally, he tires so easily, as I have experienced to my cost during palavers [séances]. The widespread practice of yoga and *dhyana* in the East is a similar *abaissement* deliberately induced for the purpose of relaxation, a technique for releasing the soul. With certain patients, I have even been able to establish the existence of subjectively experienced levitations in moments of extreme derangement.[40] Lying in bed, the patients felt that they were floating horizontally in the air a few feet above their bodies. This is a suggestive reminder of the phenomenon called the 'witch's trance', and also of the parapsychic levitations reported of many saints.

ROSARIVM
ANIMÆ EXTRACTIO VEL
imprægnatio

Hye teylen sich die vier element/
Aus dem leyb scheydt sich die sele behendt.

De

Figure 8.7 The ascent of the soul.
Source: From the *Rosarium philosophorum* (1550); reproduced in Jung's *Collected Works*, Vol. 16.

482   The psychological interpretation of this process leads into regions of inner experience which defy our powers of scientific description, however unprejudiced or even ruthless we may be. At this point, unpalatable as it is to the scientific temperament, the idea of mystery forces itself upon the mind of the inquirer, not as a cloak for ignorance but as an admission of his inability to translate what he knows into the everyday speech of the intellect. I must therefore content myself with a bare mention of the archetype which is inwardly experienced at this stage, namely the birth of the 'divine child' or – in the language of the mystics – the inner man.[41]

8 PURIFICATION

Here falls the heavenly dew, to lave/
The soiled black body in the grave.

483   The falling dew is a portent of the divine birth now at hand. *Ros Gedeonis* (Gideon's dew)[42] is a synonym for the *aqua permanens*, hence for Mercurius.[43]

484   The whitening (*albedo* or *dealbatio*) is likened to the *ortus solis*, the sunrise; it is the light, the illumination, that follows the darkness.

488   The alchemists seem to have perceived the danger that the work and its realization may get stuck in one of the conscious functions. Consequently they stress the importance of the *theoria*, i.e. intellectual understanding as opposed to the *practica*, which consisted merely of chemical experiments. We might say that the *practica* corresponds to pure perception, and that this must be supplemented by apperception. But this second stage still does not bring complete realization. What is still lacking is heart or feeling, which imparts an abiding value to anything we have understood. The books must therefore be 'destroyed' lest thinking impair feeling and thus hinder the return of the soul.

489   These difficulties are familiar ground to the psychotherapist. It often happens that the patient is quite satisfied with merely registering a dream or fantasy, especially if he has pretensions to aestheticism. He will then fight against even intellectual understanding because it seems an affront to the reality of his psychic life. Others try to understand with their brains only, and want to skip the purely practical stage. And when they have understood, they think they have done their full share of realization. That they should also have a *feeling-relationship* to the contents of the unconscious seems strange to them or even ridiculous. Intellectual understanding and aestheticism both produce the deceptive, treacherous sense of liberation and superiority which is liable to collapse if feeling intervenes. Feeling always binds one to the reality and meaning of symbolic contents, and these in turn impose binding standards of ethical behaviour from which aestheticism and intellectualism are only too ready to emancipate themselves.

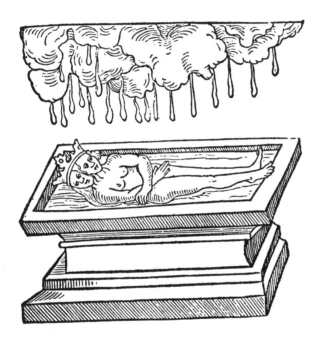

PHILOSOPHORVM

ABLVTIO VEL
Mundificatio

Hie felt der Tauw von himmel herab/
Vnnd wascht den schwartzen leyb im grab ab-

K iij

Figure 8.8 Purification.
Source: From the *Rosarium philosophorum* (1550); reproduced in Jung's *Collected Works*, Vol. 16.

9 THE RETURN OF THE SOUL

> Here is the soul descending from on high/
> To quick the corpse we strove to purify.

494   Here the reconciler, the soul, dives down from heaven to breathe life into the dead body. The two birds at the bottom left of the picture [Figure 8.9] represent the allegorical winged and wingless dragons in the form of fledged and unfledged birds.[44] This is one of the many synonyms for the double nature of Mercurius, who is both a chthonic and a pneumatic being. The presence of this divided pair of opposites means that although the hermaphrodite appears to be united and is on the point of coming alive, the conflict between them is by no means finally resolved and has not yet disappeared: it is relegated to the 'left' and to the 'bottom' of the picture, i.e. banished to the sphere of the unconscious. The fact that these still unintegrated opposites are represented theriomorphically (and not anthropomorphically as before) bears out this supposition.

496   The coronation picture that illustrates this text[45] proves that the resuscitation of the purified corpse is at the same time a glorification, since the process is likened to the crowning of the Virgin.[46] The allegorical language of the Church supports such a comparison. . . . Again and again we note that the alchemist proceeds like the unconscious in the choice of his symbols: every idea finds both a positive and a negative expression. Sometimes he speaks of a royal pair, sometimes of dog and bitch; and the water symbolism is likewise expressed in violent contrasts. We read that the royal diadem appears *in menstruo meretricis* (in the menstruum of a whore),[47] or the following instructions are given: 'Take the foul deposit [*faecem*] that remains in the cooking-vessel and preserve it for it is the crown of the heart.' The deposit corresponds to the corpse in the sarcophagus, and the sarcophagus corresponds in turn to the mercurial fountain or the *vas hermeticum*.

505   Here I must point out that very different rules apply in feminine psychology, since in this case we are not dealing with a function of relationship but, on the contrary, with a *discriminative* function, namely the *animus*. Alchemy was, as a philosophy, mainly a masculine preoccupation and in consequence of this its formulations are for the most part masculine in character. But we should not overlook the fact that the feminine element in alchemy is not so inconsiderable since, even at the time of its beginnings in Alexandria, we have authentic proof of female philosophers like Theosebeia,[48] the *soror mystica* of Zosimos, and Paphnutia and Maria Prophetissa. From later times we know of the pair of alchemists Nicolas Flamel and his wife Peronelle. The *Mutus liber* of 1677 gives an account of a man and wife performing the *opus* together,[49] and finally in the nineteenth century we have the pair of English alchemists Thomas South and his daughter, who later became Mrs Atwood. After

PHILOSOPHORVM

ANIMÆ IVBILATIO SEV
Ortus seu Sublimatio.

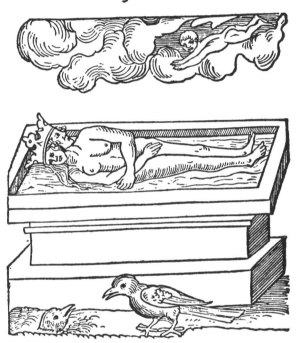

ᚻie ſchwingt ſich die ſele hernidder/
Vnd erquickt den gereinigten leychnam wider-

L iij

Figure 8.9 The return of the soul.
Source: From the *Rosarium philosophorum* (1550); reproduced in Jung's *Collected Works*, Vol. 16.

busying themselves for many years with the study of alchemy, they decided to set down their ideas and experiences in book form. To this end they separated, the father working in one part of the house and his daughter in another. She wrote a thick, erudite tome while he versified. She was the first to finish and promptly sent the book to the printer. Scarcely had it appeared when her father was overcome with scruples, fearing lest they had betrayed the great secret. He succeeded in persuading his daughter to withdraw the book and destroy it. In the same spirit, he sacrificed his own poetic labours. Only a few lines are preserved in her book, of which it was too late to withdraw all the copies. A reprint,[50] prepared after her death in 1910, appeared in 1918. I have read the book: no secrets are betrayed. It is a thoroughly medieval production garnished with would-be theosophical explanations as a sop to the syncretism of the new age.

519   I would like to draw attention to the curious pictures of the *arbor philosophica* in the fourteenth-century Codex Ashburnham.[51] One picture shows Adam struck by an arrow,[52] and the tree growing out of his genitals; in the other picture the tree grows out of Eve's head. Her right hand covers her genitals, her left points to a skull. Plainly this is a hint that the man's *opus* is concerned with the erotic aspect of the *anima*, while the woman's is concerned with the *animus*, which is a 'function of the head'.[53] The *prima materia*, i.e. the unconscious, is represented in man by the 'unconscious' *anima*, and in woman by the 'unconscious' *animus*. Out of the *prima materia* grows the philosophical tree, the unfolding *opus*. In their symbolical sense, too, the pictures are in accord with the findings of psychology, since Adam would then stand for the woman's *animus* who generates 'philosophical' ideas with his member, and Eve for the man's *anima* who, as Sapientia or Sophia, produces out of her head the intellectual content of the work.

523   In John Gower's *Confessio Amantis*[54] there is a saying which I have used as a motto to the Introduction of this book: *Bellica pax, vulnus dulce, suave malum* (a warring peace, a sweet wound, a mild evil). Into these words the old alchemist put the quintessence of his experience. I can add nothing to their incomparable simplicity and conciseness. They contain all that the ego can reasonably demand of the *opus*, and illuminate for it the paradoxical darkness of human life. Submission to the fundamental contrariety of human nature amounts to an acceptance of the fact that the psyche is at cross-purposes with itself. Alchemy teaches that the tension is fourfold, forming a cross which stands for the four warring elements. The *quaternio* is the minimal aspect under which such a state of total opposition can be regarded. The cross as a form of suffering expresses psychic reality, and carrying the cross is therefore an apt symbol for the wholeness and also for the passion which the alchemist saw in his work. Hence the *Rosarium* ends, not unfittingly, with the picture of the risen Christ and the verses:

After my many sufferings and great martyry
I rise again transfigured, of all blemish free.

524   An exclusively rational analysis and interpretation of alchemy, and of
the unconscious contents projected into it, must necessarily stop short at
the above parallels and antinomies, for in a total opposition there is no
third – *tertium non datur*! Science comes to a stop at the frontiers of logic,
but nature does not – she thrives on ground as yet untrodden by theory.
Venerabilis natura does not halt at the opposites; she uses them to create,
out of opposition, a new birth.

10 THE NEW BIRTH

Here is born the Empress of all honour/
The philosophers name her their daughter.
She multiplies/ bears children ever again/
They are incorruptibly pure and without stain.

532   From the foregoing we can see how the *opus* ends with the idea of a
highly paradoxical being that defies rational analysis. The work could
hardly end in any other way, since the *complexio oppositorum* [combina-
tion of opposites] cannot possibly lead to anything but a baffling paradox.
Psychologically, this means that human wholeness can only be described
in antinomies, which is always the case when dealing with a transcendental
idea. By way of comparison, we might mention the equally paradoxical
corpuscular theory and wave theory of light, although these do at least hold
out the possibility of a mathematical synthesis, which the psychological
idea naturally lacks. Our paradox, however, offers the possibility of an
intuitive and *emotional* experience, because the unity of the self, un-
knowable and incomprehensible, irradiates even the sphere of our dis-
criminating, and hence divided, consciousness, and, like all unconscious
contents, does so with very powerful effects. This inner unity, or experience of unity, is expressed most forcibly by the mystics in the idea of
the *unio mystica*, and above all in the philosophies and religions of India,
in Chinese Taoism, and in the Zen Buddhism of Japan. From the point of
view of psychology, the names we give to the self are quite irrelevant, and
so is the question of whether or not it is 'real'. Its psychological reality is
enough for all practical purposes. The intellect is incapable of knowing
anything beyond that anyway, and therefore its Pilate-like questionings are
devoid of meaning.

533   To come back to our picture: it shows an apotheosis of the Rebis, the
right side of the body being male, the left female. The figure stands on the
moon, which in this case corresponds to the feminine lunar vessel, the *vas
hermeticum*. Its wings betoken volatility, i.e. spirituality. In one hand it
holds a chalice with three snakes in it, or possibly one snake with three
heads; in the other, a single snake. This is an obvious allusion to the axiom

PHILOSOPHORVM.

hie ift geboren die eddele Keyferin reich/
Die meifter nennen fie jhrer dochter gleich.
Die vermeret fich/gebiert kinder ohn zal/
Sän vndötlich rein/vnnd ohn alles mahl.

Die

Figure 8.10 The new birth.
Source: From the *Rosarium philosophorum* (1550); reproduced in Jung's *Collected Works*, Vol. 16.

of Maria and the old dilemma of 3 and 4, and also to the mystery of the Trinity. The three snakes in the chalice are the chthonic equivalent of the Trinity, and the single snake represents, first, the unity of the three as expressed by Maria and, secondly, the 'sinister' *serpens Mercurialis* with all its subsidiary meanings.[55] Whether pictures of this kind are in any way related to the Baphomet[56] of the Templars is an open question, but the snake symbolism[57] certainly points to the evil principle, which, although excluded from the Trinity, is yet somehow connected with the work of redemption. Moreover to the left of the Rebis we also find the raven, a synonym for the devil.[58] The unfledged bird has disappeared: its place is taken by the winged Rebis. To the right, there stands the 'sun and moon tree', the *arbor philosophica*, which is the conscious equivalent of the unconscious process of development suggested on the opposite side. The corresponding picture of the Rebis in the second version[59] has, instead of the raven, a pelican plucking its breast for its young, a well-known allegory of Christ. In the same picture a lion is prowling about behind the Rebis and, at the bottom of the hill on which the Rebis stands, there is the three-headed snake.[60] The alchemical hermaphrodite is a problem in itself and really needs special elucidation. Here I will say only a few words about the remarkable fact that the fervently desired goal of the alchemist's endeavours should be conceived under so monstrous and horrific an image. We have proved to our satisfaction that the antithetical nature of the goal largely accounts for the monstrosity of the corresponding symbol. But this rational explanation does not alter the fact that the monster is a hideous abortion and a perversion of nature. Nor is this a mere accident undeserving of further scrutiny; it is on the contrary highly significant and the outcome of certain psychological facts fundamental to alchemy. The symbol of the hermaphrodite, it must be remembered, is one of the many synonyms for the goal of the art. In order to avoid unnecessary repetition I would refer the reader to the material collected in *Psychology and Alchemy*, and particularly to the *lapis*–Christ parallel, to which we must add the rarer and, for obvious reasons, generally avoided comparison of the *prima materia* with God.[61] Despite the closeness of the analogy, the *lapis* is not to be understood simply as the risen Christ and the *prima materia* as God; the *Tabula smaragdina* hints, rather, that the alchemical mystery is a 'lower' equivalent of the higher mysteries, a sacrament not of the paternal 'mind' but of maternal 'matter'. The disappearance of theriomorphic symbols in Christianity is here compensated by a wealth of allegorical animal forms which tally quite well with *mater natura*. Whereas the Christian figures are the product of spirit, light and good, the alchemical figures are creatures of night, darkness, poison and evil. These dark origins do much to explain the misshapen hermaphrodite, but they do not explain everything. The crude, embryonic features of this symbol express the immaturity of the alchemist's mind, which was not sufficiently developed to equip him for the difficulties of his task. He was underdeveloped in two

senses: first, he did not understand the real nature of chemical combinations; and, secondly, he knew nothing about the psychological problem
of projection and the unconscious. All this lay as yet hidden in the womb
of the future. The growth of natural science has filled the first gap, and the
psychology of the unconscious is endeavouring to fill the second. Had the
alchemists understood the psychological aspects of their work, they would
have been in a position to free their 'uniting symbol' from the grip of
instinctive sexuality where, for better or worse, mere nature, unsupported
by the critical intellect, was bound to leave it. Nature could say no more
than that the combination of supreme opposites was a hybrid thing. And
there the statement stuck, in sexuality, as always when the potentialities of
consciousness do not come to the assistance of nature – which could hardly
have been otherwise in the Middle Ages owing to the complete absence of
psychology.[62] So things remained until, at the end of the nineteenth
century, Freud dug up this problem again. There now ensued what usually
happens when the conscious mind collides with the unconscious: the former
is influenced and prejudiced in the highest degree by the latter, if not
actually overpowered by it. The problem of the union of opposites had been
lying there for centuries in its sexual form, yet it had to wait until scientific
enlightenment and objectivity had advanced far enough for people to
mention 'sexuality' in scientific conversation. The sexuality of the
unconscious was instantly taken with great seriousness and elevated to a
sort of religious dogma, which has been fanatically defended right down
to the present time: such was the fascination emanating from those contents
which had last been nurtured by the alchemists. The natural archetypes that
underlie the mythologems of incest, the *hieros gamos*, the divine child, etc.,
blossomed forth – in the age of science – into the theory of infantile
sexuality, perversions and incest, while the *coniunctio* was rediscovered in
the transference neurosis.[63]

534   The sexualism of the hermaphrodite symbol completely overpowered
consciousness and gave rise to an attitude of mind which is just as
unsavoury as the old hybrid symbolism. The task that defeated the
alchemists presented itself anew: how is the profound cleavage in man and
the world to be understood, how are we to respond to it and, if possible,
abolish it? So runs the question when stripped of its natural sexual
symbolism, in which it had got stuck only because the problem could not
push its way over the threshold of the unconscious. The sexualism of these
contents always denotes an unconscious identity of the ego with some
unconscious figure (either *anima* or *animus*), and because of this the ego
is obliged, willing and reluctant at once, to be a party to the *hieros gamos*,
or at least to believe that it is simply and solely a matter of an erotic
consummation. And sure enough it increasingly becomes so the more one
believes it – the more exclusively, that is to say, one concentrates on the
sexual aspect, and the less attention one pays to the archetypal patterns.
As we have seen, the whole question invites fanaticism because it is so

painfully obvious that we are in the wrong. If, on the other hand, we decline to accept the argument that because a thing is fascinating it is the absolute truth, then we give ourselves a chance to see that the alluring sexual aspect is but one among many – the very one that deludes our judgement. This aspect is always trying to deliver us into the power of a partner who seems compounded of all the qualities we have failed to realize in ourselves. Hence, unless we prefer to be made fools of by our illusions, we shall, by carefully analysing every fascination, extract from it a portion of our own personality, like a quintessence, and slowly come to recognize that we meet ourselves time and again in a thousand disguises on the path of life. This, however, is a truth which only profits the man who is temperamentally convinced of the individual and irreducible reality of his fellow-men.

535 We know that in the course of the dialectical process the unconscious produces certain images of the *goal*. In *Psychology and Alchemy* I have described a long series of dreams which contain such images (including even a shooting target). They are mostly concerned with ideas of the mandala type, that is, the circle and the quaternity. The latter are the plainest and most characteristic representations of the goal. Such images unite the opposites under the sign of the *quaternio*, i.e. by combining them in the form of a cross, or else they express the idea of wholeness through the circle or sphere. The superior type of personality may also figure as a goal-image, though more rarely. Occasionally special stress is laid on the luminous character of the centre. I have never come across the hermaphrodite as a personification of the goal, but more as a symbol of the initial state, expressing an identity with *anima* or *animus*.

536 These images are naturally only anticipations of a wholeness which is, in principle, always just beyond our reach. Also, they do not invariably indicate a subliminal readiness on the part of the patient to realize that wholeness consciously, at a later stage; often they mean no more than a temporary compensation of chaotic confusion and lack of orientation. Fundamentally, of course, they always point to the self, the container and organizer of all opposites. But at the moment of their appearance they merely indicate the possibility of order in wholeness.

537 What the alchemist tried to express with his Rebis and his squaring of the circle, and what the modern man also tries to express when he draws patterns of circles and quaternities, is wholeness – a wholeness that resolves all opposition and puts an end to conflict, or at least draws its sting. The symbol of this is a *coincidentia oppositorum*, which, as we know, Nicolas of Cusa identified with God. It is far from my intention to cross swords with this great man. My business is merely the natural science of the psyche, and my main concern to establish the facts. How these facts are named and what further interpretation is then placed upon them is of secondary importance. Natural science is not a science of words and ideas, but of facts. I am no terminological rigorist – call the existing symbols

'wholeness', 'self', 'consciousness', 'higher ego' or what you will, it makes little difference. I for my part only try not to give any false or misleading names. All these terms are simply names for the facts that alone carry weight. The names I give do not imply a philosophy, although I cannot prevent people from barking at these terminological phantoms as if they were metaphysical hypostases. The facts are sufficient in themselves, and it is well to know about them. But their interpretation should be left to the individual's discretion. 'The maximum is that to which noting is opposed, and in which the minimum is also the maximum',[64] says Nicolas of Cusa. Yet God is also above the opposites: 'Beyond this coincidence of creating and being created art thou God.'[65] Man is an analogy of God: 'Man is God, but not in an absolute sense, since he is man. He is therefore God in a human way. Man is also a world, but he is not all things at once in contracted form, since he is man. He is therefore a microcosm.'[66] Hence the *complexio oppositorum* proves to be not only a possibility but an ethical duty: 'In these most profound matters every endeavour of our human intelligence should be bent to the achieving of that simplicity where contradictories are reconciled.'[67] The alchemists are as it were the empiricists of the great problem of the union of opposites, whereas Nicolas of Cusa is its philosopher.

From: 'Epilogue' to *The Practice of Psychotherapy* (*CW* 16)

538   To give any description of the transference phenomenon is a very difficult and delicate task, and I did not know how to set about it except by drawing upon the symbolism of the alchemical *opus*. The *theoria* of alchemy, as I think I have shown, is for the most part a projection of unconscious contents, of those archetypal forms which are characteristic of all pure fantasy products, such as are to be met with in myths and fairy-tales, or in the dreams, visions, and the delusional systems of individual men and women. The important part played in the history of alchemy by the *hieros gamos* and the mystical marriage, and also by the *coniunctio*, corresponds to the central significance of the transference in psychotherapy on the one hand and in the field of normal human relationships on the other. For this reason, it did not seem to me too rash an undertaking to use an historical document, whose substance derives from centuries of mental effort, as the basis and guiding thread of my argument. The gradual unfolding of the symbolic drama presented me with a welcome opportunity to bring together the countless individual experiences I have had in the course of many years' study of this theme – experiences which, I readily admit, I did not know how to arrange in any other way. This venture, therefore, must be regarded as a mere experiment; I have no desire to attribute any conclusive significance to it. The problems connected with

the transference are so complicated and so various that I lack the categories necessary for a systematic account. There is in such cases always an urge to simplify things, but this is dangerous because it so easily violates the facts by seeking to reduce incompatibles to a common denominator. I have resisted this temptation so far as possible and allow myself to hope that the reader will not run away with the idea that the process I have described here is a working model of the average course of events. Experience shows, in fact, not only that were the alchemists exceedingly vague as to the sequence of the various stages, but that in our observation of individual cases there is a bewildering number of variations as well as the greatest arbitrariness in the sequence of states, despite all agreement in principle as to the basic facts. A logical order, as we understand it, or even the possibility of such an order, seems to lie outside the bounds of our subject at present. We are moving here in a region of individual and unique happenings that have no parallel. A process of this kind can, if our categories are wide enough, be reduced to an order of sorts and described, or at least adumbrated, with the help of analogies; but its inmost essence is the uniqueness of a life individually lived – which nobody can grasp from outside, but which, on the contrary, holds the individual in its grip. The series of pictures that served as our Ariadne thread is one of many,[68] so that we could easily set up several other working models which would display the process of transference each in a different light. But no single model would be capable of fully expressing the endless wealth of individual variations which all have their *raison d'être*. Such being the case, it is clear to me that even this attempt to give a comprehensive account of the phenomenon is a bold undertaking. Yet its practical importance is so great that the attempt surely justifies itself, even if its defects give rise to misunderstandings.

539   We live today in a time of confusion and disintegration. Everything is in the melting-pot. As is usual in such circumstances, unconscious contents thrust forward to the very borders of consciousness for the purpose of compensating the crisis in which it finds itself. It is therefore well worth our while to examine all such borderline phenomena with the greatest care, however obscure they seem, with a view to discovering the seeds of new and potential orders. The transference phenomenon is without doubt one of the most important syndromes in the process of individuation; its wealth of meanings goes far beyond mere personal likes and dislikes. By virtue of its collective contents and symbols it transcends the individual personality and extends into the social sphere, reminding us of those higher human relationships which are so painfully absent in our present social order, or rather disorder. The symbols of the circle and the quaternity, the hallmarks of the individuation process, point back, on the one hand, to the original and primitive order of human society, and forward on the other to an inner order of the psyche. It is as though the psyche were the indispensable instrument in the reorganization of a civilized community

as opposed to the collectivities which are so much in favour today, with their aggregations of half-baked mass-men. This type of organization has a meaning only if the human material it purports to organize is good for something. But the mass-man is good for nothing – he is a mere particle that has forgotten what it is to be human and has lost its soul. What our world lacks is the *psychic connection*; and no clique, no community of interests, no political party, and no State will ever be able to replace this. It is therefore small wonder that it was the doctors and not the sociologists who were the first to feel more clearly than anybody else the true needs of man, for, as psychotherapists, they have the most direct dealings with the sufferings of the soul.

NOTES

1 I use the word 'consciousness' here as being equivalent to 'ego', since in my view they are aspects of the same phenomenon. Surely there can be no consciousness without a knowing subject, and vice versa.

2 Cf. *Rig-veda*, X, 31, 6 (trans. from Deussen, *Geschichte der Philosophie*, I, 1, p. 140):

   And this prayer of the singer, continually expanding,
   Became a cow that was there before the world was,
   The gods are foster-children of the same brood,
   Dwelling together in the womb of this god.

   Vajasaneyi-samhita, 34, 3 (trans. from Deussen, *Die Geheimlehre des Veda*, p. 17):

   He who as consciousness, thought, decision,
   Dwells as immortal light within man.

3 Save as a child, one goes not in where all
   God's children are: the door is much too small.
                                        (*Cherubinischer Wandersmann*, I, no. 153)

4 I am God's child and son, and he is mine.
   How comes it that we both can combine? (I, 256)

   God is my centre when I close him in;
   And my circumference when I melt in him. (III, 148)

   God, infinite, more present is in me
   Than if a sponge should soak up all the sea. (IV, 156)

   The hen contains the egg, the egg the hen,
   The twain in one, and yet the one in twain. (IV, 163)

   God becomes 'I' and takes my manhood on:
   Because I was before him was that done! (IV, 259)

5 Consciousness consists in the relation of a psychic content to the ego. Anything not associated with the ego remains unconscious.

6 This ever-repeated psychological situation is archetypal and expresses itself, for instance, in the relation of the Gnostic demiurge to the highest God.

7 The conjunction symbolism appears in two places: first, at the descent into the darkness, when the marriage has a nefarious character (incest, murder, death); second, before the ascent, when the union has a more 'heavenly' character.

8   Come then, to higher spheres conduct him!
Divining *you*, he knows the way.
                (*Faust II*, tr. MacNiece, p. 303)

9 *Art. aurif.*, II, p. 294f. Cf. *Aurora consurgens*, pp. 53f.

10 In Freud this is done by making conscious the repressed contents; in Adler, by gaining insight into the fictitious 'life-style'.

11 This sentence needs qualifying as it does not apply to all conflict situations. Anything that can be decided by reason without injurious effects can safely be left to reason. I am thinking, rather, of those conflicts which reason can no longer master without danger to the psyche.

12 There were, nevertheless, some who would have liked to have the Holy Ghost as a familiar during their work.

13 In late antiquity Pan was no longer a grotesque pastoral deity but had taken on a philosophical significance. The Naassenes regarded him as one of the forms of the 'many-formed Attis' (*Elenchos*, V, 9, 9) and as synonymous with Osiris, Sophia, Adam, Korybas, Papa, Bakcheus, etc. The story of the dirge is in Plutarch. 'The Obsolescence of Oracles', 17 (*Moralia*, V, pp. 401ff.). (Cf. 'Psychology and Religion', para. 145). Its modern equivalent is Zarathustra's cry 'God is dead!' (*Thus Spake Zarathustra*, p. 67).

14 'In the midst of the Chaos a small globe is happily indicated, and this is the supreme point of junction of all that is useful for this quest. This small place, more efficient than all the entirety, this part which comprises its whole, this accessory more abundant than its principal, on opening the store of its treasures, causes the two substances to appear which are but a single one. . . . Of these two is composed the unique perfect, the simple abundant, the composite without parts, the only indivisible hatchet of the sages, from which emerges the scroll of destiny, extending evenly beyond the Chaos, after which it advances in ordered fashion to its rightful end' ('Recueil stéganographiqué', *Le Songe de Poliphile*, II, f.) In these words Béroalde de Verville describes the germ of unity in the unconscious.

15 [These mottoes, where they appear, translate the verses under the woodcuts in the figures. Figs 8.1–8.10 are full pages reproduced from the Frankfurt first edition (1550) of the *Rosarium philosophorum*. The textual quotations, however, are taken from the version printed in *Art. aurif.*, II (Basel, 1593), except for the poem at par. 528. – EDITORS.]

16 The 'Cons. coniug.' (*Ars chemica*, p. 147) says: 'Et locus generationis, licet sit artificialis, tamen imitatur naturalem, quia est concavus, conclusus' etc. ('The place of gestation, even though it is artificial, yet imitates the natural place, since it is concave and closed'). And (p. 204): 'Per matricem, intendit fundum cucurbitae' ('By matrix he means the root of the gourd').

17 Cf. Ruska, *Turba*, p. 163.

18 Cf. Hortulanus (Ruska, *Tabula smaragdina*, p. 186): 'Unde infinitae sunt partes mundi, quas omnes philosophus in tres partes dividit scil, in partem Mineralem Vegetabilem et Animalem. . . . Et ideo dicit habens tres partes philosophiae totius mundi, quae partes continentur in unico lapide scil. Mercurio Philosophorum' (Hence the parts of the world are infinite, all of which the philosopher divides into three parts, namely mineral, vegetable, animal. . . . And therefore he claims to have the three parts of the philosophy of the whole world, which parts are contained in the single stone, namely the Mercurius of the Philosphers). Ch. 13: 'Et ideo vocatur lapis iste perfectus, quia in se habet naturam mineralium et vetetabilium et animalium. Est enim lapis triunus et unus, quatuor habens naturas' (And this stone is called perfect because it has in itself the nature of mineral, vegetable, and animal. For the stone is triple and one, having four natures).

19 Cf. the alchemical doctrine of the *increatum: Psychology and Alchemy*, paras. 430ff.

20 The union of 'like with like' in the form of homosexual relationships is to be found in the 'Visio Arislei' (*Art. aurif.*, I, p. 147), marking the stage preceding the brother–sister incest.

21 Cf. *Two Essays*, paras 296ff. [Also 'Concerning the Archetypes, with Special Reference to the Anima Concept' and *Aion*, ch. 3– EDITORS.]

22 It may be helpful to remind the reader that in Rider Haggard's *She* there is a description of this 'royal' figure. Leo Vincey, the hero, is young and handsome, the acme of perfection, a veritable Apollo. Beside him there stands his fatherly guardian, Holly, whose resemblance to a baboon is described in great detail. But inwardly Holly is a paragon of wisdom and moral rectitude – even his name hints at 'holy'. In spite of their banality both of them have superhuman qualities, Leo as well as the devout 'baboon'. (Together they correspond to the *sol et umbra eius*.) The third figure is the faithful servant, who bears the significant name of Job. He stands for the long-suffering but loyal companion who has to endure both superhuman perfection and subhuman baboonishness. Leo may be regarded as the sun-god; he goes in quest of 'She' who 'dwells among the tombs' and who is reputed to kill her lovers one by one – a characteristic also ascribed by Benoît to his 'Atlantide' – and to rejuvenate herself by periodically bathing in a pillar of fire. 'She' stands for Luna, and particularly for the dangerous new moon. (It is at the *synodus* of the *novilunum* – i.e. at the *coniunctio* of the Sun and Moon at the time of the new moon – that the bride kills her lover.) This story eventually leads, in *Ayesha*, another novel of Haggard's, to the mystical *hieros gamos*.

23 An Arabic treatise whose origin is still obscure. It is printed in *Ars chemica*, and (with scholia) in *Bibl. chem. curiosa*, I, pp. 400ff.

24 This passage is rather different in the original text (*Ars chemica*, p. 14): 'in quo est nisus tuae dispositionis, et adunatio cuiuslibet sequestrati'. Cf. *Psychology and Alchemy*, para. 385 and n. 87.

25 *Art. aurif.*, II, pp. 227–8.

26 Cf. Cant. 5:3: 'I have put off my garment.'

27 Illegible original.

28 Dorn, 'Speculativae philosophiae', p. 303: 'Studio philosophorum comparatur putrefactio chemica. . . . Ut per solutionem corpora solvuntur, ita per cognitionem resolvuntur philosophorum dubia' ('The chemical putrefaction can be compared with the study of the philosophers. . . . As bodies are dissolved through the *solutio*, so the doubts of the philosophers are resolved through knowledge').

29 Cf. 'De arte chimica', *Art. aurif.*, I, pp. 584ff., and Mylius, *Phil. ref.*, p. 9.

30 Cf. 'Turba', *Art. aurif.*, I, p. 180: 'Spiritus et corpus unum sunt mediante anima, quae est apud spiritum et corpus. Quod si anima non esset, tunc spiritus et corpus separarentur ab invicem per ignem, sed anima adiuncta spiritui et corpori, hoc totum non curat ignem nec ullam rem mundi' ('The spirit and the body are one, the soul acting as a mediator which abides with the spirit and the body. If there were no soul, the spirit and body would be separated from each other by the fire, but because the soul is joined to the spirit and the body, this whole is unaffected by fire or by any other thing in the world').

31 Cf. Winthuis, *Das Zweigeschlechterwesen*.

32 Cf. Frobenius, *Das Zeitalter des Sonnengottes*.

33 'Visio Arislei', *Art. aurif.*, I, p. 148: 'Manismus in tenebris undarum et intenso aestatis calore ac maris perturbatione' ('We remained in the darkness of the waves and in the intense heat of summer and the perturbation of the sea').

34 Cf. the birth of Mithras 'from the sole heat of libido' (*de solo aestu libidinis*). Jerome, *Adversus Jovinianum* (Migne, *P.L.*, vol. 23, col. 246). In Arabic alchemy, too, the fire that causes the fusion is called 'libido'. Cf. 'Exercitationes in Turbam'.

35 See the inscription to *Rosarium*, fig. 5a:

But here King Sol is tight shut in,
And *Mercurius philosophorum* pours over him.

The sun drowning in the mercurial fountain (*Rosarium*, p. 315) and the lion swallowing the sun (p. 367) both have this meaning, which is also an allusion to the *ignea natura* of Mercurius (Leo is the House of the Sun). For this aspect of Mercurius, see 'The Spirit Mercurius', Part III, sec. 3.

36 Hence the ambivalent saying in Mylius, *Phil. ref.*, p. 182: 'In habentibus symbolum facilis est transitus' ('For those who have the symbol the passage is easy').

37 Cf. Kalid, 'Liber trium verborum', *Art aurif.*, I, pp. 355f.

38 'Tractatulus Avicennae', *Art. aurif.*, I, p. 426.

39 Cf. *Aurora*, I, ch. XII (after John 12: 24). Hortulanus (Ruska, *Tabula*, p. 186): 'Vocatur [lapis] etiam granum frumenti, quod nisi mortuum fuerit, ipsum solum manet' etc. ('It [the stone] is also called the grain of wheat, which remains itself alone, unless it dies'). Equally unhappy is the other comparison, also a favourite: 'Habemus exemplum in ovo quod putrescit primo, et tunc gignitur pullus, qui post totum corruptum est animal vivens' ('We have an example in the egg: first it putrefies and then the chick is born, a living animal sprung from the corruption of the whole') (*Rosarium*, p. 255).

40 One such case is described in Meier, 'Spontanmanifestationen', p. 290.

41 Angelus Silesius, *Cherubinischer Wandersmann*, Book IV, p. 194: 'The work that God loves best and most wants done/ Is this: that in you he can bear his son'; Book II, p. 103: 'There where God bends on you his spirit mild/ Is born within the everlasting child.'

42 Cf. Judges 6: 36ff.

43 Cf. 'The Spirit Mercurius', II, sec. 2.

44 Cf. Lambspringk's *Symbols*, *Mus. Herm.*, p. 355, with the verses:

Nidus in sylva reperitur	(A nest is found in the forest
in quo Hermes suos pullos habet,	In which Hermes has his birds.
Unus semper conatur volatum,	One always tries to fly away,
Alter in nido manere gaudet,	The other rejoices in the nest to stay
Et alter alterum non dimittit.	And will not let the other go.)

This image comes from Senior, *De chemia*, p. 15: 'Abscisae sunt ab eo alae et pennae et est manens, non recedens ad superiora' ('Its wings are cut off and its feathers, and it is stationary, not returning to the heights'). Likewise Stolcius de Stolcenberg, *Viridarium chymicum*, fig. XXXIII. In Maier, *De circulo*, p. 127, the opposites are represented as *vultur in cacumine montis et corvus sine alis* (a vulture on the peak of the mountain and a raven without wings). Cf. 'Tractatus aureus', *Ars chem.*, pp. 11–12, and 'Rosinus ad Sarratantam', *Art. aurif.*, I, p. 316.

45 The style of the pictures dates them to the sixteenth century, but the text may be a century older. Ruska (*Tab. smarag.*, p. 193) assigns the text to the fourteenth century. The later dating, fifteenth century (Ruska, *Turba*, p. 342), is probably the more accurate.

46 *Psychology and Alchemy*, para. 500.

47 Philalethes, 'Introitus apertus', *Mus. herm.*, p. 654.

48 She is the Euthicia of the treatise of Rosinus (= Zosimos) in *Art. aurif.*, I, pp. 277ff.

49 The *Mutus liber* is reproduced as an appendix to Vol. I of the *Bibl. chem. curiosa*, 1702. For illustrations from the *Mutus Liber*, see figs. 11–13 of the present volume, and *Psychology and Alchemy*, index. We might mention John Pordage and Jane Leade (17th cent.) as another pair of alchemists.

50 *A Suggestive Inquiry into the Hermetic Mystery.*
51 Florence, Ashburnham 1166, 14th cent. They are reproduced as figs 131 and 135 in *Psychology and Alchemy.*
52 The arrow refers to the *telum passionis* of Mercurius. Cf. 'Cantilena Riplaei', ibid., par. 491, and *Mysterium coniunctionis*, pp. 285ff. Cf. also 'The Spirit Mercurius', Part II, sec. 8, and St Bernard of Clairvaux, *Sermones in Cantica*, XXX, 8 (Migne, *P.L.*, vol. 183, cols. 932–3): 'Est et sagitta sermo Dei vivus et efficax et penetrabilior omni gladio ancipiti . . .. Est etiam sagitta electa amor Christi, quae Mariae animam non modo confixit, sed etiam pertransivit, ut nullam in pectore virginali particulam vacuam amore relinqueret', ('God's word is an arrow; it is lively and effective and more penetrating than a double edged sword . . .. And the love of Christ is a choice arrow too, which not only entered, but transfixed, the soul of Mary, so that it left no particle of her virgin heart free of love'). Trans. by a priest of Mount Melleray, I, p. 346.
53 Cf. the Alaskan Eskimo tale 'The Woman Who Became a Spider,' in Rasmussen, *Die Gabe des Adlers*, pp. 121ff., and the Siberian tale 'The Girl and the Skull,' in Kunike (ed.), *Märchen aus Sibirien*, No. 31, where a woman marries a skull.
54 Ed. Macaulay, II, p. 35: motto of Book I. Cf. St Bernard of Clairvaux, *Sermones in Cant.*, XXIX, 8 (Migne, *P.L.*, vol. 183, col. 933) (of Mary): 'Et illa quidem in tota se grande et suave amoris vulnus accepit' ('And she indeed received a great and sweet wound of love in all her being').
55 Cf. 'The Spirit Mercurius'.
56 Possibly from βαφή (*tinctura*) and μῆτις (skill, sagacity), thus roughly corresponding to the Krater of Hermes filled with νοῦς. Cf. Nicolai, *Versuch über die Beschuldigungen, welche dem Tempelherrenorden gemacht wurden*, p. 120; Hammer-Purgstall, *Mysterium Baphometis*, pp. 3ff.
57 Cf. *Psychology and Alchemy*, fig. 70, showing a snake ritual. There is no certain connection of snake worship with the Templars (Hammer-Purgstall, *Mémoire sur deux coffrets gnostiques*).
58 Anastasius Sinaïta, *Anagogicae contemplationes:* 'Et cum vel suffocatus esset et perisset tenebrosus corvus Satan' ('And when the dark raven Satan [or: of Satan] was suffocated or had perished'). St Ambrose, *De Noe et Arca*, I, 17 (Migne, *P.L.*, vol. 14, col. 411): 'Siquidem omnis impudentia atque culpa tenebrosa est et mortuis pascitur sicut corvus' ('If indeed all shamelessness and guilt is dark and feeds on the dead like a raven'). Again, the raven signifies the sinners: St Augustine, *Annotationes in Job*, I, xxviii, 41 (Migne, *P.L.*, vol. 34, col. 880): 'Significantur ergo nigri [scl. corvi] hoc est peccatores nondum dealbati remissione peccatorum' ('They signify the black [raven], i.e. the sinners not yet whitened by remission of their sins'). Paulinus of Aquileia, *Liber exhortationis* (Migne, *P.L.*, vol. 99, col. 253): 'anima peccatoris . . . quae nigrior corvo est' ('The soul of a sinner . . . which is blacker than a raven').
59 *Art. aurif.*, II, p. 359. See *Psychology and Alchemy*, fig. 54.
60 For further pictures of the Rebis, see ibid., Index, s.v. 'hermaphrodite'.
61 The identification of the *prima materia* with God occurs not only in alchemy but in other branches of medieval philosophy as well. It derives from Aristotle, and its first appearance in alchemy is in the Harranite 'Treatise of Platonic Tetralogies' ('Liber Platonis quartorum', *Theatr. chem.*, V). Mennens ('Aureum vellus', *Theatr. chem.*, V, p. 334) says: 'Nomen itaque quadriliterum Dei sanctissimam Trinitatem designare videtur et materiam, quae et umbra eius dicitur et a Moyse Dei posteriora vocatur' ('Therefore the four-letter name of God seems to signify the Most Holy Trinity and the Materia, which is also called his shadow, and which Moses called his back parts'). Subsequently this idea crops up in the philosphy of David of Dinant, who was attacked by Albertus Magnus. 'Sunt quidam haeretici dicentes Deum et materiam primam et νοῦν sive mentem idem esse' ('There are

some heretics who say that God and the *prima materia* and the nous or mind are the same thing'). – *Summa theologica*, I, 6, qu. 29, memb. 1, art. 1, par. 5 (*Opera,* ed. Borgnet, vol. 31, p. 294). Further details in Krönlein, 'Amalrich von Bena', pp. 303ff.

62 The idea of the hermaphrodite is seemingly to be met with in later Christian mysticism. Thus Pierre Poiret (1646–1719), the friend of Mme Guyon, was accused of believing that, in the millennium, propagation would take place hermaphroditically. The accusation was refuted by Cramer (Hauck, *Realencyklopädie* XV, p. 496), who showed that there was nothing of this in Poiret's writings.

63 It is interesting to see how this theory once more joined forces with alchemy in Herbert Silberer's book, *Problems of Mysticism and its Symbolism.*

64 *De docta ignorantia*, II, 3: 'Maximum autem est, cui nihil opponitur, ubi et Minimum est Maximum.'

65 'Ultra hanc coincidentiam creare cum creari es tu Deus.'

66 *De conjecturis*, II, 14: 'Homo enim Deus est, sed non absolute, quoniam homo. Humane igitur est Deus. Homo etiam mundus est, sed non contracte omnia, quoniam homo. Est igitur homo μικρόκοσμος.'

67 *Of Learned Ignorance* (tr. Heron), p. 173: 'Debet autem in his profundis omnis nostri humani ingenii conatus esse, ut ad illam se elevet simplicitatem, ubi contradictoria coincidunt.'

68 Of these I would draw attention only to the series contained in *Mutus liber*, where the adept and his *soror mystica* are shown performing the *opus*. The undisguisedly psychic character of this portrayal of the *opus* is probably due to the fact that the book was written comparatively late – 1677.

Index